RETURN

RETURN

THE SPIRITUAL ODYSSEY OF A SOVIET SCIENTIST

HERMAN BRANOVER

Translated by
Ilana Coven Attia
and
Mika Tubinshlak

JASON ARONSON INC.
Northvale, New Jersey
London

This book was set in 10 pt. Times by AeroType, Inc.

Part I of this book was translated from the Russian by Ilana Coven Attia. The afterword to Part I and Parts II and III were translated from the Russian by Mika Tubinshlak.

Library of Congress Cataloging-in-Publication Data

Branover, Herman, 1931–
   [Vozvrashchenie. English]
   Return / by Herman Branover
     p. cm.
   Previously published: Jerusalem : New York : Feldheim, 1982.
   ISBN 1-56821-529-0
   1. Branover, Herman, 1931- . 2. Jews—Latvia—Riga—Biography.
  3. Jews, Soviet—Israel—Biography. 4. Hasidim—Israel—Biography.
  5. Riga (Latvia)—Biography. I. Title.
  DS135.L33B73313 1996
  947.43—dc20   95-23256

Manufactured in the United States of America. Jason Aronson Inc. offers books and cassettes. For information and catalog write to Jason Aronson Inc., 230 Livingston Street, Northvale, New Jersey 07647.

To the memory of my parents,

Hertz *and* Devorah

הערץ בן אליעזר

דבורה בת אליהו

ע"ה

ת נ צ ב ה

Contents

Contents

Foreword

Herman Branover's intensely personal memoir, *Return,* is an impressive Jewish document. It records the physical and spiritual battles of a leading Soviet Jewish scientist to free himself from the bondage of Communist rule, and from the atheism that is the official view in Marxist lands, and the prevalent view in much of free Western society. He won both struggles.

With appalling difficulty, Professor Branover made his way to Israel. As one of the world's authorities in the recondite field of magnetohydrodynamics, he now serves on the faculty of the Ben-Gurion University of the Negev in Beersheva. His pioneer work in the energy field has brought him contracts with the United States government as well.

Parallel to this distinguished life in science, Herman Branover has penetrated deeply into Jewish religious thought and tradition, especially in the field of *Chabad* Chasidism. He works ceaselessly, in Israel and the United States, as he did in the Soviet Union, to restore to the Jews of our time the love for our heritage that is his own source of strength. As a small part of this unending selfless effort, he arranged for the translation into Russian of my simple work on Judaism, *This Is My God.*

I admire the man and his deeds. I hope that *Return* will inspire many readers to share the powerful Jewish vision of this bold scientist and man of God.

HERMAN WOUK

Preface

A lthough the sections of this book were written at different times over a period of more than thirty years, all of them have one leading motive – The Return – *Ha-Teshuvah* – return to Jewish roots, to Jewish lifestyle, return to the Almighty and His Holy Torah. On the personal level, the return was and still is the most important of my accomplishments. Moreover, I believe this is the only accomplishment that really counts. On the national level, the return is the most vital necessity. It will solve all the problems of my long-suffering people. The return of the entire people of Israel is inevitable. Ultimately, it will certainly happen. The question is, however, how much time it will take. As the Torah teaches, that depends on us, on how we will exercise the free will we possess.

Some parts of this book have been published before and even translated into English and other languages. Some appear in English for the first time. One large section was written especially for this edition.

Chronologically, I wrote first "From the Depths," which constitutes Part II of this book. It was written in Riga in 1963. Later I supplemented it with "Fragments" (Part III of the present book). The "Fragments" also were written in Riga during the years 1968–1970. In 1976 after I succeeded in leaving the Soviet Union and came to the Holy Land, I wrote the "Return" – a biographical essay, that constitutes Part I of the present book. Finally, I supplemented the almost twenty-year-old "Return" with an updated afterword, presenting my reflections on the latest events in Israel and in the world. This afterword was written in May, 1995.

I will be deeply satisfied if my modest work will contribute a tiny drop to the sea of worldwide efforts to bring Jews closer to *Teshuvah* and to bring about the coming of the *Moshiach*.

I am deeply grateful to the Almighty for all the good He did for me, and I pray and hope that He will not withdraw His favor from me and all children of Israel. By His boundless grace He will disclose to the world the righteous *Moshiach* speedily, in our days!

I
Return

1

Introduction

T his book was originally written as an autobiographical introduction to the philosophical notes I wrote while I was living in Riga in the Soviet Union. These notes served as conversations with myself. Having been educated in the spirit of atheism and dialectic materialism and being thus completely ignorant of Jewish philosophy, I was nevertheless driven by an unquenchable need to find an alternative world outlook to harmonize with my views on nature and humanity as well as to explain the unique place and mission of my long-suffering people in this world.

At first I had absolutely no intention of giving anyone my sketches to read. And I did not dare dream of sending a manuscript outside the Soviet Union. Yet when a possibility of doing so suddenly arose, I jumped at the chance, for I hoped that my thoughts could help others struggling with doubts and longings similar to mine. This decision caused a great deal of unpleasantness for me with the Soviet authorities. Nevertheless, my manuscript reached *Eretz Yisrael,* the Holy Land, almost ten years before I myself was able to. In Israel, my Russian-language manuscript was translated into Hebrew and published under the title *Mima'amakim* (From the Depths).

The conclusions of my philosophical search led me to see that now, as ever, it is both necessary and inevitable for the Jews to return to living by the eternal, unchanging commandments of the Torah, the *mitzvot.*

Natural science is my craft, and I was educated from childhood on a basis of rational thought. Naturally, then, I devoted much attention in my notes to the analytic methods and findings of natural science. It would be completely untrue to say that science brought me to belief. However, my search did help me clarify the limits and restrictions of rational thinking, thus helping me overcome my skepticism. One of the attributes of science today, as opposed to a century ago, is that now its limitations, the relativity and nonexactness of its judgments, are plainly evident.

Probably the only conclusions of rational thinking that can be strictly proven are estimations of its own limitations. Therefore, while it is absurd

3

to claim that rational science leads to irrational belief, at the same time there is no reason to hold on to the nineteenth-century assumption that science negates belief.

In the Jewish world, the first carriers of the view that science can negate belief were the *Maskilim* of the "Enlightenment." After them came Jewish socialists of all shades. Today, the majority of the Jewish people no longer feels that belief must be disproved through universal analysis of science or philosophy. Instead, most Jews have simply adopted a rote formula minimizing God, the Torah and the *mitzvot* as "impossible in today's world."

Here the moral obligation of the Jewish scientist is clear. Anxious about the universal spiritual deterioration of his people, the contemporary Jewish scientist must tirelessly explain the absurdity of the opinion that the modern age is special. He must prove that the penetration of advanced electronics into life and industry has not changed the properties of the soul. Human desires, virtues, and vices remain the same.

Someone who understands this will not return automatically to faith and to a Jewish way of life. But at least a major obstacle against doing so will be dissolved. An honest person, in whom the voice of conscience and duty has not been stifled, will not feel that he has to behave differently from his grandfather and great-grandfather. This pretext for pitilessly smashing tradition has laid bare the tender souls of Jewish children to the onslaught of foreign vices. It has doomed our people to forget its mission, to turn instead to assimilation and destruction. To build upon or to restore these ruins, we must first make a clearing.

Belief springs spontaneously in the human spirit. There occurs a moment in everyone's life when the presence of the Creator is felt. When one is overcome by the power of the Creator, then one involuntarily and naturally prays. For belief to become a firm, constant reality, though, the soul must be freed from the chains of prejudice, the coercions of general opinion and of self-deceit. The soul must be fertilized with deep Torah study and observance of *mitzvot*.

Belief is as natural as breathing and drinking. It does not need an apologia, and by no means do I want what I have written here to be considered as such.

All these ideas were analyzed and discussed in my philosophical sketches written in the Soviet Union during the early 1960s. As already mentioned, these writings of mine were first published in Hebrew in Israel, before I myself was finally allowed to go there in 1972. Several years after my *aliyah*, when I was preparing a new edition of *Mima'amakim*, I realized from my experience of living in Israel and visiting Europe and America that most people would interpret my philosophy by assuming that my passion for Torah is merely an intellectual hobby rather than the basis of my life. By that time, I had delivered hundreds of lectures on "Torah in the Age of Technology." And hundreds of times, members of my audience, representing the broad public of Western Jewish intellectuals, had put to me their standard question of belief: "But do you really put on *tefillin* every day and pray? Does your wife prepare kosher food and light *Shabbat* candles? All this, while living in a modern world?!"

At first such questions infuriated me. People in my audiences were inclined to be favorably disposed to Judaism as long as it remained a beautiful theory alongside many other modern "isms." They couldn't and wouldn't imagine Judaism woven into their lives, making demands upon them.

Yet, fortunately, my listeners have included a few individuals who genuinely wanted to know more about what I meant. They would ask me, "How did you come across this?" For them, a life story is more convincing than theoretical conclusions or abstract proofs. And so I decided to preface my philosophical notes with a description of my life, showing how and why "I came across this." The first part of the present book consists of the English translation of this autobiographical introduction.

I do not find it pleasant to publicly discuss my life. Naturally, I tried to shorten descriptions of personal, family, and daily life, while concentrating more on my search for Judaism, for faith, for Torah. Nevertheless, to answer "how I came across this," I had to deal with personal concerns, for which I beg the reader's pardon.

2

Happy Childhood

M y childhood was very happy. My earliest and most idyllic memories go back to when I was three years old. We lived in Riga, the capital of Latvia. This small country was independent during the years between the First and Second World Wars. The house in which we lived stood on a quiet little street situated between two old parks. Here silence reigned, but now and then was broken by the thunder of hoofbeats and the rumble of a phaeton. From the porch of our house we often heard the squeaks of a beggarly musician or the shouts of a junkman collecting rags. Our home was on the third floor of a large apartment house which belonged to my mother's father, Ilya Michlin, a well-known pediatrician.

In the mornings my older brother and sister ran off to the Hebrew Gymnasium while I remained with my mother, bustling about the house. After taking me for a walk in the park, she would do her shopping on the way home. Once home, she would light the big wood stove and start to prepare supper, with me always between her feet, exhausting her with my endless stream of questions.

I was a very sickly and shy child, a real "mama's boy." I avoided friends and noisy children's games but adored books, forcing my mother to read aloud to me for hours.

Later, when I was nearly five, I began to read by myself. I read in Russian, as both my parents had finished a Russian Gymnasium and spoke only Russian with us at home. Many of the children's books which I read were published in Moscow and Leningrad. Through them I first became acquainted with Lenin, Stalin, and the Red Army, although what lay hidden behind these words I did not yet understand.

Every Thursday my father came home. He was an agronomist and directed an agricultural school for Jewish youth who were preparing to emigrate to Palestine. Set on a farm fifty kilometers east of Riga, the school was organized on the model of a *kibbutz*. My father stayed there most of the time, coming back to the city only on Thursday and staying until Sunday. He was in love with his profession and had an encyclopedic knowledge of biology and of agricultural techniques. He was constantly fascinated by selection experiments, breeding new types of plants. In addition, he was acquainted with many other branches of the natural sciences. Paleontology and archaeology especially excited him.

When I was only about five or six years old, he began to draw me into his circle of interests. I worshiped his stories about the plant and animal kingdoms. For hours he would read aloud to me from Brem's *Encyclopedia of the Life of Animals*. Together we set up an aquarium, collected beetles and butterflies and cultivated cactuses. My sister, who was four years older than I, also liked animals. Together we bought a pet puppy.

Among my father's many skills was his ability to draw well. During the breaks between our natural science projects, he would try, unsuccessfully though, to teach me to draw. He also made things from cardboard, paper, and plywood—marionettes and all kinds of tricks that brought as much happiness to him as to us, his children. He was an exceptionally quiet and shy man: I never heard him raise his voice. He could not bear to hear curse words. Even expressions like "fool" or "the devil" upset him.

True delight would begin for us in the summer when our whole family went out to the farm. It was situated in one of the most picturesque corners of Latvia, not far from the little town of Sigulda. Its hilly landscape and rich virgin forests concealing many small lakes and clear rivers gave this area its nickname, "Lettlandish Switzerland." Its soil is not very fertile and is difficult to cultivate, but the forests abound with every possible kind of berry and mushroom. Bathed by the rain, the air is constantly full of the deep aroma of wild grasses and flowers, all of which the subdued northern sun colors in pastel tones and puts into quiet, dreamlike order.

Here my dear sister and I had several dogs, our own "experimental" furrows in the vegetable garden, and our own corners in the greenhouse and hothouses. Captured from nearby woods and fields, and kept in our house, were hedgehogs, hares, field mice, lizards, and often poisonous snakes, kept in bottles capped with gauze. Outside, two domesticated goats would persistently accompany us.

The Hebrew language was constantly heard here. The young people, who called themselves *chalutzim* (pioneers), studied not only agriculture but also the language needed in preparation for their move to Palestine.

I don't remember, though, that Hebrew, which I began to study in school at age seven, or any other Jewish subject, aroused any particular interest or feeling in me then. Of course, I knew that we were Jewish and somehow different from other people. Our school was called the *Zhid* City School, as the Latvian authorities had legitimized in their language the term *zhid* rather than the more respectable *evreye*.

In our school we put on performances on Chanuka and Purim, when we were told about the *Chashmona'im,* Achashverosh and Queen Esther. Our family always spent the Passover *seder* at the home of my grandfather, Doctor Michlin. Although he did not observe the daily laws of Jewish life, he tried to mark the major annual Jewish holidays. He often went to the synagogue on Saturdays and made an effort to take me with him.

In this way I gained certain, quite disconnected, notions about Jewish history and holidays. I heard that there was a ceremony for Jewish boys at age thirteen called *bar mitzvah.* I knew that a long time ago the Jews had come out of Egypt and that they had had strong kings, David and Solomon, and so forth. But I did not have the slightest inkling about most of the Jewish laws. For example, I never heard about *tefillin* (phylacteries) or the holiday of Shavuot, somehow considered secondary in our half-assimilated Jewish circles.

Sometimes I heard the adults talking about someone they called Dubin or, affectionately, Dubinka. From these discussions it emerged that he was very influential, close to the President of the Republic. He helped Jews with various difficult life matters while at the same time teaching them, convincing them of the necessity to observe some special Jewish laws of behavior. In particular, he requested women to visit a special institution called *mikveh.*

I also heard a little about Zionist parties. But this was basically represented to me through the image of my brother, ten years older than I. He was attracted to sports: gymnastics, swimming, and bicycle riding. Sometimes he came home with a bruised face, the result of either night skirmishes with Latvians or Germans or of battle between certain groups which bore names little understood by me, such as Betar, Hashomer Hatzair, and others.

3

Soviet Tanks Are Coming

In 1939 our unclouded, measured existence was darkened with apprehension. On the first of September the war began. This was to become the Second World War, and one of the most terrible catastrophes of Jewish history.

Several years earlier, Jewish emigrants from Germany had appeared in our area. Frightened and weary, they had knocked at the doors of Jewish homes and begged for help in burred German speech. They brought a sense of foreboding and warning into the complacent and comfortable atmosphere of the local Jewish community. But they evoked disbelief and anger rather than sympathy. The life of the Jewish middle class was entirely unaffected. Everyone was busy with his own cares of "business" or service. In the evenings people would sit in cafés or gather at friends' houses to play cards.

Even when war broke out in Poland, it was still far away from us psychologically. I remember the day that war was proclaimed. We were at the farm. The *chalutzim* were excited and seemed to be happy. With pitchforks and shovels on their shoulders, they acted out war pantomimes enthusiastically.

Endless debates and discussions concerning the future of the Baltic states began. Everyone tried to foresee who would occupy Latvia—the Russians or the Germans. Property owners like my grandfather, who remembered the German occupation in the First World War, preferred the Germans. Others, particularly those who wanted to check the increasingly pro-German and anti-Semitic Latvian government, favored the Russians.

My father was somehow considered a leftist, although he was probably completely apolitical. Indeed, he was doubtlessly attracted by the stories about the flourishing of the sciences and the extensive opportunities open to Jews in Soviet Russia. He held onto this attraction even though in 1937 two of his brothers in Moscow had been sent to concentration camps on the accusation of "betraying the homeland." Although he knew German fluently, the Russian language and culture were closer to him. As a result he apparently preferred the arrival of the Russians.

On a June night in 1940, Russian troops occupied the Baltic states. Open-hatched tanks came, with soldiers in forage caps and pointed Budenny helmets sitting on the armor. Crowds of people with flowers and red flags met the Red Army. If not the majority, at least many of the welcomers were Jews. Latvians looked upon these Jews with a twofold hatred.

The Latvian president, Ulmanis, addressed his people on the radio, affirming that he would remain at his post and appealing for law and order. This was the last statement of his life.

At first almost nothing changed. Soviet army officers swept into town, bringing along their families. The officers' wives wildly attacked the stores, which were still full of merchandise. Soon, however, queues appeared for products—an utterly strange phenomenon for us, eliciting, therefore, surprise rather than irritation.

A little later more basic changes began to take place. The farm on which my father worked was reorganized from a preparatory *kibbutz* into a regular agricultural school for the local population. My father, however, remained in his former position.

The school where we children studied was also transformed—from a Hebrew Gymnasium to a Russian secondary school, although the pupils and even most of the teachers remained the same. My schoolmates and I welcomed the new slogans and songs.

I became an Octobrist, my sister a Pioneer, and my brother a member of the Komsomol. Excitedly we sang "Vast Is the Homeland of Mine," "The Morning Brings a Tender Light to the Walls of the Old Kremlin," "Higher, Higher," and other songs. Eventually, I also became a Pioneer, solemnly taking oath "to honorably and steadfastly struggle for the cause of Lenin and Stalin and for the victory of Communism throughout the world."

There appeared new popular books about the origin of the species and the theory of evolution, as well as science-fiction novels about interplanetary travel and superintelligent creatures on the moon and Mars. Darwin's theory so captured my imagination that, with my father's help, I prepared a two-hour report on the subject. I began to pester my teacher to allow me to deliver my lecture to my classmates. I dreamed of initiating a circle of young Darwinists or at least young Michurinists. My teacher vacillated for a long time. After all, I was only nine years old and in the second grade.[1] But I was so persistent that she finally relented.

My disappointment was very deep when, after the first quarter of an hour, most of my audience were either dozing off, making paper airplanes, or stubbornly concentrating on picking their noses. After half an hour my teacher intervened, and I, pitilessly mangling and crumpling my carefully prepared report, finished my lecture in three-quarters of an hour. There were no questions, alas, outside those asked by my teacher, who was always gentle with me.

In the beginning of 1941 the Soviet regime started to expropriate property. My grandfather was deprived of everything he had accumulated during nearly fifty years of a very intensive medical practice. I remember that as I looked upon his sorrowed countenance, in the depths of my soul I condemned him as a former bourgeois discontented with the Soviet regime. My conflict with my

---

1. In the U.S.S.R. children started the first grade at age seven. After ten years of public school, if they wished to continue, they entered a five-year course of university studies similar to a combined B.A. and M.A. program in the U.S.

grandfather was further aggravated on Passover when, on the morning following the *seder,* he tried to convince me not to go to school.

Of course I went to school, supplied with a few sweet buns by my tender-
hearted grandmother. As I was a Pioneer, it was unthinkable that I would bring
matzah to school with me for breakfast.

That evening my grandfather dragged me to the synagogue, but on the way
home I started up a cruel argument, "proving" that religion was nonsense from
the position of Darwin's theory of the origin of the species.

4

Soviet Army Kills My Father

On June 22 the war rolled in on us. We were at the farm at the time.
Within one or two days after the outbreak of war it became evident that
the Germans were moving forward so quickly that it was possible that within a week they would reach us. My father deemed it imperative for us to
make our way into the depths of Russia, but the lack of a Soviet passport
held him back. He was originally from Bessarabia, which had once belonged
to Rumania. Thus, at the time of the Soviets' entry into the Baltic states,
he was not a Latvian but a Rumanian subject. While Latvian citizens had
automatically become Soviet citizens, for a whole year my father had been
turned down persistently. Even his former reputation as "leftist inclined" didn't
help him.

Now that the war had started, he was convinced that without a Soviet
passport we would not be allowed to cross the old Soviet-Latvian border. On
the third or fourth day of the war he went to Riga and rushed about to every
possible office, but panic, chaos, and desertion reigned everywhere. Depressed
and distraught, he returned to the farm. In the city he had met with my
grandfather, who adamantly stated that he was not going to go anywhere. At
that time my older brother was also in Riga and had joined the Komsomol
volunteer militia.

One day we picked up a radio broadcast from the Lithuanian city of
Shiauliai, already occupied by the Germans. The announcer read, in German,
decrees of the new regime concerning Jews. We were only 140 kilometers from
Shiauliai. To wait any longer would be madness, but my father, running his
finger across the map, still expressed the hope that the Dvina River could hold
the Germans back for a while.

A day later it was finally decided to load a wagon with our most essential things and to set off in the direction of Pskov. A horse was even chosen—an old mare named Mayga, which had a wall-eye but was unusually hardy and devoted.

A wide unpaved road crossed the farm about a hundred meters from the main building where we lived. Here, for two days around the clock, Soviet troops had been moving uninterruptedly, retreating from west to east. They were traveling by foot, in vehicles, on horses. Occasionally units passed with someone in command keeping something resembling order, but there were hours when ragged and often unarmed soldiers moved along in a kind of disorderly mob. From time to time German planes attacked, and the soldiers ran into the fields, seeking shelter in ditches, behind bushes and ridges.

My parents were getting ready to leave. As daylight was waning, I was standing by the window of the veranda, watching the avalanche of soldiers slowly moving eastward. Suddenly I heard the rumble of approaching planes, just as a column of trucks was passing by. The trucks stopped and the soldiers started to jump down and scatter over the fields. It was already beginning to get dark, and I noticed that the rifle of one of the soldiers jumping off the truck accidentally fired. A commotion began, and within a few minutes I saw a semicircle of soldiers close in on our house with their rifles raised.

I called to my parents, and my father, seeing what was going on, ordered us to lie on the floor in case the soldiers started shooting and bullets passed through the window into the room. We lay on the floor, listening to the approaching tramp of the soldiers. We knew that the Latvians in the cities were shooting at the retreating Russians from their roofs and windows. So we guessed that they were assuming that the careless shot of one of their own soldiers was an attack from the farm.

Soon their boots were pounding on the porch. The door was flung open and a shout resounded, "Who's there? Don't move!"

Keeping on the floor, we answered, "We're on your side!" We were brought out into the yard. They brought out also all the Latvians, the students of the school. They separated the men and asked, "Who's in charge here?" My father gave his name. Then they took all the men away. As he was leaving, my father cried to my mother, "Take the children and go!" A soldier struck him on the back and shouted, "What's all this talking going on?"

The next day all the Latvians returned. To all our persistent questions about my father they only answered evasively that they had been brought to the next town and then my father was separated from them. My mother stubbornly waited another day or two. She was trying to call somewhere by telephone. Finally, somehow, comprehension dawned, and for the first time in my life I saw my mother weep. I also came to understand that my father had died, but just the same I was not in a condition to feel it. The events of those few days seemed to me to be occurring in a remote, unreal world. They didn't arouse any strong emotions in me. It was as if I was experiencing just another of the high fevers of my frequent child-hood illnesses.

That very afternoon — it was the first of July — we found out that the Germans were already in Riga. My mother made up her mind and went to harness the faithful one-eyed mare, Mayga. She gathered several blankets and a coat for each of us, and we set off. I brought a book along with me which I valued more than all else. Called *Traces on Stone,* it discussed paleontological theories and how on their basis the history of evolution of the plant and animal kingdoms of the earth was reconstructed.

For five days and five nights uncomplaining Mayga pulled the cart bearing a defenseless, just-widowed woman, inexperienced with life's difficulties, and her two children — a thirteen-year-old girl and a nine-year-old boy.

The roads were jammed with soldiers and refugees. Everywhere people said that the Germans were within ten to twenty kilometers. We could hear the explosion of close-range fire and frequent airplane attacks. On the fifth day we reached the former Soviet-Latvian border. A border post control was still functioning, but everyone was allowed through with no difficulty.

In several hours we were at Pskov. We brought Mayga to a courtyard, giving her a quarter sack of oats and kissing her farewell.

At the train station, pandemonium and panic reigned. My mother managed to get us a place on one of the open platforms of a long freight train which, according to rumor, would be leaving for the east at nightfall.

We lived on that platform for twenty-three days. The train went slowly, winding around cities and standing for hours at nameless stations. It was hot in the daytime and cold at night. The engine sprinkled us with coal powder, and we ate and drank very rarely, when members of some sort of railway committee brought soup and tea.

The sounds of the war were left far behind as we went deeper into immense Russia. We became acquainted with her through the faces of the ragged, barefoot children who surrounded our train in the out-of-the-way stations. The monotony of all this was emphasized further by the ever-present sign "Boiling Water" under which stood a queue equipped with kettles and buckets.

We passed the Ural mountain range, and our railroad journey ended in Omsk. There we refugees (or officially "evacuees") were assigned to neighbor-hoods in the Omsk region.

5

Wedding Ring for a Loaf of Bread

W e were brought to the village of Tsherlak, 150 kilometers south of Omsk on the shore of the Irtish river.

We were settled into a clay hut, a cob-house, in one room together with an old landlady. All that she could share with us was head and clothing lice. From that time until the end of our four-year stay in Siberia, we constantly were covered with infections from bites and scratches. Every evening before going to bed we spent one to two hours inspecting the seams of our clothing where we would pick the lice out and then burn them in the flame of a smoky lamp.

My mother started to work as a bookkeeper in the office of the *Zagotzerno* warehouses, which supplied us with coupons to purchase products. We hadn't brought any belongings with us and had nothing to sell.

When we became completely famished, my mother exchanged her wedding ring and watch at the market for some loaves of bread and milk. Winter already was setting in, and milk was sold in the form of big frozen discs, shaped like the basin in which it had been frozen.

At that time we moved to a sort of lean-to, two-thirds occupied by an enormous Russian stove for which we had absolutely no firewood.

Forty-below-zero frosts began. Snow drifts reached the height of the rooftops, and inside our room water froze. From time to time my mother procured a few logs, but this was enough only to boil tea, not to add warmth to the room.

I studied at the local school, but most of the time I was ill. It was beyond my strength to withstand the Siberian frosts. Moreover, we were becoming hungrier and hungrier. On the rare days when I did go to school, I was seized by panic at having to face the older pupils. They stopped me on the street and shouted, "Jew-boy! Jew-boy! String him up, ahoy!" Ordering me to say "kukuruza," they laughed at my burred "r." Then they snipped off all the buttons from my torn jacket and, giving me a knee kick in the behind, graciously let me go home.

For a short time my older brother showed up in Tsherlak. The Latvian Komsomol militia had been disbanded. He worked first teaching German at school, then playing violin at the community hall, and finally driving a tractor in a *kolkhoz*. Soon he was called into the regular army, but he had succeeded in earning and leaving us with several sacks of wheat, which saved us from the cold and hungry winter of 1942, the second winter of the war.

6

Hunger Pushes Us to a Kolkhoz

To save ourselves from hunger, we moved to a *kolkhoz* bearing the high flown name "The Red Banner." But hunger soon caught up with us there, too. People ate carrion, digging up from pits the carcasses of animals dead from a Siberian plague. Children became swollen from hunger.

Summer always brought relief. Vegetables ripened, wild strawberries covered the steppes, and the beneficent Siberian rivers abounded with fish. But winter would bring back cruel hunger.

Finally, my mother decided to move to the Kazakh village. Alongside the "Soviet" law there existed the unofficial "Kazakh" law based on "one hand washing the other." As a result, the inhabitants succeeded in keeping a part of their wheat and lambs for their own use.

But on the other hand here was another scourge. Countless diseases spread from the filth. Children's hands were mottled with itch, their eyes were dimmed and blinded by trachoma, and their heads were deprived of hair and sprinkled with white, flourlike tetter. All this frightened and shocked me.

There was no Russian school, but my mother obtained textbooks for me. I learned them almost by heart and solved all the problems. Thus I finished the fifth and sixth grades. In the remaining time, I did all kinds of daily writing—about the weather, about food, and so forth. I also began to write stories. I remember that the first story which I wrote was about people making a flight to Mars and returning to Earth. I held my heroes in great reverence.

I reached my thirteenth birthday at the Kazakh village. There is no need to point out that I did not celebrate a *bar mitzvah*. But perhaps it is proper to point out that then I did not even recollect that, for a Jewish boy, turning thirteen had a particular significance.

The oppression of hunger was ended by our move to the village. But cold, lice, and malaria tormented us as before. Malaria tortured all three of us, but for each one it had a different form—the one-day, the two-day, and the tropical form. I was cured by yellow tablets of quinine which my mother provided, through some miracle.

My mother had been transformed from a delicate bourgeois daughter into a fearless Siberian woman. Even the local inhabitants were amazed at her courage when, in the performance of her bookkeeping duties, she would set off to the district center thirty kilometers away by sleigh, completely alone in minus-forty-degree frost. It was not rare for her to return home deep into the night. More than once she told us how wolves had pursued her. As I lay on a wooden cot in an unheated room, shivering from the cold and from malarial chills, I would imagine across the boundless steppes white from snow, covered by a black endless sky, a sleigh moving forward. The horse gallops. In the sleigh sits a small woman wrapped in a giant sheepskin coat. Behind the sleigh, now gaining on it, now falling back, a pack of wolves is moving. Their howls freeze the heart, their green eyes flash. . . .

7

Our Entire Family Is Killed by Nazis

In November of 1944 a letter came from my brother at the front, in which he reported that he had been in Riga. He wrote that he had not found any of the relatives and that, although it was not yet entirely clear, it should be assumed that they had been killed by the Germans.

Until that time we had known almost nothing about the annihilation of a large part of European Jewry. We received newspapers fairly regularly, although usually many days late. But it was impossible to get an adequate presentation from the Soviet press of the essence and scale of the Jewish tragedy. Much time had yet to pass until the words "ghetto," "*aktion*," "gas chamber," and "mobile gas chamber" were known to us and their terrible meaning became clear.

On May 9, 1945, the war ended. Two months later we returned to Riga. Externally nothing had changed there. It was summer, and the city parks were just as dense, green, and carefully tended as four years before. In the old city there were, in truth, some ruins, but otherwise the external appearance of the city betrayed nothing of the past war. Carriages and taxis traveled about, trams clanged, and in the famous Riga bazaar, Latvian women in starched white aprons sold aromatic garden strawberries and thick yellowish sour cream.

All our close relatives had perished. However, many acquaintances and some of our more distant relatives gradually returned from the depths of Russia.

A large number of Jews who had been living in various parts of Russia, the Ukraine, or Belorussia before the war were settling in Riga. Thus the number of Jews in the city started to approach the pre-war level.

On Rosh Hashana and Yom Kippur my mother took me to the synagogue. Of all the big synagogues in Riga only one had been preserved—in the old city, on Paytavas Street. The others had been destroyed, burned (in many cases with Jews having been locked inside them).

In those first Jewish high holy days after the war, the synagogue and the courtyard between it and the street were packed full with people. Many wore military uniforms, some with shoulder straps of high officer rank. Most of them came to meet acquaintances, to ask about the fate of near ones. But inside the building nearly everyone was praying, some in ecstasy with tears pouring forth.

I stood close to the cantor, listening to his chanting and the hum of the congregational prayer, which rose in a rich rumble and then subsided. I did not understand a word, but was possessed by a feeling of belonging to something great, penetrated by wisdom unknown and inaccessible to me. I felt that these people surrounding me in a tight ring were united by ties which transcended all I had known previously and that I inexplicably belonged to them.

I was then barely fourteen years old. I resumed my studies at school in the seventh grade. Personal contact with teachers and visits to the library and to bookstores stirred up anew my attraction to the natural sciences.

Soon I joined the Komsomol. I sincerely believed in communism and even more in the "great leader and teacher of all peoples" — Yosef Vissarionovich Stalin.

This was the time that American atom bombs had just been dropped on Hiroshima and Nagasaki, and nuclear science and technology were rapidly coming into style.

I avidly read all that concerned nuclear physics, and after every newspaper article or popular brochure my confidence was strengthened in my calling — atomic research. I was in a hurry to get to university and therefore, having finished the seventh grade, during the two summer months I conducted an uninterrupted study of all the textbooks for the eighth grade. In the fall I did the eighth-grade curriculum as an extern at evening school and went on like this to the ninth grade.

I spent, then, from six o'clock in the evening until ten or eleven at night at school, but during the day I absolutely didn't know what to do. Preparing my lessons took only one or two hours, and I spent time reading, but my day was still not filled. From having nothing to do, the completely preposterous idea entered my head to enroll at the children's ballet school at the Riga Choreographic Academy. I spent several hours a day training on the crossbars, executing upon command intricate movements of the arms and legs called by strange French names. We also learned how to do classical dances — waltz, polonaise, polka. Upon completion of half a year, we began to prepare for a students' variety show on the stage of the Riga Theater of Opera and Ballet. Waiting for my rehearsals to start, I spent long hours in the dark and empty audience section of the auditorium, watching ballet or opera rehearsals sometimes ten or twenty times. I was chosen to participate in the program of the variety show in a chorus performance of

Chopin's Polonaise, and with that my ballet career, fortunately, came to an end.

Upon graduating from the ninth grade, I once again studied at the regular day school. The man who taught physics there was considered the best in the city. Whenever he was sober, his classes were really captivating, and, as a result, my partiality toward physics was even further strengthened.

At that time I began to be particularly interested in the theory of relativity. I would sit in the municipal public library for long evenings right up until its closing time, persistently taking notes on all that I succeeded in understanding from the more or less popular books on the subject. The philosophic aspects of Einstein's theory particularly fascinated me. Some of the authors made detailed excursions into a realm of questioning dealing with worlds of four or more dimensions. Reflecting on the possibilities or impossibilities of perceiving or imaging such hypothetical worlds especially excited me.

At last, with my matriculation diploma in hand, I firmly decided to go to Leningrad to enroll in the physical-mechanical faculty of the Polytechnical Institute. Deciding on that step had not been very easy because I was sixteen-and-a-half years old and still a mama's boy, completely untrained and inexperienced in independent living. In everything, outside of my scientific passions, my mother took care of me and directed me. I shared all my thoughts with her and followed all her instructions. So well did she know and understand me that often in a conversation I did not manage to utter more than the first word and she was already able to complete my whole sentence. She taught me honesty and straightforwardness; she tried to instill in me diligence and a sense of compassion and readiness to help others. She herself had always been modest and shy, and therefore was not able to teach me the boldness so necessary for the independent life into which I was entering.

8

I Move to Leningrad to Study Science

Thus I departed for Leningrad, full of optimistic expectations and dreams of scientific pursuits and other lofty subjects. I was then, as has been said already, sixteen-and-a-half years old.

At the platform of the Warsaw railroad station I was met by Uncle Naum, a cousin of my mother. He was a widower whose wife had died of hunger during the seige of Leningrad. They had never had any children.

He received me like a son. He had a room in a large communal apartment on the Petrogradsky side. This once-splendid dwelling was now occupied by five families, with shared kitccen and hallways, presenting a classic example of a communal apartment. There I saw for the first time a kitchen with five tables and five primus burners. Even more amusing: in the bathrooms there were five separate lights. Next to the light switches on the wall hung a homemade placard on which was written: "Seat! Don't flood it and don't dirty it! Respect yourself and others!"

Leningrad caught me by surprise and won me over. I arrived there in the second half of June when the white nights were already coming to an end. But something of them still remained to excite the soul.

Having come to Leningrad while still a young man, Uncle Naum, like most Leningrad old-timers, was unrestrainedly proud of his city and in love with it. He took me to the great boulevards and squares, to the bridges crossing the silvery brilliance of the Neva River. He took me to Peterhof and to the Tsarkoye Selo Village and showed me the Hermitage, deriving unspeakable delight from the deep impression which these places made upon me. Even more marked than the clear aesthetic impression of the city was the contact it gave me with history. For the first time in my life I met things about which I had read in textbooks, in the works of Pushkin and Dostoevsky—places and events that until then I had thought were separated from me by the barriers of irreversible time. The possibility of crossing the bridge over the Winter Ditch, of walking along the casemates of the Petropavlovskaya Fortress, of going right up to the Bronze Horseman, seemed to me, somehow, wondrous.

Leningraders impressed me. Many of them—at least at the time—were distinguished by erudition, by readiness to help one another, and by very touching sentiments toward their city.

However, there wasn't much time for enjoying interesting sights. My entrance examinations were approaching, and I had to prepare for them.

The exams began. That was in the summer of 1948. Stalin had already delivered his famous toast to the "great Russian people." Mikhoels had been murdered already.[1] The epoch of Jewish newspapers, theaters, and publishing houses was reaching its last days. The era of the Stalin-Zhdanov ideological decrees against "cosmopolitanism" was beginning. Rumors spread that institu-

---

1. Shlomo Mikhoels was a famous actor and producer of the Jewish theater in Moscow. In 1942 he was chosen to be the president of the Jewish Anti-Fascist Committee, a group of prominent Soviet Jewish intellectual and literary figures who organized to help fight against Hitler. This committee was sent by the Soviet government to Britain and the United States to raise money for the faltering postwar Russian economy. The $2 million which they collected was given to the Kremlin, but in the persecutions of 1948 the committee was accused of "Zionism" and "sabotage." Mikhoels was killed in an "accident," and all the other leading members of the committee—except Ilya Ehrenburg—were arrested.

tions of higher learning were going to be restrictive about accepting Jews, particularly in schools of nuclear physics.

I did well in the examinations. True, in the oral examination on Russian literature an unpleasant incident occurred. After I had thoroughly answered all the questions on the examination form, plus several additional ones, the woman examiner threw this question at me: "At what time of day and to whom did Korobochka go after Chichikov visited her?" I, honestly, had read Gogol's *Dead Souls* all the way through more than once, but when and to whom this Korobochka had gone I couldn't recall. "You have shown disrespect to *my* national writer," the examiner angrily accused me, emphasizing the word "my"—and struck me down with a three.

Despite this unpleasantness, my average mark was on the level of the best students taking the examination. Moreover, my three was in literature, and I was applying to the physical-mechanical faculty. Yet when they posted the lists I found myself among those rejected. After the tears in my eyes dried, I started to study the lists in greater detail, and I found nearly fifty obviously Jewish names among those not accepted. I could not find a single such name among those that were accepted. My discovery not only did not console me, but it shocked me even more.

I was ashamed to tell Uncle Naum what had happened, and there was no one else with whom I could share my feelings. The tram ride home from the end of the Viborgsky site of the Polytechnical Institute to Uncle Naum's apartment took close to an hour. But this was not enough time for me to calm down sufficiently to feel able to talk with anybody.

I didn't drink vodka, and therefore all I could do was go to the grocery and buy two pieces of pastry and eat them. Finally, all the same, I had to go home and tell Uncle Naum what had happened. To my great surprise, my news didn't shock him very much. First of all, he just naturally didn't understand what it meant to me to see my dreams of being a physicist wrecked. Secondly, it did not strike him as either impossible, surprising, or new that I had been rejected because I was a Jew.

The next morning I went to the Institute to protest and plead my case. I knew that the vice rector of the Institute was Professor Levy. I had seen him once. He had a definitely Jewish appearance and spoke in an unusually thin voice, pronouncing the "r" more gutturally than most Jews. True, I didn't know then that he was called Ivan Ivanovitch and that his father had been baptized.

The secretary didn't let me see Levy, but I firmly resolved to wait for him at the door of his office. Evening had set in already when he appeared, making his way to the exit. I followed him. I was very agitated since I had never spoken face to face with a professor before. We left the building. There was a strong thunderstorm, pouring rain. We jumped over puddles, and the wind muffled my voice. "Tell me," I pleaded, "tell me just one thing. They didn't accept me because I'm a Jew, right?" He replied something about the equality of all nationalities in the Soviet Union and added that the next day they were going to suggest that those who had not been accepted should enroll in other faculties. Then he disappeared in the wet, lightning-blazed darkness.

I remained standing there drenched, humiliated, and miserable, not yet knowing then that, possibly, this moment—when I deeply and painfully understood that I was not like all the others around me because I was a Jew—was the start of the most important and fortunate turning point in my life. I was not able to know then that three thousand years ago the Almighty had said to the Jews: "Here I give you a blessing and a curse, life and death. Choose life." Naturally I did not realize yet at that moment the blessing and therefore far from feeling the happiness of being a Jew, I deeply felt the curse. But this was great progress in comparison to the time when I was certain that I was the same as everybody.

9

First Thoughts about Being Jewish

In the end they accepted me into the hydro-energetics department. Although this was not at all the answer to my dreams, the studies captivated me. The first lectures on differential calculus made an enormous impression on me. The elegance of the thought, the dynamics of the presentation, and the deep philosophy of this subject seemed to me to be a genuine revelation. I would spend a lot of time thinking about what I had heard in these lectures and I bought many books on mathematics, going far beyond the limits of our modest required course. I spent long evening hours reading these books, delighting in the process of comprehending what was written in them and experiencing great happiness when a difficult point finally became clear. These were hours, it seemed to me, filled with profound thought and meaning.

I derived pleasure from the lectures on physics and analytical geometry, less so from chemistry. And having to study mechanical drawing and geodesy was very tortuous. These subjects repelled me by their particular practicality and by reminding me that I was not in the physics department.

Our bachelor's quarters at Uncle Naum's filled with one more tenant. This was Misha Gurevich, the brother of Uncle Naum's late wife. He had just been demobilized from the army in which he had served during all the war and for three more years after it. Well past forty, he had neither a wife nor a place to live, so tender-hearted Uncle Naum gave him shelter.

We all three of us would return home late in the evening, and then Uncle Naum began to prepare our bachelor supper. We sat until long after midnight, drinking tea that was brewed with solemnity by Uncle Naum. There was no end to our conversation, and over and over they returned to two central themes: the falseness and cruelty of the Soviet regime and the unique fate of our long-suffering Jewish people.

Even though I had already lived under Soviet rule for eight years, all I knew about it was what was written in the newspapers, which knocked themselves out in their servility to Stalin, and what I had been forced to learn in school from *The Short Course on the History of the All-Union Communist Party of the Bolsheviks,* reprinted yearly in millions of copies. Moreover, I of course had read *Virgin Soil Upturned* by Sholokhov,[1] *The Young Guards* by Fadeyev,[2] and other books in the same spirit. Here, in Naum's room in Petrogradsky, I first heard about the N.E.P. and the subsequent persecution of the N.E.P. men,[3] about the confiscation of farm land and property, about the bloodcurdling methods of the Cheka,[4] starting from the time of Uritsky[5] and Dzershensky[6] up to the apotheosis of 1937[7] when millions were murdered or sent to labor camps without trial or inquest—through the verdict of "troika"[8] courts.

But if all this was disturbing and depressing, the stories of my mentors about the past and present of the Jewish people excited and aroused my soul. I found out about the heroic period of the Judean and Israelite kingdoms, and about the tragedies of the Babylonian captivity and the Roman slavery. From these ancient times we proceeded to the life of the Jews in the Pale of Settlement, to the pogroms, to the Beilis affair,[9] to the hardships and

---

1. Novel about the establishment of collective farms.

2. Novel about an underground movement of young people organized to fight fascism.

3. Abbreviation for the New Economic Policy adopted by Lenin in 1921 to try to save the collapsing economy of the country by allowing private industry and trade. Later, thousands of people who had cooperated with this plan (the "NEPmen") were arrested and brutally persecuted.

4. Russian abbreviation for "Extraordinary Commission," the first name given to the secret police system that was founded in November 1917 to wipe out counter-revolution, speculation, and sabotage in the new Communist regime through refined methods of murder, detention in concentration camps, and confiscation of property.

5. First chairman of Petrograd Cheka.

6. First head of the Soviet national Cheka.

7. The climax of mass arrests, fixed trials, murders, and concentration camp convictions through which Stalin "purged" the Communist party and secured his despotism.

8. Three-man commissions, appointed by the Cheka, that condemned political prisoners and used absolutely no ordinary tribunal processes.

9. Public trial held in Kiev in 1913 against a Jew, Mendel Beilis, accused of having murdered a Christian boy in order to use his blood for Jewish ritual purposes. Although Beilis was acquitted, the trial gave vent to the virulent anti-Semitism of Czarist Russia.

persecutions during the civil war between the Reds and the Whites, to the rise of Jews within the arts and sciences with the Soviet regime, and, finally, to the new period of persecution just starting. Our conversation hardly touched upon the State of Israel, proclaimed half a year earlier. It must be said that for me this event had occurred almost unnoticed. I, naturally, had read about it and about the subsequent war, in which the Soviet Union at first had taken the side of the Jews and had even denounced the "Arab nationalists" in the press. However, the proclamation of the Jewish state had not seriously excited either myself or anybody around me. In any case, I had not felt that this event had direct bearing on me. Now, in the course of our nocturnal discussions, it gained greater importance and immediacy in my imagination.

Both of my interlocutors were unusually proud of the wisdom of the Jewish people. Yet the Prophets and the compilers of the Talmud, although mentioned in part, did not serve as much as a measure of this wisdom for them as did the innumerable names of Jewish scientists, writers, and musicians. They received great pleasure in compiling long lists of names in which were found Einstein and Disraeli, Spinoza and Karl Marx, Tarle the Soviet academician and historian, Joffe the physicist, Ilf the writer, Dubnov the historian, Feuchtwanger the writer and many, many more. Paradoxically, neither Maimonides nor Yehudah Halevi, nor the Baal Shem Tov, nor Rabbi Yochanan ben Zakkai, nor even Mosheh Rabbeinu found themselves on this list. However, at the time I did not notice this tragi-comic paradox.

Naum and Misha often had long arguments analyzing this or that dubious case, for example whether the composer Bizet was Jewish. They composed a separate list of revolutionaries and Communist leaders: Trotsky, Sverdlov, Uritsky, Kautsky, Rosa Luxembourg, Martov, Mekhlis, Volodarsky, Kaganovich, Kamenev, Zinoviyev, etc. Strangely, their clear picture of what Russian Communism was did not exclude the possibility of taking pride in famous Jewish Communists.

In this connection it should be mentioned, moreover, that for them, as for most of other Soviet citizens, the conviction that "the newspapers all lie" did not exclude the belief that there "must be something" in what was written in the newspaper.

Uncle Naum adored newspapers and magazines, and his room was filled with all kinds of collections of complete annual sets, new as well as yellowed by time. He read all kinds of books with great interest, sometimes reading the whole night through. Thanks to his extraordinary memory he was truly encyclopedically informed about the history of Soviet Russia and the Civil, Soviet-Finnish, and Second World Wars; about Soviet literature; about Leningrad, past and present; and, of course, about all questions connected with Soviet Jewry.

10

Attempt to Study Hebrew

A fter a while Uncle Naum obtained for me a book about the Beilis affair (published in the early twenties) and two volumes of a prerevolutionary edition of Dubnov's *General History of the Jews*. By some wonder these books had remained intact at a friend's house, surviving the domestic purges of the dreadful nights of 1937 and 1948.

Dubnov took hold of me, and I read his books several times in succession. This brilliant author's account of the three-thousand-year history of my people stood before me, evoking the events of the present day.

Needless to say, I unqualifiedly accepted all the author's conceptions, not understanding that there is a difference between the traditional Jewish attitude to the holy books and the biblical criticism invented by the Germans and so willingly adopted by the Jewish "enlighteners" – the *Maskilim*.

Following the author, I was convinced that the Five Books of Moses were a literary work, compiled from the creation of many authors living in different epochs, that not King Solomon but an anonymous writer living many hundreds of years later was the author of the Song of Songs, and so forth.

The idea especially pleased me that the numerous strict laws regulating every step of a religious Jew were invented by the authors of the Talmud in order to protect the people, dispersed after the destruction of the ancient Hebrew state, from assimilation and annihilation. This idea so captivated me that I wrote a poem, the last verse of which I remember to this day:

> Praise, praise to the Talmud's creation,
> Able to save us by its sages,
> And to the mortal sons of an eternal nation,
> Showing the way through the darkness of ages.

My sensitivity to everything Jewish sharpened remarkably. At that time there appeared in *Pravda* an article by Ilya Ehrenburg, which unfortunately later became famous. Taking a full page, he argued that there is no Jewish problem in the Soviet Union and that, moreover, according to Leninist-Stalinist doctrine the Jewish people simply doesn't exist. "All the unity of the Jews of other countries," it said, "is based on their oppression. This is the same as if the whole world started to persecute redheaded or snub-nosed people. . . . " Hence it follows that as no one oppresses the Jews in the

Soviet Union, then that which unites them with Jews in other countries no longer exists.

In no way could I reconcile myself with the role of a member of a community of redheads or snub-nosed persons. With even more persistence now I tried to understand what my people was and what was its nonpareil uniqueness, which I was sensing more and more.

At that time anti-Semitism from "above" was increasing, agitating and strengthening anti-Semitism from "below." It became more and more difficult for Jews to enter certain departments of institutes of higher learning and to advance in work. There were cases of arrests and expulsions. There were many rumors about lists of Jews wanting to go to Israel which were given to Stalin by Golda Meyerson [Meir], the first ambassador of the State of Israel to the U.S.S.R. Many terrible stories were told about the fate of the people mentioned on the lists.

About that time I initiated a desperate attempt to renew and to further my knowledge of Hebrew. I was limited to what I remembered from the first grade of the Hebrew Gymnasium nine years before, and this was hardly more than an uncertain knowledge of the alphabet.

I went to the Saltikov-Schedrin Library and, wasting much time roaming through the catalogues, finally found a few textbooks on ancient Hebrew for Russian readers, published in Vilna before the revolution. I spent many hours filling notebook pages with grammatical exercises while also compiling my own Hebrew-Russian dictionary. After hesitating and suffering doubts, I decided to ask a fellow student to join me in these studies. He agreed, and for the two of us the work became a real joy. Whenever we tired, he would take out a book of lyric poetry and I— of the theory of relativity and quantum mechanics.

Soon, however, our work came to an end. One day, when we came to the library and submitted our book order forms, they asked us to follow one of the library workers.

We walked for a long time along dim corridors, through depositories with the heavy smell of old volumes inducing a solemn harmony. Finally, we came to an anonymous office. The man sitting behind the desk was very courteous and smiled a lot. He wanted to know why and with what purpose we were studying ancient Hebrew. Our answers were incoherent—the more so as we ourselves didn't really understand why we were doing this. I simply felt an internal need for it and this feeling had been transferred gradually to my friend.

All this was very displeasing to our interrogator. His face took on a reproachful expression while sweetly and ingratiatingly he requested us to stop the studies.

When I told Uncle Naum about this, he panicked. For him there was no doubt that the danger was serious and that now we had to be quieter than water and lower than grass.

11

Encounter with Philosophy

My study of Hebrew was arrested, but my attraction to all things Jewish grew even stronger. Our nocturnal conversations in the communal apartment on the Petrogradsky side became yet more lengthy and ardent.

On Passover there appeared at our home *matzah,* which, true, we ate alongside bread. On the eve of Yom Kippur I went to the synagogue and then fasted the whole day, continuing to study at the Institute. In the evening, to break the fast, I bought white bread, which I ate while waiting for the tram home from the Institute.

Apart from the technical courses at the Institute everyone was required to study the history of the party. In the *Short Course on the History of the All-Union Communist Party of the Bolsheviks* was a special chapter on dialectical materialism, which was taught in particular detail and depth. We heard lectures and prepared seminars, making abstracts on "Sources," "Questions of Leninism" by Stalin, "Materialism and Empirical Criticism" by Lenin, and so on.

In "Materialism and Empirical Criticism," Kant, Mach, and other philosophers were mentioned. But we were able to discern them only through fragmentary quotations or through the words of instructors who also, of course, did not possess their own copies of the original works of Kant.

From our Institute library, celebrated for its rich collection of books and journals, Mach, Descartes, and Leibnitz had disappeared long ago. I saw with my own eyes how from time to time trucks loaded with shredded and trampled books would pull away from the rear entrance of the library. In these transports the library got rid of, among others, the sixteen-volume *Jewish Encyclopedia* which had still been available during my first days of study at the Institute.

Thus, we stubbornly mastered dialectical materialism. After the mathematics and physics books it was very difficult for me to get used to the Leninist style, where abuse and derision of other opinions replaced proofs.

Gnoseology, the theory of knowledge, seemed to me to be the most vulnerable part of Marxist philosophy. I struggled for a long time over its claim that our sensory organs give us the true representation of things. This claim provoked many questions. For example, where is the guarantee that two different people can experience identical feelings when perceiving the very same thing? The argument against the Marxist theory of knowledge that seemed to be the most important and irrefutable was this: if we assume that the totality of our sensations gives us the complete and true representation of an object, then there must be some sort of higher arbiter who knows beyond sensation what this object is. Thus, one of the main tenets of the materialist theory of knowledge contains an admission of a Higher Being.

I began to hunt for philosophy books. Often I couldn't get hold of the work of a certain philosopher, so I had to make do with books about him—or more often books against him. Whether in depth or superficially, I became acquainted with Plato, Socrates, Heraclitus, Aristotle, Lucretius, Philo of Alexandria, Avicenna, Bacon, Spinoza, Pascal, Descartes, Leibnitz, Fichte, Kant, Hegel, Feuerbach, Mach, and others.

The strength of abstraction and refinement of thought of some philosophers fascinated and delighted me, while the inconsistency and naïveté of others annoyed and perturbed me, but it was always stimulating to read. Without even suspecting it at first, I was searching in philosophy not just for an alternative to dialectical materialism, which had become unacceptable to me. I was searching for a system of views, a world outlook which would give me, among other things, a key to understanding the unique essence and unmatched historical fate of the Jews.

I understood, or rather instinctively felt, that the answers to my questions lay in the realm of the irrational. I was realizing more and more that my searches were bringing me to God, Who chose the Jewish people. Toward this end, reading philosophers could give me only indirect help.

These studies helped me to reject dialectical materialism as a system. But materialistic and atheistic views, criteria, and measures still controlled me. Their basis lay in my belief, absorbed since childhood, in the theory of evolution and in the omnipotence of twentieth-century science.

Books and lectures on physics, astronomy, biology, science-fiction, and paradoxically Dubnov's *General History of the Jewish People* were the real sources feeding my materialistic outlook. How could I have known then that physics, astronomy, biology and, even more so, Jewish history, were by no means identical with materialism and atheism, but—on the contrary—allowed for a directly opposite interpretation—with great success even!

Thus I already understood the absurdity of materialism. I saw through not only the part dealing with gnoseology, but also through its fundamental premise, its desire to turn spirit into a function of material. But I still remained a materialist-atheist, believing that science and modernity itself negate religion.

However, influenced by my strong desire to understand everything Jewish, I gradually became aware of a stronger and stronger need to examine this last thesis. I began to delve into the newest theories in various scientific fields (except for, of course, genetics and cybernetics, which were forbidden by Stalin), searching for clear and direct arguments against religion.

It soon became evident that such arguments don't exist. Already it was becoming clear to me that there is a difference between science, which deals only with the interrelationships of phenomena, and religion, which reveals the essence and purpose of things.

Realizing this difference brought me closer to the conclusion that, as the approaches of religion and science are absolutely different, in principle they cannot contradict one another. I was close then to discovering for myself the difference between "creation from things created" — accessible to science and technology — and *"creatio ex nihilo"* — accessible only to the Most High. Of course, I didn't know these terms then. Only twenty years later was I to learn them from studying Chasidism.

Whatever it was, one of the serious obstacles on the way leading me to Judaism and to Torah was beginning to crumble.

12

Joys of Sciences and of the Arts

F ive years of study at the Polytechnical Institute passed. All these years I studied hard and enthusiastically. During the long winter nights I would sit in the Institute library until it closed. Neither the student drinking parties nor the then so popular evening dances interested me. On the eve of Soviet holidays and the official New Year I found myself the only reader in the enormous reading room.

However, as has been mentioned already, I snatched a great deal of time from my regular studies for philosophic and additional scientific pursuits. In addition, all my group at school was very carried away by art. This was a small group of eleven students, seven of whom were Jews. Together we went to lectures on the history of the fine arts and musicology. We spent innumerable days at the Hermitage and did our best never to miss a concert either in the large or small auditorium of the Philharmonic. For several years we attended fascinating weekly lectures on classical music given most successfully by Entelis the musicologist.

It goes without saying that I stayed in the Komsomol. One school year I was even elected to be my group's organizer. I spoke at meetings and repeated trite phrases dug up from the latest newspaper.

I cannot say that the dishonesty of my behavior upset me in particular. Everybody lied. Lying had long ago become a learned habit. The only alternative was to stand up and declare in front of everyone: "I don't want to pretend, I want to leave the Komsomol," and . . . go to Siberia. Alas, I didn't stand up and declare and, I admit, it never even entered my mind to do so.

While in my third school year I began to work in a hydraulics laboratory. Although at first my role was auxiliary, the very fact of participating in scientific research excited me.

I remember how once in the process of work I planned a simple facility, designed it, and gave the draft to the shop. After several days I received my creation prepared. This impressed me as a miracle. It seemed wondrous that my thought, having been transformed first into a conditional drawing of linear design, suddenly became tangible, existing in reality. My work in the laboratory also brought me greatly needed earnings, which together with a scholarship secured for me a modest but fully comfortable existence.

The oral examinations, which were a calamity for many students, were taken by me as a holiday, as a game of chance. I loved to be examined by instructors with whom an exam was turned into a competition, into single combat on the field of the depth of knowledge and quickness of wit.

In the summer we went for engineering practice in building hydrotechnical structures. These constructions were in vogue as Stalin, "the great architect of Communism," had just decreed the commencement of "great constructions of Communism." This included a number of large scale hydroelectric power stations and also the Volga-Don shipping canal.

I spent the entire summer of 1951 on the construction of this canal. I was in the section adjoining the Don River. To this day I see before my eyes the boundless, sun-scorched dusty steppe on which Kazakh convoys with dogs drove colonies of working convicts stretching out to the very horizon. The heat was over 40 degrees centigrade, but the men worked furiously as one day of labor counted as three regular days of their sentence. I became closely acquainted with many of the convicts and heard hundreds of heart-rending stories. I learned something there about hydrotechnics. But undoubtedly the face-to-face collision with this side of life, hitherto unknown to me but so typical of the Stalinist era, was even more important and instructive.

13

The Doctors' Trial

I completed my studies at the Institute in 1953. Six months before that, a crisis had broken out for Soviet Jewry: the famous "Doctors' Trial."[1]

I remember well the morning ride on the tram—with its windows thickly covered with hoarfrost—on the 13th of January in the year 1953. Every-

---

1. The January 13, 1953, Tass dispatch in *Pravda* "unmasked" nine Jewish doctors for conspiracy. The charges against them included: "espionage" and "terrorist" work as Zionist, American, and British agents; "murder" and "attempted murder by poison" of seven top-ranking military officers; "damage to the health of the Supreme Soviet leaders"; and guilt of having "monstrously trampled on the sacred flag of science." Two of the doctors died under the torture of their "interrogations," but the others were forced to yield the "confessions" planned for them by the secret police. The "Doctors' Trial" set the stage for even more internecine conspiracy and purges within the Kremlin. But all this was abated by the sudden death of Stalin on March 3, 1953.

thing was as usual. The tram crawled through the Viborsky side, squeaking on the curves. I was writing my thesis already and therefore could allow myself to go to the Institute later, after the rush hour had passed. There was even a place for me to sit. I plunged into a book. However, soon I noticed that the heavily wrapped passengers were neither dozing nor reading as usual but were in a state of extreme excitation. Many were conversing heatedly. Through the clangor of the tram the words "Jews" and "Zhids" kept flying at me. I was not able to understand what had happened until I got out at the Institute. Stopping at the first newspaper stand, I found in *Pravda* the notorious communiqué from Tass.

And then it began. . . . Meetings condemning the "doctor-killers" and the "Jewish bourgeois nationalists." Newspaper articles. Newer and newer exposures. If anti-Semitism had prevailed previously with the word "Jew" slyly camouflaged in the expression "rootless cosmopolitan," now suddenly the word was flashing from the newspaper columns.

Quickly, rumors spread about trains being prepared for a mass expulsion of Jews to Siberia. The masses revelled more and more in the permissibility of open anti-Semitism.

Once when I was traveling home late in the evening from the Institute, I was thrown out of the moving tram, accused of trying to stop it with the emergency brake. By a miracle I succeeded in staying on my feet.

Then Stalin died months later, and the "Doctors' Trial" subsided. Undoubtedly the "trial" and its preceding prolonged struggle against "rootless cosmopolitans" promoted a strengthening of my Jewish feelings. At the time of Stalin's death my fondest dream was to reach the promised land of Israel. I remember in that winter of 1952–53 Jaffa oranges arrived at the food store where Uncle Naum worked. He said that the store employees labored deep into the night, destroying the paper coverings in which the oranges had been wrapped. He did not succeed in bringing papers, but he did bring some oranges. It seemed sacrilege to me to eat fruit grown under the sky which was beckoning and calling so. Even though being able to go to Israel some day was not simply unrealizable but even totally naïve to dream about, nevertheless I was returning incessantly in my thoughts to this subject.

During my vacations, spent in Riga, these sentiments were strengthened still more. No matter how strong the official forced standardization in all the provinces of the Soviet Union, in Riga it was still possible to find Jews who were not so brainwashed. Some of them, in a small group of confidants cautiously glancing at a portrait of the "Great Leader," sometimes dared to relate the contents of the last B.B.C. broadcast and sometimes even to talk about Israel. I talked a lot about this subject with my sister's husband, Mark Israeli, a survivor of the ghetto and a German concentration camp. I was very friendly with him.

Once, while in Riga, somehow I got hold of a prayerbook—a *siddur* with Russian translation. Behind the words of the prayers, as I struggled to make out the Hebrew text letter by letter, clarifying its meaning with the help of the Russian translation only when absolutely stuck, a world of cosmic conceptual depth, immense thought, and eternal truth were intimated to me. In this old Vilna edition there were not only translations of the prayers but also some Jewish laws and rules were given. I began to feel discomfort that whereas in theory I was so devoted to the ideas and the spirit of Jewish learning, in practice I hardly fulfilled any of the instructions of this teaching. I began to try to carry something out. My conceptions about the Jewish laws were confused and contradictory, drawn sometimes even from such sources as the stories of Sholom Aleichem. As a result, at the student dining hall I stopped ordering pork schnitzel and requested that butter not be put on the potato puree served with beef goulash. Little did I suspect then that in Jewish law this beef in itself was no less unkosher than the pork which I had turned down.

14

The Diploma of an Engineer

Not long before school finished, we were assigned to places of work. A special commission, headed by a high-ranking official from the Ministry of Higher Education, conducted the assignment. Beforehand, a list had been compiled with the names arranged in decreasing order of the student's scholastic and social achievements. In corresponding order to the list, we had to enter the hall where the commission sat. Supposedly, everyone had the right to choose from the number of places of work left at the moment that his turn came. I was second on the list. Since they had informed us that there were four places open for doctoral studies, I was confident that I would remain as a graduate student in the department of hydraulics. However, when they started calling the students, something strange happened. They didn't call me, not second and not third. I burst into the hall. Stuttering from excitement, I began to explain that probably through a misunderstanding they had forgotten to call me. No one said anything, but two husky fellows seized me by the shoulders and threw me back into the corridor.

They called me seventh and told me that I was being offered work at the all-union institute of the paper industry, Giprobum. I started to protest, and a corpulent man in a military uniform with shoulder straps of a lieutenant-general, looking at me with disdain and condemnation, said: "Offer him Vorkuta, [Siberia]; then he'll agree quickly to Giprobum."

I did not agree to or sign anything. Nevertheless it turned out later that my appointment as an engineer at Giprobum had been confirmed without my consent. The only thing that I could gain at this institute was that Riga was among the many cities in which it had branches.

In the middle of the summer of 1953, when the white nights were waning, I defended my thesis on "The Two-Hundred-Thousand Kilowatt Kopchagaysky Hydroelectric Station on the Ili River," received a diploma "with distinction," and went to Riga. Of all the thesis projects on electric power stations proposed to us, I had chosen the one on the Ili because this river flows through a desert. I wished to believe that by working on this project I was acquiring experience which I would someday be able to make use of in my homeland. . . .

15

I Go Ahead with Research

T he university was behind me and a diploma "with distinction" was in my pocket, but this did not bring me much satisfaction. Ahead of me lay the sweat of Giprobum—planning the construction of paper factories—whereas my thoughts and dreams were riveted toward two alluring summits. One was called science, creation, discovery; the other—Israel. A way to Israel didn't exist. And the way to science was blocked by many barriers.

I ran to various seminars at the Latvian University, enrolled in correspondence courses at the physics-mathematics department, and took innumerable examinations. At work, putting the sketches aside, I would fill piles of paper with hydrodynamic equations, trying to solve a practical problem which engrossed my attention: the flooding of a hydraulic jump.

Somebody gave me the results of an experiment, the theoretical solution of which was yet to be found. All at once it dawned on me; with a very simple and logical assumption, the solution was obtained. With a palpitating heart I began to substitute the experimental data into the formula obtained. The agreement was perfect. My head was spinning and everything inside me was singing. I felt myself a master of nature; it was obediently subjugated to the offspring of my reason. I was reminded of the words of LaPlace: "When a mathematical solution, proven by experiment, becomes a law of nature, this brings the highest delight available to man."

I wanted terribly to continue the work, to expand it, and to conduct additional experiments. In an abandoned basement hydraulics laboratory at the Latvian University I was allowed, for a certain fee, to conduct experiments. I managed to leave Giprobum and to be appointed an instructor in a college. In order to pay for the experiments, I took on additional work. But with two jobs I could make it to the laboratory only late in the evenings.

16

I Meet Fania and We Share Zionist Aspirations

A little while before this I had become acquainted with Fania, my future wife. On the first days of our acquaintance I flooded her with discourse about Jews, Judaism, and Israel. She received it all favorably, with interest— even my philosophic profusions. Thus she passed the principal test, as I saw it, and soon the question of our marriage was decided. True, as I shall narrate later, this marriage was postponed for many years, and the reason was again our longing for Israel.

Fania was studying medicine, but in the evening she would selflessly assist in my experiments on hydrodynamics, sitting in the damp, dank basement sometimes until dawn.

In keeping with an old Leningrad custom, I began to accompany Fania to the museum and to symphony concerts. Her parents, who were as far from Zionism as they were from symphonic music, started to call me "the symphonist."

After a while I summarized all the theoretical and experimental data of my research into a long article, which was published in the scientific journal of the Latvian Academy. It was a joy to hold my first printed work in my hands. I made poor Fania read the entire article. She heroically did this, wishing to please me. From the professional point of view, the article was quite well received. Continuing the experiments and preparing subsequent articles, I proceeded toward writing a dissertation. In this way, it was becoming possible actually to receive a degree without being enrolled in graduate school.

However, before I had time to complete the dissertation, events of an entirely different nature overwhelmed me. 1956 was the year of Israel's Sinai Campaign. It was also the year of the Hungarian revolt against the Soviet regime, which was so brutally suppressed.

In that same year, there convened in Moscow the famous Twentieth Congress of the Communist Party at which Khrushchev spoke for the first time about the "cult of the personality" of Stalin. Whether in connection with these events or independent of them, the end of 1956 was marked by a sharp intensification of interest in Israel among a certain segment of Jewish youth in Riga.

In November or December of 1956 Fania and I were invited for the first time to a gathering at someone's house where the main subject of the evening was Israel. What went on there threw us into a state of great excitement. This was so unlike the usual parties of young people always so repulsive to me, where they drank, danced and joked. Here reigned an idea, an outburst of spirit. We heard tape recordings of Israel radio broadcasts about the Sinai Campaign. We dreamed aloud about going to Israel. We also heard records of Yiddish songs and somebody recited a Shalom Aleichem story from memory.

An argument began. Most of the people present considered "*galut* melodies" and the Yiddish language to be obsolete and devoid of significance in an age when the history of the Jewish people was being created in the State of Israel and written in Hebrew.

The very possibility of discussing these subjects in a large—albeit carefully chosen—company evoked in us delight and giddiness. We dispersed intoxicated by the whole experience. It is true though that anxiety was mixed with our happiness and that every unexpected knock on the door aroused highly unpleasant feelings. However, as time went on and nobody came to arrest us, we became bolder and more resolute.

Rumors soon cropped up that Gomulka, who had then come into power in Poland, had made an agreement with Khrushchev allowing former Polish citizens who had gotten stuck in the Soviet Union during or after the Second World War to return to Poland. Allegedly, the agreement pertained also to Jews who had once been Polish citizens. Not long afterward, the agreement was actually published. This was staggering! Walking on the streets side by side with us were people who had the official right to leave Soviet Russia. It was known also that Poland at that time hardly hindered the departure of Jews to Israel. Who could have imagined this a year before?

The only misfortune was that neither Fania nor myself ever had even the most remote connection with Poland.

It didn't take us long to decide what to do. As a first step it was resolved that our wedding would be put off indefinitely. Instead, each of us would register a marriage with a former Polish citizen and go with our fictitious husband and wife to Poland, so that in the end we could reunite in our homeland.

We were breathtaken by these plans. Everything changed. All our commitments were reevaluated. In particular, my dissertation, which was already prepared by then, became the first sacrifice of the new initiative. I made this sacrifice without regret. The problem consisted of how to find a suitable bride and groom. Fania had barely reached twenty years of age. Her parents especially feared that we would lose each other in the big world, so they insisted that the bride and groom be sister and brother. This complicated the search for candidates even more.

Despairing of finding someone suitable in Riga, I decided to set forth to Vilna—a city that had belonged to Poland before the war. Having acquired the address of some Vilna Jews with whom I could start my search, and having received a few days' leave from my college, I set out on my way. In the city I was introduced to some Vilniusites, and as they were all connected to a circle of people thinking about Israel, I got the impression that all of Vilna was taken over by departure fever.

Families already preparing for the journey disappointed me. In my opinion, they should have been rejoicing, singing, and taking interest only in getting the official papers faster and in finding themselves on the other side of the border. When I imagined someone crossing the despicable armed border unhindered, my heart stopped beating and was filled with an inexpressibly sweet quivering. But these people for the most part were depressed and irritated. From morning to night they were running to stores, buying, and packing.

I visited dozens of families, but having gotten nowhere, I returned to Riga. After a week I went again. In the course of two months I visited Vilna no less than ten times. A few times I went together with Fania. The "fiancés" we found were not at all suitable: either they asked for sums of money that I wouldn't be able to scrape together in twenty years, or they declared that they were ready to marry Fania and take her away, but the marriage had to be "for real." I went to Kovno a few times also, but again to no avail.

Unexpectedly, a suitable choice turned up in Riga. One of our Rigan acquaintances was married to a pure-blooded Polish woman. In the time being described here—the early spring of 1957—her brother Yusek came to visit her. He was not yet thirty years old. As it turned out, he lived in the province of Koshalin in the town of Slupsk, together with his mother and unmarried sister Rufina. I could not have dreamed of a better choice. Yusek had come to Riga not only to see his sister. He dreamed of buying an automobile in Russia and taking it back to Poland. Therefore he was looking for a way of earning money.

We quickly came to an agreement. The plan was simple. Fania and I would immediately stop seeing each other and allow rumors to spread among all our acquaintances and relatives about our quarrel. Fania would start to appear in public with Yusek and go with him to the evening dances at the medical institute where she studied. Afterward Yusek would return to Poland and send his sister Rufina to Riga, and then I would play at falling in love at first sight. For all this, I would pay Yusek a sum of 22,500 rubles—enough to buy a car plus some other little things.

Everything went as planned. Fania got "married," appeared everywhere with Yusek, was photographed with him a lot, and incessantly shared her raptures with her girlfriends. Eventually, taking with him a brand-new auto-mobile, he left—and letters started coming. The letters were clumsy and primitive, but we were satisfied that the KGB was registering the mere fact of their arrival. As none of Fania's friends knew Polish, these letters could be displayed fearlessly, and they made their impression.

Soon my bride Rufina arrived. I promenaded her through all the boulevards and parks of Riga, dying to run into acquaintances and colleagues. Finally we went to register our marriage. After the registration I moved into the apartment of Rufina's sister. Her relatives were exasperated by my excessive caution and anxiety. They considered the marriage registration quite enough and that acting out a play was unnecessary. I did not yield, and they did not want to give me a bed. So I started to pass the night in their hallway on the floor, fully dressed, stretched out over newspapers.

17

The Collapse of the Polish Epopee

In October 1957, Rufina left. I ran along the platform after the departing train enacting the part of the tormented separated lover. However, I quite sin-cerely did dream of the time when I would once again see that annoying Polish woman, but on the other side of the border. From that day on I wrote innumer-able letters, taking great pains to describe in many lines my unbounded passion. Fania had long since received an invitation from Yusek, but she had not submitted an exit application as it had been decided that I must try to leave first. Finally, an invitation arrived for me from Rufina. By then I had already informed my superiors and fellow teachers at the college that my young wife was pregnant and despite all my reluctance to leave Russia, I was compelled to hasten to Poland so as not to miss the birth.

The director easily gave me the recommendation required for submitting an exit application. I handed in the papers, but somehow I was not totally confident and did not feel any triumph. After a few months they summoned me by telephone, but alas not to the same department of the police where applications are handed in, but to the KGB.

At the appointed hour I traveled to the KGB building by trolley-bus. This was to be my first personal acquaintance with this legendary institution, and, I confess, the prospect did not delight me. Before the stop where I had to get off, a woman standing behind me asked if I was getting off. I thought to myself: "With what pleasure I would let you get off here, while I travel as far away as the eye can see—as long as it is away from that dreadful house." However, taking myself in hand, I got off the trolley-bus. The not-so-warming but bright March sun was shining as I walked. . . . I wondered when I would see it again.

I was received by an employee whom I recognized without difficulty as an old fellow student from the tenth grade of high school. He had a funny last name—Riyabokon ("spotted horse" in Russian). As a classmate he had been distinguished by tempestuous behavior and insolence and especially had vexed our mathematics teacher.

Another employee quickly joined Riyabokon, and they began to vie with one another in interrogating me. They started round-about, but gradually they focused entirely on Rufina. They obstinately insisted that the marriage was fictitious. "You wanted to take advantage of her, she wanted to take advantage of you, and she outsmarted you," one of them told me. I categorically denied all the accusations and tried desperately to figure out what they were aiming at. The interrogation went on for many hours—right up until evening, and the next day—the same thing over again. They started to suggest that my so-called "wife" had lost her passport before leaving Riga and in receiving a new one had not indicated on it that she had gotten married in Riga.

I was convinced that they were trying to provoke me, and I continued to deny everything. In the end they made me write out a written explanation and released me. Riyabokon went with me to the corridor. He took me gingerly under the arm and, whispering in my ear, said: "Please, I talk out of friendship toward you. If there is anything not so—admit it. It will be better for you." I again repeated that I knew nothing and demanded that they put me in touch with my wife.

Leaving the KGB, I rushed to Rufina's sister. How great was my surprise and despair when it became evident that Rufina actually had lost her passport and, receiving a new one, had not indicated that we were married. "She was afraid that after returning to Poland, Mama would see it registered in her passport," her sister explained.

Thus, our grandiose plot collapsed in a most foolish manner. Nevertheless, psychologically, I simply was not able then to reduce myself to being resigned to the necessity of living out all my days in the Soviet Union, breathing the suffocating air of lies—never to see the Holy Land.

I went out of my way to write love letters to Rufina, and, in accordance, I continued to pretend a total break with Fania. It should be mentioned that ever since the beginning of our "Polish epic" we not only did not meet in public, but we did not even speak together on the telephone. We saw each other once every two weeks in a basement laboratory of the college where I worked. This basement accommodated the student physics laboratory, which I directed. The key to it was held only by me. In order to agree upon the day and hour of a meeting, we worked out a whole conspiratorial system. I would call Fania from a public telephone on the street. Changing my voice, I delivered a message which had nothing to do with our rendezvous. She would hang up the receiver, and then I would call again. Instead of lifting it up again, she would count the number of rings. Thus I would relay the day, and then the hour of our meeting.

We made our ways separately to the basement laboratory, under the cover of darkness, and checking that no one was following. In this same basement I buried large polythene wrapped packages of my manuscripts on philosophical and Jewish subjects. The wrapping, incidentally, did not work. Some years later when I extracted the manuscripts, it turned out that the dampness had seeped in and all the letters had run together, making it impossible to read.

Now, after our fiasco, we still continued to see each other only in secret in the basement, as we were afraid to put an end to what at first had seemed to be a hope of being freed from slavery. It went on like this until 1961 when all hope for the Polish alternative was lost and Fania and I acted out a farce in front of our friends of making up. At this time we were married, secretly, according to Jewish law—nearly five years later than we had intended to when the delusive ray of hope had flashed, seemingly opening the way to the Holy Land.

The *chuppah* was held in the town of Dvinsk. We flew there and back all within a few hours. By that time I already knew that the Rogachev Gaon, one of the greatest Jewish minds of our time, had lived there before the war. This was one of our reasons for wanting to have the wedding ceremony there.

Tshernov, the "*shammes*" of the Dvinsk synagogue, and his aide performed the wedding at the *shammes*'s home. Several more Jews were collected from the street and thus we had a *minyan*. We shared with these unknown people the wine and cake we had brought from Riga. They presented us with all their warmth and a most cordial *mazal tov*. We only registered our marriage officially, according to Soviet law, one and a half years later.

18

Hebrew Studies and Beauty of Nature Comfort Me

The wreck of our hopes of emigration brought me to a most difficult spiritual crisis. I was in a state of deepest depression. Everything seemed meaningless, pointless, hopeless. Going on with life in the Soviet Union became simply unthinkable, but to devise a new utopian loophole did not appear possible. There were hours when, as if dreaming, I pictured us in Israel. Nothing could be sweeter than these hours, imagining myself a proud citizen, forgetting about anti-Semitism and above all physically perceiving the Holy Land! But even more bitter was waking up each time to find myself enveloped in a fog of hopelessness, obscuring not only the horizons but also the things closest to me. Desperately wallowing in the fog, I would break out of it only to have it thicken and close in on me again.

It perplexed me how people around me were able to live quiet philistine lives, being happy, laughing. It shocked me how comfortably they adjusted themselves to the all-pervading lies, how with serious mien they were able to read Soviet newspapers and to listen to official radio broadcasts instead of howling like wild animals in insult and disgust. In no way could I understand why the human stomach reacts immediately with indigestion at the smallest quantity of spoiled food, whereas the brain day after day digests tons of thoroughly rotten information with impunity.

A few factors, however, kept me from falling into madness. There were, first of all, the wise and good exhortations of my mother, who, herself a staunch pessimist, always found words of encouragement for me. The countenance of my ever-patient wife Fania kept me from complete frustration. Furthermore, my philosophical work and my communion with nature saved me.

I was brought closer and closer to Judaism. Questions of gnoseology continued to occupy me. As before, I pondered and read much about the correlations between the rational and the transcendental. But it was becoming increasingly clearer that it was impossible to separate the Jewish people and Judaism from the fundamental and seemingly abstract problems of philosophy. On the contrary, the answer to all questions decisively lay in their profound interconnection.

I had an abysmal lack of knowledge about Judaism. I started to go to the synagogue every Saturday. What I saw and heard there spoke to my heart, although to a great extent it remained incomprehensible. In particular, I did not have the slightest notion about the internal construction of the prayers. I remember that I was so struck by the harmony and order of the service and by how flawlessly the participants knew the responsibilities and times of their performances that I was convinced that the services were preceded by special rehearsals.

At this time I was still riding on public transportation on the Sabbath and turning lights on and off, but nevertheless I tried to devote my free hours on Saturday to studies that seemed to me to be connected with a Jewish theme. I read books on Jewish history or even simply lingered over the letters of the Hebrew alphabet.

I obtained a teach-yourself textbook, and Fania and I began to study Hebrew. I also continued to hunt for prayer books and other Jewish religious books with Russian translation. It was terribly difficult to procure such books, but, even worse, the translations helped very little. I felt that the clumsy language of these translations—much resembling Church Slavonic—revealed only the exterior meaning of these holy books. Their true content, their living soul, seemed to have been hopelessly lost.

Therefore I persistently continued to reread ten or twelve times the original ancient Hebrew text. Even though I understood only one word out of ten, and that with difficulty, this clarified more for me than the translation. Here every simple and modest word bore, besides a practical and worldly meaning, a whole world of profound associations and philosophical categories. An aroma of simple wisdom and pure holiness wafted from these words, whereas in the Russian translation the depth was lost, the holiness turned into sanctimoniousness and the purity and uprightness into hypocrisy.

I also became more and more keenly aware of the need for commentaries, for someone wise and perceptive of the depth of Torah to help me and guide me. Not having such a teacher, I would struggle for hours with a single phrase, not perceiving its connection and correlation with the other parts of the teaching.

Contact with the Torah healed my desperation. It raised me above time, space and borders and united me with Israel in a unity over which the KGB had no control.

Ever since childhood, when I would walk with my father through the forests and fields surrounding the farm, I have felt a deep affinity for nature. Nature was for me not an ornament, not a work of art summoning delight, but a living partner in mutual love. And every time that people offended me, this love would be especially strengthened. The dense mossy forests, saturated with moisture and the scent of mushrooms, called me; the meadows motley with flowers and butterflies beckoned. Every year as soon as spring awakened, a deep yearning for nature would drive me away from the lifeless and apathetic stones of the city to the fields and gardens—to where life was being born and triumphing, where the scents of the reviving earth inebriated and melted the soul, releasing exultant hymns to the Creator. Fear of being late for the festival of spring would overcome me. This festival was composed of many events— each one more meaningful than the next. It seemed to me a crime not to witness every one of them.

One morning the trees awake from their slumber amidst the finest lace of sticky baby leaves, and then the bird-cherry tree blossoms in a frenzy, and then the nightingales sing, starting as they ought at night, but, carried away, they continue on the whole day through, and then the lilac blooms, and then the very last to turn green are the pensive, solid oaks, and then . . . Thus spring ends, flying away with the poplar down. The linden trees then burst into blossom and their honeyed aroma penetrates into the cities, flooding the streets, streaming into windows and prevailing over soot and stench.

Now the frenzy in nature yields its place to efficiency—there is so much to be done, you see, in the short northern summer. At sunrise work begins for the birds and the insects, and for those people who still understand that bread grows in the fields and that rain does not just ruin outings but is primarily a blessing for the harvest.

Especially I loved the twilight hours, when the rays of the low sun, setting through the leaves of the emerald-saturated trees, suffused the earth with quietude and subdued light. The last breezes calm down. For some time the lowing of cows returning from pasture and the barking of dogs are heard from a nearby farm and then these voices, too, subside. The earth pulsates, pacified, tired from the day's accomplishments and satisfied with them. In a while, hiding in the cold low places of the dark, tree boughs start to quiver from the awakening night winds, arousing secret nocturnal rustles. And then—silence. And it seems that the world is meditating on the harmony and wisdom of creation.

Autumn evokes the same quiet and peace of the summer twilight hours, extended for many weeks. Weakened from its summer labors, the sun begins to caress and redden the seasoned apples. Long threads of gossamer float in the air until the red-golden carpet of fallen leaves, smelling like strongly brewed tea, is covered by hoarfrost.

The chasteness and purity of nature healed my soul from the poison of cynicism, cruelty and lies which I had to breathe day after day. Moreover, contemplation of the forests and fields led me to thoughts of their Creator and engendered infinite thankfulness and a need to pray to Him.

In the course of a few years, to the extent that I slowly became liberated from my feelings of depression, meaninglessness, and hopelessness through the help of these curative influences, so did I progress in the practical observance of Jewish laws. In particular, I finally came to understand the basic rules of *kashrut.* I bought some new plates, spoons, and forks. For a long time I abstained entirely from meat. Finally, I found an underground butcher who sold kosher meat from time to time. Keeping kosher, despite all the inconveniences connected to it, brought me great moral satisfaction and the feeling of honestly and voluntarily fulfilling my obligations.

19

Beginning of Jewish Activities

T oward the beginning of the sixties there were already several dozen Jews in Riga who displayed their interest in Israel quite openly. They exchanged

Israeli books, brochures, calendars. They reproduced copies of old books by Chaim Nachman Bialik and Ze'ev Jabotinsky. They gathered together to hear Israeli records or to learn Hebrew.

Fania and I participated in numerous meetings of that nature, although we were put off by their salon style, by their mixing of the holy and the eternal with exhibitions of awful Philistinism and sometimes with the most banal flirting.

The capture and trial of Eichmann had great influence upon the consciousness of many Jews. Memories of the still-recent tragedy of the Jewish people were stirred up strongly anew. Many Jews who had been listening regularly to Israel radio now did not budge from their receivers while the trial was on. For entire evenings they would listen to the Hebrew, Yiddish, Russian, and English broadcasts in succession.

About that time the Rumbula episode came to light. Rumbula is the name of a small railroad station twelve kilometers east of Riga. This name is one of a dreadful series of words like Auschwitz, Treblinka, Babi Yar, Ponari.

In the fall of 1941, in the pine grove opposite the station, the Germans, with the enthusiastic participation of Latvians, exterminated the entire population of the Riga ghetto. Nine abysmal graves hold nearly fifty thousand victims. This place remained absolutely abandoned and was known to very few. Finally, a group of Jews took it upon themselves to bring some order to this fraternal burial ground. With the help of Bella Michelson who miraculously had survived and crawled out of one of these graves almost twenty years before, they searched for the site. Only the extraordinarily thick, high grass growing on them marked out the graves.

At first the group was small in number. It included the lawyer Garber and his wife; the engineer Getz; the young, ardent and unrestrainable Marek Bloom (who appropriately changed his last name after arriving in Israel to "Lapid" – meaning torch); the architect Rachlin and his son (a clever boy, passionately in love with Israel, who was later the victim of Soviet secret-police persecution that led to his tragic death); the artist Kuzkovsky (of blessed memory); Ezra Rusinek, and others.

The true spirit and motivating force of all this was Samuel Tzeitlin, whom everyone called "Bubi." Bubi was connected with Zionism when yet a youth, before the Soviets entered Latvia. Then, fighting the war in the ranks of the Red Army, he was badly wounded. He was arrested while still in hospital and "resettled" in a Soviet camp for many years. Finally returning to Riga, Bubi remained a bachelor. He worked as a dental technician, which, without burdening him too much, secured him a modest subsistence. He knew absolutely everyone and would sit almost until daybreak visiting with friends and acquaintances, endlessly telling concentration camp stories, debating urgent Jewish topics, and consuming an entire bottle of vodka each night. Reputed to be a great eccentric, he made fun of everyone, himself included. He went about in a torn and threadbare coat and maintained touching relationships with his former camp inmates, including several priests. And he knew how to help dozens of Jewish families and to disseminate hundreds of Jewish books.

Rumbula became his lifework. He endeavoured to obtain the maximum possible support from the Soviet authorities. Wondrously, he convinced them to allow the construction of a memorial, and even obtained some money for the project.

The work at Rumbula became a weekly activity. Every Sunday a few hundred people would gather together, a great many of whom were young boys and girls born after the war. They paved walk-ways, cleared the site, and leveled the earth. A wonderful atmosphere of solidarity, brotherhood, and spiritual uplift reigned. At first it depressed me to be at this terrible place where at each step the earth turned up a bone, a child's shoe. The squeak of the pine trees swayed by the wind seemed to me to be the anguished sighs of those shot down. Even hours after coming home, I was not in a condition to return to ordinary activity. Dragging heavy barrows of gravel, I thought: with what joy would I be working within this circle of brothers if we were not unearthing a cemetery but, for example, building a synagogue. It shocked me how these tender boys who had not yet sprouted beards could be singing songs, here at this grove of death and despair. Sometimes they even nibbled apples carelessly while standing right on a grave. But gradually I got used to this, learning to suppress my feelings. The fact was that these boys working here were progress- ing rapidly in developing Jewish feelings. This seemed to me to be a compensa- tion for the tragedy of the ghetto. It was a fitting memorial for the annihilated.

Having finished work, the people would congregate. Someone would read or chant the memorial prayer for the dead, another would deliver a short improvised speech, a third read his own poetry. From time to time the speeches grew bolder. The spirit of the Rumbula Sundays prevailed over many Jewish families in Riga and gradually—through relatives and friends—it was spread to Moscow, to Leningrad.

It didn't take much time until Rumbula drew the attention of the authorities. Henceforth we worked under the strict surveillance not only of the secret police but also of the regular police, as well as of cadets from military academies. The after-work meetings were broken up. The homemade monuments on the graves—often an enormous star of David twisted out of barbed wire—were destroyed.

A special storm was raised by the attempt to place a tombstone upon which was written in Yiddish: *"Di korbones foon Fascism"* (the victims of fascism). The authorities demanded that the inscription be done in Russian and that the slain be called "Soviet Citizens." It was rumored that a special ideological commission of the Central Committee of the Communist Party came from Moscow to Riga just for this.

The finished stone with the Jewish inscription was confiscated. However, Bubi and his friends stole the stone from the engraver's at night, placed it on its prepared site, and photographed it. The next day these photographs were seen in foreign newspapers, and the authorities decided to give in.

This stone is still standing.

Twice a year—in autumn at the anniversary of the extermination of the ghetto and in spring at the anniversary of the victory over the Germans—thousands of Jews congregate at the Rumbula cemetery. The authorities break up these meetings, arresting the speakers. Policemen wail into loudspeakers set up all around so that the speakers can't even hear their own voices. They surround the entire grove with tanks and cannons and then tell anyone who tries to approach that war exercises are being conducted.

But in every instance the authorities are the losers. Their opposition inflames the feelings of even the most apathetic Jews.

There is no doubt that Rumbula was one of the most important factors in the awakening of the "Silent Jews" of Soviet Russia, an awakening which subsequently led many thousands of them toward emigration to Israel.

20

Institute of Physics and My Ph.D. Work

To the extent that I recovered from the shock caused by the failure of our attempt to escape through Poland and began to reconcile myself with the thought that we still had many more years in the Soviet Union, I began to remember my abandoned scientific work. I started to think about a new dissertation to replace the previous one, sacrificed to the hope of leaving the country. A friend told me that in the Physics Institute of the Latvian Academy of Sciences they were beginning to develop a new field of study—magnetohydrodynamics. This term was absolutely new for me, but as it included the word hydrodynamics, it seemed quite likely that I could fit into this field. When I went to the library to clarify what magnetohydrodynamics is, it turned out that this term did not yet appear in even the large encyclopedic dictionaries. Nevertheless, I finally found out that magnetohydrodynamics is the study of the movement of electroconductive fluids in the presence of a magnetic field. Based on the two classical sciences of hydrodynamics and electrodynamics, it can be applied to astrophysics, geophysics, flow-measuring techniques, to different aspects of metallurgy, and finally to the production of electrical power.

I went to the Institute of Physics and told them of my earlier experience in measuring the velocity of flows and turbulent pulsations. To my great surprise, the head of one of the laboratories and director of the Institute literally grabbed me. Certain that because of the blots on my personal record they would not accept me for work at the Academy, I told them that at present I could not leave the technical college, but consented to work at the Physics Institute part-time at half salary. And that is what was agreed.

As a new branch of science, magnetohydrodynamics was full of yet unexplored problems with wide ranges of opportunity for research initiative. When I began the work, I didn't at all expect that within a few months my experiments would yield such abundant results. In less than a year I published more than ten articles and presented lectures at several conferences.

In early 1962 I defended a dissertation on turbulent magnetohydrodynamic flows at the Moscow Institute of Aviation. I was spending more and more time at the Academy. I was becoming acquainted with more and more dignitaries of the scientific world of Moscow and Leningrad.

In connection with my work I had to read not only about hydrodynamics, but also about various fields of physics and astrophysics. All this brought me back again to an analysis of the mission and limitations of the natural sciences. I contrasted and compared "world culture and science" with the teaching of my people, illustrious figures of science with the sages and luminaries of Judaism.

I was drawing closer and closer to formulating my own unified world outlook. But it was necessary to collect and systematize my disparate thoughts, to make a written account of my philosophy. On one hand I didn't have time to do this, and on the other it was a pity to write something only to burn it or to bury it in the basement to be ruined by dampness. It seemed quite risky to keep at home manuscripts full of disproof of Leninism, now that at the insistence of the director I had become a regular employee of the Physics Institute, which was cooperating with security-cleared facilities. It seemed especially risky when my Polish escapade was taken into consideration, as well as my participation in pro-Israel evenings, my working at Rumbula, and going to the synagogue on Saturdays.

In early 1963 I broke my leg and found myself on a forced leave of absence for several months. At that time the temptation to pour out the fruits of my many years of reflections finally won out.

I wrote night and day, crossing out, tearing up what was written and writing again. I finished all the work in a few weeks. When I had almost finished writing, we received notice that one of my relatives living in Tel Aviv was intending to come for a visit. Soon we learned that a relative from Fania's side was also coming, later. The prospect of meeting with Israelis, relatives at that, was very exciting. But as all my thoughts were riveted on my manuscript, the temptation overcame me to make use of the coming visits to send it to Israel. Just the thought of it made my heart stop beating. My reverence toward the Holy Land and everything connected to it was immeasurable. Religiously I collected not only stamps and postcards from Israel, but even candy wrappers that accidentally fell into my hands. And now suddenly it became possible that my beloved, long-nurtured creation could reach the Promised Land! Copying my work into a thick notebook, I waited eagerly for the relatives to arrive.

21

My First Essay on Philosophy, Science, and Judaism

And so the quintessence of years of searching, doubting, and transcending lifelong prejudices found independent existence in the form of a thick notebook with a dark-blue leatherette cover, filled with fine handwriting. The main question to which I addressed myself was the truth or falseness of the thesis that the brilliant modern natural sciences and technology disprove and preclude religious faith.

From early childhood, long before I became fascinated by physics and even before my familiarity with Darwinism turned into zealous belief in evolution, I had assumed this thesis to be self-evident. All the people around me, of all ages and walks of life, regardless of their level of education or station in society, adamantly accepted this thesis as true. Whether staunch Communists or former sympathizers who had become literally fed-up with Communism (as was more often the case), the people around me all concurred in the belief that atheism is both inevitable and necessary "in our enlightened times." Yet no one bothered to think about the origin of this blind belief. No one was ready to go to the trouble of finding out whether this belief was justified. Although so many of the concepts and theses of Communism had turned out to be nonsense when applied to life, it did not occur to anyone to question the notorious thesis that science replaces religion.

It is interesting to note that at the time when I was writing all this, I did not yet know that Ben-Gurion had often claimed that "science makes us atheists." Not only had he often repeated this wretched thesis, but he constructed the State of Israel and its system of public education upon its basis.

The first goal of my philosophical study was to explain how modern man forms a world outlook which leads him on to blind atheism and materialism. Examining the various methods of how consciousness is formed in my contemporaries, I reached the conclusion that materialism and atheism are foisted upon us. Most people are brainwashed into becoming materialistic atheists from a very young age, through their upbringing and education, and never make any effort to ascertain the truth. But as even the most conditioned and submissive human mind nevertheless retains a minimal amount of curiosity, sufficient to ask a question or two, the initiation into atheism occurs simultaneously with the deification of science.

"Science has proven that . . ." sounds so solid, so imposing, so comfortable, so contemporary and useful in building up our self-satisfaction as representatives of this enlightened age. It does not matter if one never actually studied science or if one studied some years ago merely to pass exams and then forgot it. It does not matter that one has no idea about religion when he renounces it. All that matters for modern man is that science exists and scientists exist who have studied everything and know everything and have answered all the questions.

My second goal was to show what the natural sciences *can do* and what they *cannot do* because of the limits of their very essence. Here I had to investigate how the basic assumptions of any given science and thus the subsequent results of this science and the world picture it provides correspond to the real world.

The most important point for me to prove was that no science is capable of even touching upon the *essence* of things. Using symbols made to correspond to actual objects, science can study interactions between things. Science can make generalizations from the *phenomena* in which these things function. But it can never answer questions like "What *is* object *x?* What is its purpose?" (questions the answers to which are given solely through Divine revelation).

Then I further demonstrated how and why these and other limitations of science do not prevent it from succeeding when applied to practical use. In exactly the same way our orientation in the world and the actions we perform in it do not alter the fact that we have absolutely no concept of what lies behind the sensual images through which we perceive the material world around us and our own corporeal envelope.

While analyzing the question of the objectiveness of our perceptions, I was struck by the revelation that the very essence of philosophical materialism spells out its own obvious disproof. The materialist theory of cognition, which categorically claims that the universe can be known, is based upon the assumption that the aggregate of our sensory organs gives us a true picture of the world. In other words, the materialist theory of knowledge maintains that the human senses enable us to know the world "as it really is." Such shortsightedness! This claim categorically requires the acknowledgment of the existence of a Higher Power, a Supreme Arbiter, Who knows for sure "how the world really is" and can pit our partial knowledge against His absolute knowledge! Thus the fundamental premise of dialectical materialism inevitably leads to the recognition of the existence of God!

A large part of my essays was devoted to dispelling the artificial aureole surrounding the hypnotizing concepts of "science" and "scientists." In reality the craft of the scientist is in principle no different from that of a shoemaker, although the former is unquestionably more complex, requiring much more training. This is why the instruments, equations, and terminology used by the craftsman of science, being so incomprehensible to the layman, are dazzling him into relating to the scientist as to a priest in a neo-pagan cult. Not only dilettantes, philistines, and laymen fall prey to worshipping the seeming all-powerfulness of science, but also many scientists blindly believe that their research brings them closer to knowing the world and themselves.

In my writings I did not attempt to explain the Torah because I myself at the time had barely been able to scratch its surface and to sense, with the heart more than with the mind, its greatness and all-embracing significance. All I could do was to try to knock down the ridiculous stone wall erected by "enlighteners" which cuts us off from the treasures of the Torah and from God Himself.

This mental wall induces people to exclaim: "In our day and age one cannot believe that the world has been in existence for only five thousand years!" or: "You can't possibly believe—in the twentieth century—that whether or not I turn on the television on the Sabbath affects the fate of the Jewish people!" or: "How can an enlightened human being today say that God created man out of the dust of the earth or that He dictated the Torah to Moses on Mount Sinai?" Talking in this vein, pleased with their ultraenlightenment, people fritter their lives away on nonsense at breakneck speed. Euphorically drifting into the abyss of irreversible assimilation and propelling their children in the same direction, they dauntlessly flit past the eternal truth and the eternal values kept by Jews for centuries.

The sum total of my notes constituted a kind of "preparing of the ground," clearing away atheistic rubbish and "enlightened" gibberish from the building site. Only after having done this was it possible to begin rebuilding the house with a Jewish world outlook. At this culminating point, I called upon my imaginary reader (or, to be more exact, myself, now freed of prejudices) to open the Book of Books—the source and repository of our distinctiveness and eternalness. I called upon him/myself to trust in the truths that have not been influenced by time, to learn them and to rise to the ultimate affirmation of Judaism—*Shema Yisrael!*

22

Meeting with Israeli Diplomats

I won't attempt to describe the excitement of my Israeli uncle's visit. Concerning my manuscript, though, my relative, guided by worldly wisdom befitting his age, said that it seemed to him a risk involving possible unpleasant consequences for me far greater than what the situation warranted. Painfully, I came to agree.

By the time that Fania's relative arrived, I had devised a new plan for transporting the manuscript. I reached the conclusion that the safest and most hopeful way was for her to pass it on to the Israeli Embassy during her stay in Moscow.

Pecking with one finger on the keys of the typewriter, I typed out the manuscript onto the thinnest paper. Now it could all fit into a regular postal envelope.

Fania and I scheduled our vacations to begin when her relative was to arrive. After receiving our guest in Riga, the two of us traveled to Moscow a few days before she joined us there.

In Moscow we visited Fania's relative several times at her hotel, where we held discussions on the most harmless, neutral subjects. Once, when she went out to the street with us to bid us farewell, I arranged to meet her at the large pharmacy on the Twenty-Fifth of October Street. The rendezvous was kept. I explained my request to her. She agreed and took the manuscript. The next day the manuscript was delivered to the Embassy.

It all went simply and smoothly. It ought to have stopped right there, but a thirst for further meetings with Israelis possessed me. Possibly, this thirst was aroused by a feeling of some sort of disappointment left by the encounters that had just taken place. Although by that time I was quite well read and informed about life in Israel, nevertheless I expected Israeli Jews to be surrounded by a halo of holiness or at least a sign of the Chosen People. Their behavior, their mode of thinking, their interests should set them apart from all other peoples. Alas, this was not so. I convinced myself that those with whom I had become acquainted were not characteristic representatives.

I had heard that many foreigners frequented the Aragvi restaurant in Moscow. In the evening of the same day that my manuscript had made it to the Embassy, we went to that restaurant. I was already not eating anything at places like that, but for appearances I ordered something and persistently pecked my fork on the plate. And suddenly—my heart missed a beat. The two couples occupying the neighboring table were speaking loudly in Hebrew. On the coats of the men were little badges with blue stars of David.

I did not dare start to talk to them in the restaurant in front of everybody. Therefore I decided that we should wait until they finished dining, and then we would meet them on the street.

While they were finishing their meal, we hastily paid and dashed into the street. I was terribly excited. Soon they also left. We said "shalom" and asked them in Hebrew if they were Israeli tourists. It turned out that they were not tourists but workers at the Embassy. This made the meeting even more interesting, but, of course, more risky. They asked us to join them. It was almost midnight and Gorky Street was quite deserted. The warm, windless night, saturated with the aroma of flowering linden trees, evoked tranquility, but inside me everything seethed with excitement. Just think of it: me strolling along the center of Moscow with an Israeli diplomat!

One of them, Moshe Z., gently led me by the arm and answered the countless questions that erupted from me. Fania was walking behind us with the second diplomat and both wives. I asked Moshe about the spiritual condition in Israel, about the education of children, and about many, many other things.

It disturbed me a little that half an hour earlier, as I had seen with my own eyes, the entire company had eaten the most nonkosher dishes with tremendous appetite. But I tried not to think about this.

I told Moshe that I had passed my precious manuscript on to the Embassy and asked him to keep an eye on its fate.

Meanwhile Fania said that I very much wanted to have a *Chumash* and *machzorim* with Russian translation. They promised her to bring all this to the synagogue on Arkhipova Street on the coming Saturday. This again puzzled me, as I already knew that it is forbidden to carry things on *Shabbat*.

When we mentioned that from Moscow we were going on to Transcaucasia to spend the rest of our vacation there, our new friends announced that they were also leaving for vacation in a few days—to Yalta in the Crimea. They suggested that we travel to Transcaucasia via Crimea so that we could see each other again. It was best and safest to meet and talk on the beach—they explained—where it is always full of people in bathing suits, making it difficult for anyone to notice or recognize us.

23

My Brainchild Travels to Israel

On *Shabbat* at the synagogue I received a *tallit* and books from the Embassy employees, as had been arranged.

Now it remained for us to decide whether to go to Yalta. We soberly deemed it to be folly, but the temptation was so great that we decided to go.

Fania was four months pregnant and felt ill traveling. Arriving in Yalta, we launched a desperate attempt to get a hotel room, but this, of course, was impossible. Then I decided to call the hotel for foreign tourists, the Ukrainia, where the Z's had to be staying. I called there anyway, not even hoping that it would work, but surprisingly it turned out that it was possible to get a "deluxe" room for two days.

It was clear that after all my former contacts and with my present work, it was forbidden for us to go to this hotel. But Fania was barely able to stand on her feet, so I decided to disregard all our fears.

The next day I caught the Z's on the hotel stairs, and we agreed to meet on the "Golden Beach" during the following day. We spent a few happy hours with the Z's that day, talking, looking at Israeli postcards. In parting, I wrote down and gave them our address and the addresses of our relatives in Israel.

When we returned to the hotel, I noticed two young men near the manager's desk. At first glance they didn't please me very much.

That evening we sailed by ship to Sukhumi. Those fellows from the hotel, however, haunted us for a long time, serving as food for all kinds of conjectures and not very pleasant suppositions.

I met the Z's two more times in Russia. Each time I tried to find out what was happening with my manuscript, but they didn't know. The first time was at a concert of the Israeli pianist Pnina Saltzman in Leningrad. The second was at an international film festival in Moscow where the Israeli film *Remember* was also shown. I should note that the film depressed me, not only by its mediocrity but even more by its blasphemous presentation of memories of the horrors of Nazi concentration camps against the background of scenes of a Jew living together with his French concubine in contemporary Israel.

At Sukhumi, I also became close friends with a family of Georgian Jews named Krikheli. In the coming years I visited them a few times during the high holy days of Rosh Hashana and Yom Kippur, in order to spend these days in Jewish surroundings and to go to the synagogue without fear.

Still, the manuscript was there, in Israel, and this heartened and quieted me. Even the thought that it was possible that I was condemned to remain until the end of my days on alien soil seemed less frightening. After all, a small part of me was already in the Holy Land.

24

First Encounter with Chasidim and Practical Commandments

I continued to go regularly to the synagogue on *Shabbat* mornings. Sometimes, as before, I stood alone in the rear corner of the large upstairs hall, but
more and more I preferred to go down to the basement to the *Chasidim*. There
my place was between two pensioners—Shmuel-Aaron Raphelson, who first
taught me how to find my way in the prayer book, in order to find the place in
the text at any given moment, and the late Nochem Besser, who patiently
answered my countless questions about Judaism, one more naïve than the other.
Besser, as I found out later, secretly taught Torah and *halachah* to dozens of
boys and girls. These magnificent, shy, and good men rendered me a priceless
service in my search for Judaism, and I am infinitely grateful to them.

One *Shabbat* at the beginning of 1964 a forty-year-old man approached me.
He had a black moustache and extraordinarily lively, pure-blue eyes with a glint
of mischief in them. Vigor and inspiration brimmed in him. He started to insist
that I come with him to his house, promising to tell me many important and
interesting things and to give me good Jewish books. Right there he wanted to
know if I put on *tefillin* daily. As I didn't know what that was, he insisted even
more that I come over. As he went away he suggested that I find out about him
from any of the synagogue congregants, as "everyone knows who Notke with
the moustache is."

He left me with mixed feelings. First of all, I was not accustomed to Jewish
books being offered in public, in the presence of witnesses. This involuntarily
alarmed me and forced me to query if he were a provocateur. On the other hand,
there was something very attractive about him.

I asked Raphelson about Notke and he replied: "He's a *Chasid*. You can go
with him."

I wondered what *"Chasid"* meant. Wasn't that section of the synagogue
called *"Chasidim"*? However, I was ashamed to ask. Thus, the gradations and
nuances of the concept of *"Chasid,"* nay the very concept, remained an enigma
to me for a long time to come.

In March, nine days before Pesach, a son was born to us. We gave him a
double name, Hertz-Daniel. The first name was in memory of my father, and
the second one pleased Fania very much. The functionary at the "Bureau of
Registration of Acts of Civilian Status" point-blank refused to register a double
name. It didn't help either appealing to a superior authority or attesting, among

other things, that the Azerbaijanis register four or five names, plus their invariable "ogli" at the end.

The boy was registered under the name Hertz. We started to call him Geka for short. But, naturally, at the circumcision we gave him both names.

The day before the circumcision I went to invite Notke. This was an appropriate occasion to take advantage of his offer finally. However, for some reason he could not come. When the baby was almost a month old, Nochem Besser told me about the *pidyon haben* ritual—the symbolic redemption of a first-born son from a *kohen,* a member of the priestly class. For this purpose he advised me to invite Notke, who was a *kohen.*

This custom seemed strange to me, possibly even absurd. Wonderfully enough, though, I had felt nothing of the kind in relation to the ceremony of circumcision. Such is human nature that the unfamiliar seems foolish and wild. Restraining my doubts, however, I invited Notke and Besser, and everything went according to *halachah.*

From then on Notke masterfully plunged into our life, often evoking the displeasure of Fania for "pushing" too much. Looking back in retrospect now, I feel tremendous gratitude toward Notke, just as I was then irrepressibly pulled toward him. He symbolized for me the quintessence of Judaism, the Torah, the Jewish way of life. Through Notke's mediation, a perfectly new world was opened up to me. Furthermore, he was a most outstanding personality, even though from the point of view of the social circle to which we belonged, he was a simple, uneducated Jew.

I was amazed at the integrity of his world outlook and the uncompromising agreement between his behavior and this world outlook.

It was a joy to see a man who was very earthy, loving all that was beautiful and savory, yet nevertheless always inspired by an ideal. He was not suffering for his ideal. He hated sacrifice. It was just that he simply could not conceive of himself outside the constant awareness of and adherence to this ideal. Therefore having to forgo something was not a sacrifice but the only possible natural way to behave.

Notke did many things daily that the average philistine would consider an unbearable burden and an enormous sacrifice to personal comfort. It amazed me that this man, without having completed high school, was able to talk for hours about philosophical difficulties in explaining the creation of matter *ex nihilo,* about time as one of the dimensions of the physical world, about the Divine soul of the Jew, and about the necessity for that soul to master and control the body, which ought not to be rejected but rather ennobled through keeping the commandments.

Once I asked him how he had arrived at all this, and he burst out laughing in reply. "I don't make this up by myself. It's all written."

"Where?"

"Here at least, in this book that I study." He showed me a pocket-sized book. "This is *Tanya,* the major book of the Old Rebbe."

"And you studied it?"

"No. I *am* learning it."

"For how long?"

"For a few decades."

This was very strange to me, used to studying several volumes in the course of a few weeks or even days in preparation for each one of the numerous exams which I had taken in my life.

Often Notke referred to the *Kabbalah,* to the *Zohar.* I admit that this frightened me and made me uncomfortable. The fact was that I had never read or even seen the books of the *Zohar.* However, I remembered a few allusions to the *Kabbalah* in Sholom Aleichem, particularly in his story "Song of Songs." From these I concluded that the *Kabbalah* was a collection of very primitive, childishly naïve mystical tales.

Things got even harder, especially when Notke "pushed" me to fulfill a few commandments that I had never heard of before. Already on one of my first visits he had presented me with a little velvet bag of *tefillin,* insisting that I put them on right there and then under his guidance and direction. He explained that these phylacteries had to be put on every morning except on *Shabbat* and holidays.

To tell the truth, it was very difficult for me to do this. Thousands of voices inside of me began to screech and resist. All that I had internalized from Soviet education shrieked: "No!" All that had sunk into my brain from Soviet universities howled: "Never!" All that had been absorbed in me from my atheistic surroundings revolted and protested: "This is primitive!"

True, I had already gone far in rejecting my past education and in adopting Judaism. But for me Judaism still seemed to be food for the soul and the mind, a sublime philosophical system. So suddenly being confronted with such material, physical duties was most strange for me. True also, I had long since understood and accepted many commandments relating to the sphere of everyday and physical things, such as kosher food, many of the Sabbath laws, circumcision, and so forth. Yet, I had been familiar with these for a long time and understood them without reflection. The commandment of *tefillin,* however, was unknown and seemed very strange. The dictum of the Pentateuch that ". . . thou shalt bind them for a sign upon thine hand, and they shall be for frontlets between thine eyes . . ." I was inclined to interpret purely allegorically.

The fact was that I did not only not know the practice and meaning of the Oral Law which elucidates the Pentateuch, but I didn't even suspect that it existed. Nevertheless, Notke's insistence and even more so a deeper internal voice compelled me to continue the daily practice of the commandment of putting on *tefillin*. I very soon started to feel extremely uneasy, to suffer from a strong sensation of nonfulfillment and of spiritual defection, if for any reason I did not manage to put on *tefillin* in the morning.

A month after I had first put on *tefillin*, I had to go to Leningrad for a conference. I arrived there by train early in the morning and rushed immediately to the synagogue where I could perform this *mitzvah*. But to my extreme disappointment, I found the synagogue already closed. So instead of attending the conference for which I had come, I spent the whole day trying to get a place in a hotel, where I could put on my *tefillin*. Neither persuasion nor bribery could help. I didn't eat anything all day, and I shivered terribly as I ran in the cruel frost from one hotel to another. But I was unaware of all this against the background of my great distress that the sun was declining lower and lower while I still had not put on *tefillin*. Miraculously, I somehow obtained a cherished key three minutes before the sun set and managed after all to do this daily obligation. What kind of irrational power controlled me that day? What had become of my scientific skepticism?

Similar experiences occurred with other *mitzvot*. For example, during the first days after I started to wear a *tallit katan* with *tzitzit* tassels on the corners, I simply felt like a clown, even though the *tzitzit* were carefully tucked under my clothes and nobody saw them. However, after a month this feeling became entirely reversed. Without *tzitzit* I simply felt naked. Sometimes, due to my absent-mindedness, these tassels would stick out from under my clothes. My colleagues at the Academy of Sciences on occasion would snatch the *tzitzit* and ask in astonishment what they were or if I wore underwear that was so threadbare that the threads were unraveling.

In the manuscript sent to Israel I had tried to convince both myself and others of the vital necessity to fulfill all the commandments of the Torah. Now I was enduring psychological difficulties in trying to actually practice what I had preached. How trying it was for Fania then, who at best was a benevolent reader of my essays! Suddenly she was confronted with a kosher kitchen and *Shabbat* candles, *Shabbat* rest, as well as monthly immersion in the *mikveh*. . . .

Albeit with hardship, the eternal triumphed over the superficial and the alien. The more I entered into this new life, the more I felt myself participating in the mission of my people. The bits of knowledge from the Torah which previously had been known to me became lit with new understanding. At that time more and more treasures appeared on my horizons—the commentaries of Rashi, the *Mishnah*, the *Shulchan Aruch*. The Talmud at that time still remained closed to me, but I managed to extract grains of information about it through quotations or references in other books.

25

Studying Torah

F inally the day came when I felt able to study Torah independently. A wonderful period began—a time of cognition, reevaluation and daily discovery.

On the surface, my life continued as usual. There was the trip every morning to the Institute of Physics at the Academy of Sciences, followed by long hours in the laboratory with endless discussions of the latest experimental results. There would be agonizing searches to find the reasons for the failure of a test that had been repeated over and over again. And there was always work with Ph.D. students and participation in scientific conferences.

As usual, books filled with formulas and schematics found their way to my desk at home. Scattered piles of written papers grew almost up to the ceiling. Some of these papers were filed, but most of them ended up in the waste basket. But in the midst of this stream of papers, the *Chumash,* the *Mishnah,* the *Shulchan Aruch,* and of course *Tanya* now invariably remained on my desk. Putting aside the hand-written pages, immediately forgetting the despicably vain attempts of human intellect reflected in them, I could plunge into the pure, life-giving, tranquil, yet passionate ocean of eternal wisdom.

Gradually and very cautiously Notke introduced me to his circle of friends. I became acquainted with self-controlled and always externally calm Yisroel Pevzner, with temperamental Shimon Gutman. For several months I studied Torah with Rashi's commentary with Avroam Godin, who before the Second World War had been the secretary of none other than Mordechai Dubin, who for years had represented the entire Jewish community to the Latvian government. With respect I observed Mordechai Aharon Friedman—a man of biblical appearance—whose seniority, erudition, and invincible will enjoyed indisputable authority among the *Chasidim* of Riga.

All his friends were as dedicated as Notke himself. For all of them, compromise or accommodation to the Soviet reality at the expense of disobeying the *Shulchan Aruch* was not just inadmissible but simply didn't exist as a possible alternative.

They searched for Jewish children who showed interest in Judaism and tried to help them. This was such an important thing to Notke and his friends that for its sake they would forget about food and drink. Under their influence, many elderly people—who when younger had been able to learn Torah and Hebrew—were transformed into secret teachers for these children. For security reasons they never taught more than one child at a time, but as most of them were pensioners with free time available, they had a total of many students.

How can we measure the contribution of these modest anonymous people to the awakening of Soviet Jewry? I have already mentioned Nochem Besser. Another indefatigable teacher was Gradus, whose first name I have unfortunately forgotten. This shy, small man feared neither hard frost nor Soviet law as he tirelessly treaded from house to house. Alas, he is no longer alive. His dream of going to Israel, which he had cherished so, was never realized. There are many others who are still alive and working. May their days be increased!

The dwellings of the *Chasidim* (which often were only single rooms within large communal apartments) were clear of all Soviet influence. Their children and grandchildren breathed, from infancy, love and devotion for the Jewish people and the Torah. They all lived in the hope of leaving for *Eretz Hakodesh*. They had absolutely no doubt about either the necessity or the hoped-for realization of this departure. Some sort of secret surrounded them that was greater than simply a conspiracy. I felt that there was a side of their life still beyond my comprehension. This feeling was confirmed all the more when I found out that every one of them contributed at least a fifth of his sometimes very modest income to a charity fund.

My donations were also accepted, but where they went remained a mystery to me. Only much later did they tell me of the existence in those years of a secret system of Jewish education and training that helped many children return and stay in the fold of Judaism. Even now it would be premature to openly discuss in more detail the hundreds of miniature *yeshivot* and *chadorim* spread all over immense Russia. Hidden in private apartments, these institutions operated under the strictest secrecy regulations, which became an easy, matter-of-fact routine for both pupils and teachers. During the Stalin era, punishment in case of discovery was death; later it was reduced to "years." But none of the participants in this underground educational movement was thwarted by this danger.

Many things distinguished my new friends from my nationalistically and Zionistically inclined acquaintances: their integrity, their deep knowledge of the Torah, their lively wisdom, their clear conception of the meaning and purpose of life. Their trustworthiness was self-evident. It would be simply inconceivable to suspect treachery or KGB collaboration in someone who, in the name of the Jewish ideal, against a great many objective difficulties, brought each of his own steps into conformity with Jewish learning and built on this a life for all generations of his family.

The fruits of their efforts were felt. They believed it was most important for a Jew to remain a genuine Jew and to help others return to Judaism. Wherever fate may have thrust them, they knew how to bring this about. Their desire to go to Israel flowed out of their world outlook, naturally and organically.

Finally, I found out that they have a spiritual leader, a rebbe. He was not only their leader, but the great Jew of the entire generation, the preceptor of all Jews, in that he taught and urged the need to study Torah more deeply and more scrupulously, to fulfill the commandments with a great spiritual uplift, and to educate oneself and one's children to love every Jew as one in whom a portion of the Lord resides. I discovered that the Rebbe is called the Lubavitcher from the name of the small town of Lubavitch in White Russia. My new friends were correspondingly Lubavitcher *Chasidim,* also called *Chabad Chasidim* from the first letters of three concepts: *chochmah*—wisdom, reason; *binah*—comprehension; *da'at*—knowledge. These were the three essential elements in the philosophical teaching of this branch of Chasidism. I discovered more and more the unusual life strength and steadiness of *Chabad* both as a teaching and as a movement. The terrible millstones of the Cheka, GPU, NKVD, MGB, KGB, names of Soviet secret police, and the Soviet propaganda apparatus, which for fifty years had been crushing all and sundry, seemed powerless to crush *Chabad,* although for a time it acted against it especially violently.

I became acquainted with many illustrious *Chabadniks* and heard amazing stories about others. These were extraordinary people—earthy, not self-denying. Thanks to a confluence of unshakable belief and a clear world outlook guiding their behavior, they were able to overcome insurmountable obstacles. I almost never heard them complaining about the difficulties facing Jews in the Soviet Union trying to keep the Jewish way of life. With their mood permanently elevated, they unequivocally reasoned that if the Almighty gave us the *Shulchan Aruch*—the Jewish Code—then He certainly also provided us with the means to obey it, regardless of the external circumstances. And miraculously enough, this approach, based on absolute *bitachon baShem,* always won against all odds.

I heard about the legendary Mendel Futerfas, who rescued thousands of Jews from Soviet captivity. He himself remained inside the Soviet Union until after the completion of this unbelievable act. Then he was captured and condemned to death. While waiting for the execution of his sentence, he sat in solitary confinement and sang Russian folk songs, which he carefully chose and imbued with deep allegorical meaning. They commuted his sentence to twenty-five years, but after ten years he was able to leave Russia and now lives in Israel.

I heard about Chaim Zalman Kozliner, nicknamed *"Chazak"* (Strong). When NKVD agents came to arrest him, he raised his arms and began to chant words from the *Kabbalah* with such strength of feeling that the police retreated.

I became acquainted with Schneer Pinsky. The tiny Moscow apartment of this small, quiet man served as both a shelter and an academy of Chasidism for scores of Jewish visitors from all corners of Russia.

Wherever I would travel, whether to capital cities or to remote corners, if there were any vestiges of Yiddishkeit—a *minyan* praying regularly, a *mikveh* still providing ritual ablution, a *melamed* still teaching children, a *sukkah* still being built for the autumn holiday of *Sukkot*—investigation revealed that all this was maintained by one or two "possessed" *Chabadniks*. Sometimes, even, the *Chabadnik* had left the area ten or so years before, but the order established by him was still functioning. This was repeated in Russia, Belorussia, the Trans-caucasus, and Central Asia.

26

Double Life

O utwardly, our life changed rather little. I continued to work at the Physics Institute. My experiments on magnetohydrodynamics were progressing very successfully. I studied the influence of the magnetic field on turbulent flows of liquid metals and electrolytes. This was then a totally unknown area. When I could ascertain which research methods should be applied, after having overcome an entire set of difficulties, I felt like a traveler on a mountain road where after every curve, after every new pass, new horizons and perspectives were opened up.

Though, of course, from a philosophical point of view I harbored no illusions about the significance of my work, I must admit that on the whole it pleased me. I published much, participated in conferences, and had under-graduate and graduate students. But real life began only on those rare, mean-ingful evenings when I managed to get to the chasidic lessons on Torah. Most of the day I spent in the "scientific world." I had occasion to meet with many professors and academicians, who five or so years before seemed to me to be standing on pedestals of inaccessible height. Now I had the occasion to observe them close up. Some of them were still modest. Others put on airs. But when I compared them to those who study Torah—who, as I now understood, really deserve the name scholar, although having neither title nor rank—all these professors seemed to me to be pitiful pygmies. The fact was that not only were most of them possessed by all possible passions and ambitions, but that science and the social status conferred by it were, to a great degree, means of satisfying these lusts. Even those who were sincerely dedicated to their science now seemed to me to be limited in comparison to the bearded Jew, who, although having never completed any university, penetrates into the very meaning of the essence of the universe through reading an ancient volume in a sing-song voice.

Not long before, the path of human history had seemed to me to be marked by the milestones of scientific and technological achievements. Now I distinctly saw and even more strongly felt that this history is unwinding according to the eternal and invariable plan set down in the Torah. Technical progress receded to the very bottom of the scale of genuine values.

My double life demanded great effort and maximum economy of time. Even previously I had never known what boredom from lack of activity was. I never understood how some people have to rack their brains to figure out how to "kill time." During my student days while associating with fellow students or while traveling by train, whenever I would allow myself to be persuaded to be drawn into a game, I would suffer deeply and wait for the moment that I would finally be released from this vacuous pastime. At such times I would always have the feeling of participating in a premeditated crime of reducing down to nothing the most precious and wondrous gift—time, intended for construction, creation, and the striving for self-perfection. Now, after my encounter with Torah and commandments the appreciation of time became even stronger.

27

Further Complications with the KGB

After meeting with the people from the Israeli Embassy and forwarding my manuscript, I constantly felt that I was being followed. As I didn't notice anything positively suspicious, I tried to convince myself that this was merely the fruit of my active imagination. However, in the end I came to be convinced that my intuition was not deceiving me.

After our baby was born, I finally received an apartment from the Academy in the "academic settlement" of Salaspils, twenty-three kilometers east of Riga. The entire settlement consisted at that time of a few four-story brick houses. Two kilometers away an experimental atomic reactor belonging to my Institute was already functioning. There the building where the magnetohydrodynamics laboratories of Riga were to be transferred was also being erected. In the meantime I commuted to Riga to work. Fania was working at the Institute of Organic Synthesis, also in Riga. My mother would come every day to the baby, but the trip, the walk, and taking care of the child were taxing her strength. Therefore, we searched persistently for a suitable nursemaid. Our happiness was boundless when we finally found a poor old woman who lived nearby. She stayed alone with the child all day. Before leaving the house in the morning I would carefully hide, beneath my underwear, my *tefillin, tallit* and the few Jewish books that I had.

One morning, just as I arrived at work, the telephone rang.

"Is Branover at work today?"

I recognized the voice of the directress of the personnel department.

"This is Branover. What's the matter?" As I answered I immediately felt anxious.

"No, no. Everything's all right. Someone here asked for you. They'll call you." She was evidently in a hurry to hang up.

It was obvious: they wanted to be certain that I hadn't stayed home for any reason. (Later, in the evening, I found out that the same thing had happened to Fania at work, but she hadn't paid any attention to it.)

The next train to Salaspils left only an hour later. That hour dragged out agonizingly. On the way home I tried to convince myself that my imagination was simply playing tricks on me. Nevertheless I ran home from the station. A gray Pobeda, parked near the house neighboring ours, immediately drew my attention. Running up the stairs, I silently opened the door, entered the little anteroom, and froze.

The door to the next room was closed. From behind it I could hear male voices. I should have stood and listened, but my nerves couldn't take it. I flung open the door.

Geka was peacefully playing on the floor. Seeing me, he started smiling and crawled to meet me. To the side stood three men talking to our nursemaid.

"What's the matter?" I asked.

"It doesn't concern you," one of them answered. "We had some questions to ask your employee. Please excuse us that we had to talk to her in your apartment."

They left almost immediately, taking the old woman with them. The next day she came and said that she refused to work for us.

There was no doubt now that we were being followed. It worried me greatly that they probably knew that I had passed something on to the Israeli Embassy. Although I was not officially connected with any secret work, I was surrounded by people and entire laboratories connected with various military departments studying questions related to rockets, submarines, and so forth. If they wished, the KGB could easily accuse me of transmitting secret information to Israel and do with me as they pleased.

Half a year went by before the assistant director of the Institute summoned me. He then contended that I was receiving packages "from the West." I truly had not received anything and therefore was quite sincerely filled with indignation. However, he stood his ground, reprimanding: "You must understand where you are working. If you were working at the Loggers' Authority, then you could receive all the packages you pleased." Arguing with him was just as impossible as with the characters at the KGB.

Finally, a year later, I was called to the "Special Department" of the Academy. I was most courteously requested to meet at my convenience with one of their members, who wished to talk to me.

The meeting took place the next day. My interlocutor showed me his permit. Written there was: "Committee of State Security, Chief of the Department— Coleman."

"Please tell me about all your meetings with foreigners," he asked with great gentility.

I tried to tell him about meetings with my first cousin once removed, who had come from Israel two years before to visit, and about some other chance encounters on the street. It was clear, however, what he was driving at.

"Please try a little harder," he insisted. Then his voice became cruel and inexorable. "Remember that your fate is being decided at this moment."

I continued to persist. Then he told me—in excruciating detail—about my meetings in Moscow on Gorky Street and in Yalta, where on the beach I wrote something on a piece of paper torn from a green notebook and gave it to employees of the Israeli Embassy.

"What was it?" he insisted.

"The address of my uncle and of my brother-in-law's second cousin in Israel. I asked to send them regards," I answered.

For several hours this idiotic dialogue was repeated over and over. When it got very late, he let me go, ordering me to come again in the morning.

At night I calmed down. Considering everything, I came to the conclusion that two years of checking apparently had convinced them that there were no really serious charges against me, and they were probably not interested in "blowing up" the matter just then. (Still, for security reasons, I curtailed my visits with Notke.)

Later I found out that the director of the Institute had insistently kept me from being kicked out.

28

Deeper into the Rebbe's Teaching

G radually I began to renew my visits to Notke and my chasidic activities. Especially moving were the chasidic evening gatherings—*farbrengen*—

and their way of celebrating the major holidays. Forty to fifty people would get together, including newcomers to Judaism. Most of these gatherings took place in the autumn and winter, and now that I look back upon them the image that comes to mind is the striking contrast between the coldness and darkness outside and the warmth and light inside the room throbbing with excited people.

But stronger than the physical contrast was the psychological contrast. People came and went one at a time as a security precaution. But once they were inside, the KGB and the Soviet regime ceased to exist for them. They became free and independent participants in something grand and eternal, subject only to the Almighty.

They sang heartening chasidic melodies—with words and without words. Some of them were like genuine symphonies, full of feeling and philosophical reflections. Everyone felt bound to one another by the *mitzvah* of love for the People of Israel, for the Holy Land, and for one's fellow Jew. This *mitzvah* was fully carried out on these holidays taking place in praise of the Almighty and under His protection. During festive meals, with tears in their eyes, people would wish one another a speedy departure for Israel. Then the readings would begin. They read *ma'amarim*—the writings of the Rebbe.

It was hard for me to understand these *ma'amarim* and to follow the stormy discussions. I was restricted by my lack of knowledge of the language, consisting of a combination of Hebrew and Aramaic and also by the abundance of references to the Talmud, the *Zohar,* the Rambam and so forth. They also read *sichot*—speeches of the Rebbe in Yiddish, and these were easier to understand, as I had picked up quite a bit of Yiddish from my friendship and studies with the *Chasidim.*

I never ceased to be amazed at the philosophic and psychological depth of the Rebbe's thought and at the strength of his foresight. Later I tried to translate some of the *sichot* into Russian so they could be accessible to the uninitiated. In particular one of the Rebbe's *sichot* on Chanukah moved me and made a deep imprint on my mind.

In it the question is asked why—out of all the events commemorated by Chanukah—does the Talmud single out precisely the seemingly modest episode of the jug of oil for the Temple lamps rather than the mighty military victories of the Maccabees over the Greeks? The Rebbe explains that the oil for the Temple lamps symbolizes wisdom. Just as the Greeks profaned the oil by their contact, so does the smallest exposure to non-Jewish influence always profane Jewish wisdom. There can be no compromise, not even the slightest adulteration in the sphere of the Jewish spirit!

It is also stated there that the world is constructed by the Creator so that, in the natural course of events, non-Jews simply should not rule over Jews, except in the case where . . . Jews give themselves and their Torah over to the control of non-Jews. It was very understandable to us since we in Soviet Russia experienced the consequences of allowing the gentiles in.

In another place the Rebbe said that it is not the possibility of *ge'ulah* (redemption) that should seem unusual. On the contrary, the prolonged *galut* (exile) should seem strange, surprising, and unnatural. All this provided much food for thought and debate.

There were periods when I set up a strict schedule of Jewish studies for myself. Especially enthralling were the lessons on the *Tanya,* which Zalman Levin—a great, quiet man and a living encyclopedia of Judaism and Chasidism—gave me. Not long before, he had been released from prison after a ten-year confinement, during which he did not once eat non-kosher food or break the *Shabbat.* Now he was working as a craftsman-electrician at a factory. With his son, Moshe Chaim, I translated an abridged Russian version of the *Shulchan Aruch*—the code of Jewish laws. Naturally while we worked together Moshe Chaim and I talked a lot about Chasidism, especially about the *Tanya.*

It amazed me when I found more and more answers in the *Tanya* or in the other book of the Alter Rebbe—*Likutei Torah*—to questions that had been troubling me so many years. I found answers to questions about the spiritual and physical worlds; about the order of creation of the material world by God from nothing; about how universal preordainment from above still allows for man's free will and his freedom of choice. Principally I learned about the higher destination of man, how man can become spiritualized by permeating his life with Torah, without resorting to asceticism. The simple, refined, and immeasurably profound teaching about the struggle of the Divine soul and the bestial soul within man gave me a completely new understanding of the concept of the Chosen People, of the commandment to love one's fellow Jew, and of various aspects of Jewish life and behavior. In contrast to this, how poor Freudian theory looked. Although of Jewish origin, Freud did not realize the prime aspect of man—the Divine spark.

Most difficult of all for me to understand and accept was the grandeur and profoundness of simplicity. As I have already said, as long as the Jewish religion and the Torah were identified in my mind as a system expressed in complex philosophical terms, then everything was all right. But crisis ensued when it became evident that the Torah is primarily a practical guide to everyday life and that the philosophy which permeates it is—both in essence and in form—absolutely unlike the university texts to which I was so accustomed.

In the textbooks everything was directed toward classification and generalization, toward showing similarities within outward differences and diversity. The Torah, on the contrary, primarily narrates things unique, exclusive and nonpareil: a chosen people—the Jews; a time set apart—the *Shabbat;* a land incomparable to any other place in the world—Israel, and its center—

Jerusalem; and singular forefathers, holy men and prophets. And only in the One and only God is all the uniqueness universally generalized, and unified.

My intellect in no way could reconcile itself to this new seemingly "unscientific" way of looking at the world. It was even harder to accept the stories of the Torah about miracles, about supernatural events.

It took me years to understand that it was not at all modern "sophistication" or the "progress" of the human intellect that stood between me and the concept of miracles, but rather certain notions and ideas absorbed almost since infancy. Until now it had never seemed necessary to check, analyze, or reconsider them.

According to these ideas, our age is a special age—the century of science. Mysticism is used as a derogatory term, and belief in the supernatural is considered to be a sign of feeblemindedness. Even much later, when I already understood that, in principle, science cannot contradict belief, and that the essence of things and the origin and development of the universe are absolutely out of the reach of science and represent an area where Torah rules supreme, still the question of miracles disturbed, troubled, and frightened me. It took me even more time to realize the simple truth that someone living one or two thousand years ago and myself are in the very same position regarding miracles. A miracle is called a miracle precisely because it occurs so very rarely. Therefore, an ancient believer, just like myself, probably never saw a miracle occur. And also, just like me, he saw only the natural course of events united by bonds of cause and effect in everyday life.

Being a student of twentieth-century natural science based on indeterminism and probability physics, I should have had a more favorable attitude toward intelligently comprehending miracles. Unfortunately, my mind was constrained by an education and psychology invented by shortsighted, arrogant, lazy people at the dawn of the so-called "Age of Enlightenment."

My internal protest and rejection of the supernatural increased if the events in question took place in the recent past or present. My "intellectualizing" mind quietly accepted the idea of One Almighty God Who chose the Jewish People. But upon being presented with the situation that this Creator—Who granted the universe existence and definable laws—sometimes changes these laws for a definite purpose, my mind would become alarmed and discomforted. My intellect also rose up against the chasidic acceptance of mind-reading and the prediction of the future by contemporary *tzaddikim*, against the idea of transmigration of souls, and against the type of dialogue with God and display of supernatural powers attributed to, for instance, the Baal Shem Tov.

It was enormously difficult for me to accept the idea of *hashgachah pratit*—that God exercises permanent supervision and control over all living beings and inanimate objects in the universe. Involuntarily attempting to imagine a human being in the role of such an overseer, our mind is convinced that such a person is impossible and hence concludes — completely contradicting elementary logic — that this is impossible for God also.

Curiously, our forefathers possessed a breadth of vision ample enough to contain a genuine idea of God. Yet, we who have been brought up in a world of man-made electronic computers which can supervise millions of objects at once — surely we ought to feel it easier to imagine the power of the Limitless Mighty One, but we don't!

The principle of continual creation formulated by the Baal Shem Tov helped me to overcome this difficulty. This principle affirms that God not only directs all things in the world, but is continuously creating them from nonexistence, renewing their existence. And if this continual creation were to cease for an instant, then everything existing would turn into nothing. This principle is even more radical than that of Divine supervision, but, possibly, it is precisely this which makes it easier for a mind educated in rationalism to grasp.

As long as I was only reading the explanations of all these phenomena in the *Kabbalah* or in the philosophy of *Chabad,* I felt totally at ease. The theory of the creation of matter from Divine emanation through successive contractions and abasement of the spiritual in favor of the material, as well as the principle of continual creation (which actually defined the possibility of the reverse influence of a righteous man upon the acts of creation by God) overwhelmed me by their rightness, wisdom, and refinement.

However, when it came to applying these theories to life, a psychological barrier went into effect. The imprint of my atheistic upbringing and education was solidly lodged within me. Psychological habits turned out to be stronger than ideology and reason.

Many years passed until I could resign myself to intellectually accept and then to genuinely feel, on a higher level of consciousness, truths such as the idea that a righteous Jew putting on phylacteries can sometimes more successfully defend the Jewish people than an armada of tanks or an escadrille of airplanes. It is impossible to prove or disprove this, but within the framework of Jewish philosophy it can be explained. In order to become imbued with these convictions, one must stop resisting them and dwell for a while within their wonderful world. The extraordinarily harmonious and profound chasidic principle of continual creation, of the provision of the universe with life energy, clearly and convincingly explains why the behavior of every single Jew determines the fate of the world, since the amount of life energy is a function of this behavior.

But it is not enough to be intellectually elated by the harmony of the tenet of the origination of the universe from a sole source. It is not enough to mentally understand the mutual relationship of all parts of the universe with this source. Only when this teaching is so deeply ingrained into one's world outlook that everything is perceived through its grace does it become a guiding and ennobling factor directing one's behavior. And then one can both understand and feel that this world—with all its materiality and corporeality—is absolutely illusory and that its existence depends upon the will of the Creator, the only true and absolute existence. The will of God is such that, in this world, humanity in general and Jews in particular, having been given freedom of choice, fiercely struggle against their baser nature in the name of serving the Creator.

Gradually I realized what it was in *Chabad* that attracted me so. *Chabad* paradoxically unites a rational approach to reality with purely irrational belief, the most realistic pragmatism with the highest idealism. This combination does not at all impair the integrity and harmony of the world outlook and attitude which are so deeply characteristic of *Chabad*. Torah and life are not purposefully and consciously united and connected, but rather are interwoven and interfused into an organic unity. Every action, step, and word of a *Chabadnik* emanates from his comprehension of God, the Torah, and the Rebbe and thus are derived from a single source. The exemplary *Chabadnik* of our generation, Ben-Zion Shem Tov, would say that our trouble is that we do not realize how good it is, how happy we ought to be that we have such a God, such a Rebbe, such wise and noble laws.

Of course this integral unity is refracted in different ways by different natures and sometimes is considerably distorted by personal idiosyncrasies. Therefore only outstanding personalities manifest this beauty and harmony. Yet if the distinctive and stable characteristics in the lives of most *Chabadniks* were to be isolated, this harmony would be clearly revealed.

29

The Six-Day War

At the end of 1966 signs of the Jewish exodus from the Soviet Union came to life. A few families received permission to get exit visas. True, most of them were elderly, but their departure evoked a new wave of excitement. We, however, still didn't have anyone in Israel to send us an invitation.

I visited all the emigrants before they left, sometimes even accompanying them as far as Moscow, plying them with requests which they probably forgot even before crossing the border. I also tried to clarify our chances of getting evicted to Rumania, as my father had been a Rumanian citizen. In 1941 the Soviet regime had given him a Nansen passport, making us in essence

Soviet citizens through illegal means. But all these plans proved to be totally impracticable.

June 1967. The Six-Day War moved not only Jews but also Russians, who suddenly discovered that Jews know how to fight. The always hostile Latvians respected the Jews as allies resisting the Soviet regime. Many Jews who previously had known only vaguely about the existence of the State of Israel or who had cautiously put this subject aside, now began to speak about it and about their need to go and live there.

The number of young people attending the synagogue on holidays increased. True, they still mainly congregated in the courtyard. On Simchat Torah there was no end to the dancing and singing inside the building and on the street. The work on the graves of our brethren of the Riga ghetto at Rumbula was intensified, along with the gatherings there.

I would spend entire evenings by the radio, listening to all the Israeli broadcasts in succession—first in Russian, then in Yiddish, Hebrew, and English—petrified that I would miss the most minute or seemingly trivial detail of this miracle of miracles which went down in history as the "Six-Day War."

Only one thing perplexed me. It seemed natural after such an obvious miracle for all Jews to immediately turn to God or at least to instinctively express some form of thankfulness to Him. Most of all I expected this from the Jews living in Israel. However, outside of a few exceptions, nothing like this happened. Moreover, Israeli statesmen stubbornly avoided using even the most natural expressions like "thank God" or "with God's help" which frequent the speeches of other leaders of other countries in the free world. I gathered the impression that most of our leaders then were pathologically protesting against God.

Skipping ahead, I might add that similar thoughts have continued to upset me every time that the Almighty performs a miracle for His people but is given neither acknowledgment nor gratitude. For example, in the beginning of the 1970s the bloodshed of the Arab terrorists trying to destroy Israel was turned against their fellow Arabs during "Black September" in Jordan. Despite the fact that it was impossible to explain this rationally by attributing it to the sophistication or strength of Jewish arms, again the miracle was not acknowledged and on the whole gratitude was not expressed.

I can't help but to contrast and compare such events with the passages from *parashat lech lecha,* where, after Abraham, our forefather of blessed memory, returns from a brilliant victory over Kedorla'omer and his allies, God suddenly says to him: "Fear not, Abram, I am a shield to you; your reward shall be very great." Rashi explains: Abraham feared that the victory which had been granted him exhausted the reward that he deserved. This feeling of being indebted to God is catastrophically lacking in the present generation.

30

Trips to Buy Chicken

In early 1968 dozens of families finally succeeded in getting permission to leave Russia. This time there were actually young people among the emigrants, as well as those with higher education and with military obligations. Some chasidic families also left. The chances for *aliyah* were demonstrably increasing. Notke took heart, and he selflessly collected ancient Hebrew manuscripts which could now be saved by being taken out of the Soviet Union. He traveled throughout Russia, and my Sunday excursions with him became more infrequent but did not cease. Those trips in my old, small car to Lithuania for chicken had become almost a habit. We would leave before dawn and then pray and breakfast somewhere in the forest after the sun rose.

These trips can show the relativity of the notion of everyday hardships. Those of my relatives who knew about the trips would say: "He's obsessed. To waste his entire day off, without sleeping half the night, to be jolted about for three hundred kilometers in a broken-down car just to haul back live, stinking hens which have to be plucked after slaughtering—all this for the sake of getting pieces of kosher meat for the family. This is too much! Only a crazy fanatic can't understand that the Jewish law allows for exceptions under such circumstances!"

But, honestly, not only was this not difficult but, on the contrary, it gave me great pleasure. I was simply fulfilling that which was required of me. In addition, Notke's chasidic stories about Yisrael Baal Shem Tov were especially inspiring when told against the background of delightful rural landscapes.

A wonderful world was revealed in these stories. This world—which by logical reasoning was so distant and strange to me—awakened secret reminiscences through which it became precious and immediate. The purity of spirit and the nobility of the people living and acting in that world, their selflessness in helping their fellow Jew and in serving God, their constant gathering of "Divine sparks" cast into the lowest spheres of life, saturated this world with unique atmosphere and moods. The Holy One blessed be He clearly showed His presence in this world.

I will not conceal the fact that at first these stories, full of miracles and the supernatural, troubled the skeptical shell of my soul. I was inclined to understand them allegorically. It took some time until I reached an understanding of their simple literal meaning and until I realized that the bustling activity of our habitual world is illusory when compared with the world possessing the greatest degree of genuine existence, the world of the Baal Shem Tov.

31

Notke Leaves for Israel

In the spring of 1969, before Pesach, Notke and his family left also. After receiving the permit, he came home and started running around the room, extraordinarily excited, repeating over and over: "Fine fellow!" When his astonished household asked him who the fine fellow was, he replied, "The Almighty of course. He made them give us the permission to leave to go to *Eretz Hakodesh.*" Thus, here too, Notke remained true to himself, expressing his unbounded faith combined with an intimate rapport with *Ha-Kadosh Baruch Hu.*

Because I didn't know anything about the fate of my manuscript in Israel, Notke suggested that I give him a copy of it. It was a serious risk he took in spiriting the manuscript out of Russia. After arriving in Israel, he helped publish the book under his suggested title of *Mima'amakim* (From the Depths), taken from the Psalms of King David.

Although I was lonely without Notke, I felt more confident knowing that my loyal friend was "over there." During that time I defended my doctoral dissertation. Shortly afterwards I was appointed a full professor. Some interesting invitations were sent to me from abroad. In particular I was invited for a university lecture tour in the United States. Not only was I not allowed to go, but I was instructed to reply that my wife was ill and I was not able to leave her. Incidentally, for a long time afterwards I continued to receive expressions of sympathy and wishes for my wife's recovery from my colleagues abroad.

I still didn't have a single concrete peg upon which to hang my request to leave the Soviet Union. I could not allow myself to embark upon a new fabrication after my Polish escapade with Rufina and Yusek and all my unpleasant experiences with the KGB. Moreover, I still didn't have any actual close relatives in Israel to invite me. Therefore I decided to wait a while, in agony that perhaps I was letting the last possibility escape.

I continued to work at the Academy, but it was increasingly difficult to concentrate on my work. My research seemed more and more meaningless and my colleagues and graduate students unbearably tiresome. These people were sincerely and firmly convinced that they were the pillars and motivating forces of human progress. The atmosphere at scientific conferences and conventions especially reinforced this self-affirmation. These were actually celebrations of the greatness of the scientific élite — from the theatrical grandeur of the festive openings, to the refined pleasure experienced through demonstrating one's erudition and mental acuity during the discussions, to the strained wit of the banquet toasts while rubbing elbows with an eminent authority—and, above all, prevailed the sweet realization of self-aggrandizement along with the historical significance of the event. I write this not to judge others but to describe how I myself once had conceived my mission as a scientist, particularly at scientific conferences.

32

High Holidays in Trans-Karpathia

In the summer of 1968 the Soviet invasion into Czechoslovakia put an end to Dubcek's unprecedented experiment of creating "Communism with a human face." At that time I was concentrating entirely on Jewish problems and was little concerned with truth and justice on a global scale. Yet this invasion provoked an inexpressible feeling of disgust and resentment that unimpeded brute strength can destroy everything noble in this world.

Time passed, but there still was no hope, not even the smallest possibility, of leaving. Nevertheless I increasingly felt that the day was coming nearer when it would be possible to go. As I have mentioned earlier, on the surface hardly anything changed, but in truth everything was bound up in the exodus. Indeed, I continued to write articles and books on magnetohydrodynamics, but it became more and more difficult to concentrate on these subjects. I gradually resumed my open participation in Jewish activities, attending the synagogue again instead of the secret *minyan,* and this gave me great pleasure. It didn't matter that the synagogue was located on the other side of town and that on Shabbat and holy days I had to walk four kilometers to get there and four kilometers back, in the heat of summer and the cold of winter, morning and evening.

I was especially moved by the month of *Elul.* This is the last month before the New Year—Rosh Hashanah—designated for the Jews as a time of spiritual stock-taking and self-improvement. In the course of the last days of this month special prayers—*selichot*—are read. They are recited in the early morning, long before the rising of the sun.

It was a wonderful sensation—rising in the middle of the night to walk to the synagogue through the dark, empty streets. The cold night would smell of the autumn dampness, of fallen leaves. I would pass groups of mushroom pickers with baskets and buckets, who were piling into trucks that were taking them from the city to the forests. And we few Jews would go forth with the knowledge that we were doing what our grandfathers and our great-great-grandfathers did at this time of the year—prepare for the days of Judgment and renewal and plead with our Creator to inscribe all our brothers from the four corners of the earth in the Book of Life.

We went to be judged before the Omniscient, and it was both awesome and joyous. Reciting and hearing the *selichot* prayers evoked in me thousands of associations, reconstructing the atmosphere of *shtetl* life in the Jewish Pale of Settlement long, long ago. I could see and feel how the old *shammes,* huddling in a tattered *kapota* against the predawn chill, would tread from house to house, knocking on closed shutters, reminding the Jews that it was time for the Almighty to bestow blessings upon His children scattered in a hostile, cold world. And the Jews would leave their dilapidated homes and hurry to the little wooden synagogue, dimly lit by flickering candles and kerosene lamps. Old men with beards and young boys with curling *pei'ot* (sidelocks) . . .

I would be filled with nostalgia and longing for the *shtetl*—physically poor but spiritually overflowing with upward ascending spirit. These reminiscences were an inexhaustible source of moral admonition and inspiration during the whole year and especially on the eve of the Day of Judgment and Repentance.

There was always the feeling at this time of the year that we were heading toward something great, joyous, a little frightening, but most of all exalted. It was somewhat similar to how I used to feel before exams when I was a student, but now this was infinitely more important and elevated. And along with the awe and the inexpressible feeling of heightened expectation, pride and even a sort of gloating overcame me when I saw that the supposedly all-powerful Soviet regime—with all its army, uniformed and secret police, ubiquitous Communist Party, tanks, airplanes and atom bombs, and gargantuan state machine—stood powerless to prevent a handful of unarmed defenseless Jews from serving their eternal God.

For the autumn holidays themselves I usually went to Transcarpathia. There vestiges of Jewish communities were still preserved. These communities were not as strong as those in Georgia, but in compensation most of their Jews were far more learned in Torah. Dozens of *minyanim* and *mikva'ot* were still functioning. During my visits there I became friends with yet another wonderful person—Yosef Mordechai Kagan, the underground rabbi for Mukachev and all Transcarpathia.

Officially Yosef Mordechai took in empty bottles at a glass collection station built in the courtyard of his house, but his real work was leading the Jewish life of Mukachev, Khust, Ujgorod, and other towns. The life story of this man was horrible. His first wife and six children were killed in Auschwitz. Miraculously he survived and, thanks to his deep faith, was able to make himself return to live and work and even to build a new family. Then, from 1950 to 1953, to avoid arrest, he hid from Stalin's bloodhounds, sent out for his arrest. There were entire days and nights that he spent buried under mud in a ditch by the road, but never once during those three years did he forgo a single *mitzvah*. While this was going on, his second wife heroically raised four little children. When I knew him, his hair was entirely gray, even though he was well below sixty. Incidentally, he was the first Jew with *pei'ot* whom I had ever seen. He now lives in Brooklyn.

In the home of Rabbi Yosef Mordechai I learned a great deal about Jewish laws and customs. Among other things I acquired the art of baking fragrant *Shabbat challot* and since then I have baked *challah* at our home for every *Shabbat*.

The time I spent in Transcarpathia was wonderful. Contact with Soviet reality was suspended, almost completely broken. Everything was devoted to God, Torah and the Jewish people (*am Yisrael*); every minute was filled with Jewish learning. During the Ten Days of Penitence between Rosh Hashana and Yom Kippur, I devoted many hours each day, in the chasidic tradition, to reading *Tehillim*, the Psalms of King David. I recited the entire book up to three times a day, and once I was able to repeat the reading a full five times in the course of a single day.

Meanwhile our son, Geka, was growing up, and this created new problems. We had to protect him from the pernicious influences of the outside environment and open the wisdom and harmony of the Torah to him as early as possible, while taking care that he not give us away. By age one-and-a-half to two years he already knew quite thoroughly the difference between *Shabbat* and weekdays, between kosher and *treif* food. By age three he not only had mastered the Hebrew alphabet, but he knew many Hebrew words and could read a few simple ones. But at the same time he had to understand that not only were there Jews and non-Jews, but that only with "good Jews" could he talk about the prayers which he was starting to read from the *siddur,* about *Shabbat* and about *Hakadosh Baruch Hu*. He adjusted well to all the rules of the conspiracy. With only rare exceptions he knew how to determine by himself with whom he could speak about what. Naturally, at home he wore a *yarmulke,* which he adroitly hid in his pocket whenever anyone came to us. And visitors came often because we were still living at the academic residences of Salaspils, so most of our neighbors were my colleagues. Neighbors were always coming to borrow kitchen utensils, to the point that we had to amass a special set of *treif* equipment for lending purposes. On *Shabbat* we had to light the candles behind the closet in a back room of our apartment. Often in the middle of our *Shabbat* meal uninvited visitors would show up. We would sit with them for hours in the front room, while the food that Fania had cooked got cold and dry. For the Pesach *seder* we would cover the windows with black curtains as if for an air raid. We would open the door only to those who knocked in a special way agreed upon in advance. Later we changed apartments, moving to the center of Riga to a house inhabited by people we didn't know, so this problem became less acute.

Geka loved hearing about Jewish history, about our forefather Abraham, about Moshe Rabbeinu and King David, about the Exodus from Egypt, about the Temple in Jerusalem. He presented many questions about the incorporeality of God, about the human soul, and about the Holy Land of Israel, which he longed for more than the most enticing toys. When he started going to school a new problem arose—how to free him from studies on Saturday. I still was not ready to sacrifice my work at the Academy, so I decided not to do as my friends the *Chasidim* did—either not to send Geka to school at all or to go to the principal and demand that our son be released from Saturday classes because we were religious. We chose the more cowardly path; we obtained a doctor's letter testifying that Geka's state of health necessitated his having two days of rest a week.

33

Different Ways That Lead to Zion

More and more Jews were leaving. The emigrants began to include nonreligious people as well as those who had not belonged to the Zionist movement before the advent of the Soviet regime, and even those who had not been recently drawn to either Judaism or Zionism. These Jews, who seemed to be indifferent to everything Jewish, apparently were being carried along by the tide. A peculiar "chain reaction" was going on. The departure of one Jew "stimulated" others to go—relatives, neighbors, colleagues.

The most important advance in the exodus movement was the entry of Dr. Mendel Gordon into the battleground. This shy, quiet, young Rigan doctor was the first Soviet Jew with a Ph.D. to get permission to leave for Israel. Mendel was the first to devise and test most of the tactics which later became the trademarks of the "refuseniks." He sent back his Soviet identification papers several times to Moscow and renounced his Soviet citizenship. This left him unemployed, homeless, and hungry. Although Mendel came from a religious family in Dvinsk, he had long been far removed from Judaism. Now, having entered into single-handed combat against the Communist regime, he at once returned to the ethics of his fathers. It must be said that at that time—in the early 1970s—the search of young Jews, especially academics, for the way back to Torah was becoming a fairly widespread phenomenon in Riga, Leningrad, and Moscow.

I was very interested in these people who were taking the same path that I had fortunately chosen earlier. This interest did not consist only of a feeling of special kinship, but of definite practical considerations as well. It was important for me to understand the motives driving these people to Judaism and Torah, so that this spontaneous process could be intensified and stimulated.

It turned out that the majority of them were not at all moved by recognizable philosophical reasons. Ethical-moral aspects held more importance for many. And there were many also who, moreover, found it difficult to analyze their reasons for turning to Torah. Sometimes negative factors played a major role: offense inflicted by a hostile environment, difficulties in getting accepted to a university or in advancing in work. But often there were positive factors contributing to the rekindling of their Jewish spark such as chance gleanings of information about the Torah and Jewish laws and customs. One person, for example, was stimulated by reading the last chapter in Deuteronomy, in which the Jewish people are warned about turning away from God and are told of the punishments and disasters that would befall them if they do. When he compared this with what was going on in the world, the realization of the total fulfillment of the prophecy made him shudder. This was the turning point of his life. Another one read *The Jewish War* by Feuchtwanger and started his return from there. There were many others who by chance (or so it seemed to them) met a *Chabad Chasid* and, through accepting an invitation to spend *Shabbat* with a religious family or even to put on phylacteries just once, they discovered a new world for themselves.

These people were all young. Most of them had a university education. Although differing in many ways, they were all equally wholehearted in their devotion to their newly discovered Torah, for which they were prepared to happily undergo any sacrifice or deprivation. Their new life-style presented numerous problems at work and in their studies. But possibly even more difficult for them were conflicts that arose with parents and wives.

It's questionable whether the Hebrew term for penitents—*baalei teshuvah* (meaning literally "returnees")—is appropriate for people who had never even heard before of anything Jewish to which they could later return. At any rate, the life history of every one of them was a moving tale. I shall mention here only a few of the dozens of *baalei teshuvah* whom I knew. For example, there was David Kajdan of Moscow University. One of the most talented mathematicians of our generation, he became an able student of *gemara* within a few years of learning almost entirely by himself. Or take Shmuel Raphaelson, a boy from Riga who became impassioned with Judaism at age twelve and spent months living on bread and water when he was unable to obtain kosher food. Or Tzvi Epstein, a teacher from Kolmna who would spend eight hours a day traveling to and from a remote school where he was allowed to teach without taking his hat off. The people mentioned here have left Russia, but hundreds of new *baalei teshuvah* are constantly springing up in Riga, in Moscow, in Leningrad, in Tashkent.

After many ordeals, Mendel Gordon won and was given permission to leave. His success bore great psychological significance which strongly influenced others. It was apparent now that the situation of young Jews holding advanced academic degrees was no longer hopeless!

The *Chasidim* were leaving one after the other. As the number of *Chasidim* in Riga declined, my personal responsibilities in helping to maintain Jewish life and education within the local community increased, as did my duties in writing and disseminating literature on Jewish and Israeli subjects. This demanded more of my time than my work at the Academy and limited my collaboration with *aliyah* activists. My friends and I considered Jewish education to be even more important in the long run than *aliyah* because any Jew who had even just an iota of Jewish education would soon be found in the ranks of those fighting to leave for Israel.

At that time, June 1970, the "National Co-ordinating Conference of Fighters for Jewish Emigration" took place. Sad to say, the politicking was so great that before the conference even opened, political quarrels had broken the assembly into factions, the number of which seemed to exceed the number of participants. This picture contrasted sharply with that of our Chasidic movement, where no one sought glory or rushed to express his opinions. *Chabadniks* preferred to concentrate on tedious mundane tasks with clear results and tremendous moral satisfaction.

And then, the famous Leningrad "Airplane Affair" occurred, followed by related court trials that agitated the entire Jewish world. On the one hand there was worry and concern for those who had been arrested, and on the other hand there was joy and pride that the *aliyah* movement had become so strong. However, even in this stormy period charged with pro-Israel consciousness, the number of Jews actually affected by this awakening remained an extremely modest minority among the total three million Jews in the Soviet Union.

There were far more Jews who only passively sympathized with those of their brothers who were finding their way back. These passive sympathizers thirsted to know what was happening on the Jewish front, as these events aroused within them sweet memories of their childhood and of their parents' and grandparents' homes. However, they clearly rejected the possibility of participating in Jewish activism because, in the final analysis, they valued Russian culture, their professional careers, and their orderly lives far more than these emotions and sentiments. There were other Jews in the Soviet Union who were openly hostile to the awakening Jewish movement, which they saw as a threat to their well-being. And finally, the vast silent majority of Soviet Jewry not only did not participate in these events, but—as unlikely as this may sound—they were hardly aware that anything was going on. All that interested these people were material matters such as a better, private apartment, a car, a *dacha,* exclusive imported clothes, enrolling their child in a university.

There is another group which could be mentioned here—the Jews who comprise the core of the "Democratic Movement," struggling to change the situation within Russia. The only thing they have in common with the *aliyah* movement is a common enemy. This small movement enjoys neither mass support nor any chances of success. It sprang up, apparently, only thanks to the success of the Jewish *aliyah* movement—the only movement during the entire Soviet regime to oppose government policy and to achieve its aims. (I doubt that anyone can provide a rational explanation for the success of the Jewish movement in Russia.)

The "Democratic Movement" presented a complication for the Jewish movement. However, the most immediate, dangerous enemy of the Jewish awakening was and still is Judeo-Christianity. The center of this movement is in a Moscow church, headed by an exceedingly enterprising convert (from Judaism to Christianity). Exploiting the fact that the Russian Jews who are now thirsting for spirituality are catastrophically ignorant of Judaism (the way back is blocked by many linguistic, cultural, and psychological barriers), this Judeo-Christian leader and his cronies lure unwary souls by the easy accessibility of their poisoned wares. For some time this group has been obsessed by a large ambition. They want to establish their church in Israel. Toward this end, they have been channeling people to Israel who are instructed to outwardly behave as Jews, even as believing, observant Jews. The tragedy is that for secular Jews both in Russia and in Israel it is very hard to sense the danger and the far-reaching consequences of this threat.

34

We Finally Apply Officially for Emigration

In the summer of 1971, the new developments finally reached us. My sister's and my brother's families left one after the other. A little later I received a *vizov* from them—a genuine, authentic invitation to come live in Israel. At last after so many years of waiting and wanting to leave, I was able to take positive action.

This did not mean that the express route to the Promised Land now lay open before me. This did not even mean that I could realistically expect that they would let us go in the near future. But it sufficed that I no longer had to sit idly by, shuddering at the thought that the door, opening ever so slightly to freedom, might be slammed shut at any moment.

During my long years under Soviet rule, I had collected papers, documents, and photographs many times for all kinds of institutions, but never had I done this with as much enthusiasm as I did now. It didn't matter that Fania and I had lost our jobs. It didn't matter that I had absolutely no idea what we would live on while waiting to receive permission to leave. And this could take years.

The day that I brought the papers to the Department of Visas and Registration (O.V.I.R.) of the Ministry of Internal Affairs was one of the happiest days of my life. Outside of the fact that this was the first step on the way to Israel, I immediately felt freed from many chains that had been restraining me for years. I no longer had to worry about my job at the Academy. I no longer had to hunt for an "underground" *minyan* in a private apartment. No longer did I have to travel to Georgia or Transcarpathia for the High Holidays. I didn't have to hide my beret in my pocket anymore. I could even let my beard grow now, obeying the Jewish law not to "round off the side-growth of your head or destroy the side-growth of your beard."

It would not be an exaggeration to say that at the time I submitted my application for permission to receive a visa, I had reached the maximum success and prosperity possible in the Soviet Union. I was earning a top salary and had a flat in the center of town, a car, and even a dacha on the shore of Riga Bay. Moreover, I had achieved recognition as an authority in my scientific field of magnetohydrodynamics. I had published many articles, monographs, and textbooks. I had students. If I had not "spoiled" my autobiography by my adventures with the Polish woman and the Israeli diplomats, then I surely would have been able to even travel abroad on business or to climb the administrative ladder.

According to any "normal" Soviet citizen, I had everything necessary for a quiet, orderly, fully satisfying and happy life. But this success only depressed me more, as it reminded me how far away I was from fulfilling my true aspirations. It was an achievement in the very opposite direction of that in which I wanted to go.

In distraction, I did everything possible so as not to feel this sweet prosperity. I deprived myself of needed sleep to spend hours poring over old Hebrew volumes which stubbornly would not yield to me. I would write and rewrite essays on Jewish-philosophical concerns. I wrote these essays only to burn them—either out of dissatisfaction with what I had written or out of lack of a place to keep them. I participated in all kinds of "illegal" Chasidic activities, free now to place my life in danger. And when and if I ever had a spare moment, I would sink into reverie about how someday I would help build the Land of Israel. Mostly I saw myself in the Negev desert seeking new ways to desalinate sea water. Sometimes my dreams linked my future with aeronautics (after all I was an expert in fluid dynamics!). I imagined myself spending sleepless weeks in Israeli laboratories working on endless experiments connected with development and defense projects.

It is no wonder, then, that when the long-awaited time came to take a stand for *aliyah,* I happily rejected my worldly achievements—my security, my prestige, and the opportunity to be scientifically creative.

About a month and a half after submitting our applications we received the expected refusal. I started to write endless letters and complaints. I made appointments with ministers and deputy ministers. I went to the Central Party Committee. The Latvian Minister of Internal Affairs told me that as I had worked in close contact under the same roof with people engaged in secret research, I couldn't help but know what they were doing, even though I never had "access" to secret work. Therefore, I would have to postpone my emigration until I forgot everything. "It's possible that they'll give you permission in five years," he said. "But then again, it might take ten to fifteen years."

I can't say that this encouraged me, but my morale was still much better than before I submitted my request. A number of *Chasidim* still remained in Riga, and they hastened to encourage me. Foremost among them was Shlomo Feigin. Studying Torah together with him became even more vital and joyful for me. I delighted also in being able to participate at the synagogue every day of the week, and I tried not to miss any of the public prayers.

It was wonderful to go to the synagogue openly, just as I would go to my own house. I have already written here that, to a great extent, ever since meeting the *Chasidim* I stopped feeling the authority of the Soviet regime, as from then on everything that happened in my life was on such a high spiritual plane that the KGB was powerless to interfere. Having to pretend and lead a double life, keeping secret everything connected with observing the *mitzvot,* had nonetheless been a terrible burden and constraint. Now I could walk proudly to the synagogue with nothing to hide.

How happy I was to get up just before daylight to ride or walk through the city, holding *tallit* and *tefillin* and talking with Jews about Torah and the Jewish destiny. On *Shabbat* after the morning prayers I would stay in the synagogue for *kiddush* and then sit for a long time, listening to explanations of the weekly *sidra* of the *Chumash* and endlessly enjoying the spiritual warmth and the atmosphere of brotherhood.

35

The Refuseniks Struggle

I continued to write complaints and to protest. Soon I started getting phone calls from abroad: from London, Paris, New York, Geneva, and many other cities. The leaders of various movements for Soviet Jewry, students, women's groups, senators, and the chief rabbis of England, France, and Israel phoned. Chief Rabbi Unterman's call from Israel especially excited me, of course. Several Nobel Prize winners and members of the Nobel Committee in Sweden also telephoned me saying that they were considering me as a nominee for my accomplishments in magnetohydrodynamics. Horrified by the idea that this could be an additional obstacle blocking my way to Israel, I begged them to leave me alone. Then again, Senator Walter Mondale called, asking me what I wished to say to the U.S. Senate.

Knowing the absolute indifference of the Soviets to public opinion, I could not see how this would help me. I would try to explain to the person at the other end of the line that I would prefer a statesman or scientist or writer on good terms with the Soviets to act on my behalf. My interlocutor was usually so intoxicated with his organizational success that he was too excited to listen to me patiently, so all I could do was to thank him cordially. All this ingratiation would take place at three o'clock in the morning, after I had already gotten up for several other calls— talking in English, no less—and knowing that the KGB was recording everything. I honestly admit that it was not very pleasant.

Eventually the KGB cut off my phone. At that time I established contact with some of the Riga *aliyah* activist groups, which were bitterly hostile to one another most of the time. I started to participate in their activities—collective letters, demonstrations, hunger strikes, mass marches to government institutions. Later I began to suggest ideas for various initiatives, a number of which were actually carried out. To tell the truth, however, this so-called struggle disgusted me. Its aim was not to bring any harm at all upon the regime that was tormenting us, but rather to simply attract attention to our demands. Moreover, this "struggle" had to be conducted very delicately so as not to cross over the fine line leading to prison.

I searched frantically for new forms of action that would truly hurt our enemies while—even more importantly—being good for us. Finally, I had it. Torah, collective study of Torah! What could be more dangerous to the Soviet powers than the study of Torah? And what could better guarantee the continuation and future of the *aliyah* movement?! Not without reason had the Torah been one of the prime targets of the Communist regime ever since 1917. On the other hand, what could be more beneficial for us, preparing to settle in *Eretz Hakodesh,* than to become accustomed to Jewish learning?

I tried to explain to the *aliyah* activists that for us, being unemployed and having so much spare time available in this interim period before our physical *aliyah* provided a wonderful opportunity to regain the Judaism that our Soviet upbringing and education had denied us. Alas, it was very hard to make these people see the necessity of becoming Jews in the full sense of the word right there, in the Soviet exile.

I submitted a request to all kinds of high government offices to permit us to set up a study circle on Jewish religion at the Riga synagogue. I did not doubt that permission would not be granted and that the authorities would simply not respond. But it was important that my request be registered. This gave us a trump card against any possible accusation that our studies were implicated with anything anti-Soviet.

While futilely waiting a month for a reply from the government, we started to meet in small groups at private homes. Starting from *aleph,* we explained the meaning of the Jewish people and the Torah, pointing out that just as it is a disgrace for an intelligent Russian not to know who Shakespeare, Repin, and Beethoven were, so is it even more a disgrace for an intelligent Jew not to know who Ezra and Nechemia, Hillel and Shammai, or Yehuda Halevy were.

I should mention perhaps that for some of my former colleagues and Jewish acquaintances, my transition to open belief and observance of *halachah* aroused slanderous talk. Following a chimeric logic, they accused me of pretension. Sometimes they tried to disrupt the studies I organized. And toward this end, alas, they stopped at nothing, not even at seeking the help of the Soviet government. This is a sad story, and I would prefer not to discuss it.

Seeing how much time and strength the refuseniks were wasting, I tried to devise more and more ways to channel their energy into Jewish self-improvement through strengthening their Jewish consciousness. It seemed strange that these people, who were so decisively breaking away from their past in order to fulfill the important *mitzvah* of *aliyah* to *Eretz Yisrael,* were disregarding the other 612 commandments as well as other Jewish responsibilities. It was painful to see that most of these people, persecuted and suffering, did not turn their thoughts to God, seeking His help and support. Only rare exceptions among them did what the grandfathers and great-grandfathers of all of them would not have failed to do.

I could not help but compare these people with my many chasidic friends who had already managed to leave Russia and become acclimatized in Israel. I realized more and more clearly that the best thing for these rootless *refuseniks* was to start to learn how to be *Jews* while still in Russia. Otherwise, after having totally broken off from their past, they stood in danger of becoming catastrophically alienated when they did get to Israel. With their immediate goal of *aliyah* achieved, what would they do without the opposition of the Soviet regime to spur their emotions?

I tried to use every opportunity possible to draw attention to the spiritual aspect of what was happening to us. Thus at a gathering at Rumbula on Lag b'Omer, I talked about the meaning of this holiday so unknown to Soviet Jews. I tried to explain that with all the greatness that Bar Kochba personified in physical military strength, in historical perspective Rabbi Akiva—who personified spiritual strength—proved to be far greater.

All these efforts were like drops in the ocean. But, nevertheless, I saw that there were some people—although few in number—upon whom my persuasions and explanations were beginning to seem effective. And this was enough to keep me from despair and to make me continue.

At this time the KGB and the police began to harass us more and more. Trying to intimidate me, they even accused me of having killed a child in a hit-and-run accident. After endless interrogations, they apologized for the "mistake." However, we continued to live in unbearable tension. Each knock at the door could mean a new arrest; every call—another interrogation by the regular or secret police. There is no sense in dwelling on this in more detail because hundreds of Soviet Jews have endured similar and often worse ordeals, which have been widely publicized in the media.

The tension was mounting, and I was getting quite anxious. I kept my brother in Israel informed of my worsening situation, and he made a tour of Europe and America in order to organize support for me from American Jews, prominent scientists, and so forth.

For the first time I was able to experience how much I had gained psychologically by acquiring faith. Dozens of times it saved me from despair. After pouring out my soul in prayer or submerging myself in Torah study, I again became uplifted and certain of our ultimate success. Geka had even more faith and was more certain than I that we would soon leave. And the anxiety only made Fania stronger. But my poor long-suffering mother could not take it. The tension drained her strength and aged her terribly.

36

The Rebbe's Blessing over the Telephone

In August 1972 the Soviet government started to demand ransom as repayment for the cost of the higher education of Jews who wanted to leave the country. At first it was hard to clarify the exact price of each diploma, but it was evident that my various diplomas were going to cost me a lot. I estimated that they would total tens of thousands of rubles. Even if I were able to continue working as before, it would take at least five to ten years—without eating or drinking—to raise the sums that were being demanded. And here I had been unemployed for a year without earning anything. (We had been living all this time by selling clothes which we received in packages from world Jewry. In particular, Notke had entrusted us to the care of the New York organization *"Ezras Achim,"* which sent us things easy and profitable to sell.)

This new obstacle of diploma ransoming, however, did not shake our unwavering belief that we would surely leave in the near future. True, there were days when it seemed hopeless. Sometimes after a routine visit to the KGB it seemed that these ordeals would never end and that the next time they called me, I would have to stay with them.

One day I gathered my courage and went to the post office to call the Lubavitcher Rebbe in New York. Although convinced that they wouldn't connect me with New York, in less than ten minutes I was talking with the Rebbe's secretary. The Rebbe gave me his blessings and assured me that we would soon receive permission to leave.

The autumn holidays came and went—our last holidays in the Soviet Union. Immediately after Simchat Torah we got permission to leave. Only a week before they had dragged me to the KGB and intimidated me, and now suddenly—they were letting us go. It was all so pitifully simple and prosaic. They called me to come in, informed me, and presented a bill for my diplomas. Throughout the many years that we had waited for this moment, it had always seemed to us that when it came, the earth would stand still, thunder would roll and lightning would flash. But nothing of the sort happened. A petty clerk simply called us to her office and told us that permission had been granted. And now, when I am writing these lines, it's even hard to remember any details outside of the fact that it was most prosaic, with no orchestras playing.

Recovering from the happy shock, we started to study the bill that had been presented to us. It came to more than thirty-one thousand rubles. This far exceeded any amount of money which I had ever held in my hands at one time.

Some people tried to convince us not to even try to raise the money. They said that we should wait and protest, and so forth. Our telephone started working again at that point, and among our callers from abroad were those who advised us to "boycott" this so-called "tax-on-education." Their advice seemed absolutely absurd to me. If the Soviet government were burning with desire to expel all its Jews while also demanding payment of this "tax," then perhaps, just out of spite, a Soviet Jew might decide not to leave and to fight to abolish this ransom. But considering that Jews had to wait years in order to receive permission to leave Russia, then the advice to protest and refuse to leave was not only stupid but, in my opinion, destructive.

Moreover, it was clear to me, now that I had finally gotten hold of the cherished permission to go to Israel, that a contemptible thing like money could not stand in the way—even if I had to work to pay it off to the end of my days.

In the end, everything worked out more simply and faster than ever anticipated. Both in Riga and in Georgia, Jews with money were found who trusted me and were willing to lend us all that we needed. Within a few days I brought a very heavy bundle to the bank. All the members of my family together with Bubi Tzeitlin (who came especially for this occasion out of his love for the extraordinary) could not count the piles of bank notes. None of us were experienced enough in money-counting.

From then on, everything went smoothly and happily. Running around to countless bureaucrats and waiting in long lines didn't bother me. It was even fun solving bureaucratic puzzles, for instance when office A doesn't give out form X until receiving form Y, given out by office B, but office B demands that it be given form X first, and so forth.

It took quite a lot of time to arrange for permission to transport my library. They made me pay the value of all my old books, even though they were my own. Furthermore, my entire collection (especially my old Hebrew volumes) had to be subjected to a thorough inspection, including leafing through pages and shaking bindings.

Yet, after two weeks we were sitting on board a train headed for the town of Brest on the Polish border. Many people had accompanied us to the railroad station. The door to our apartment had not been closed for twenty-four hours straight the day before we left. Relatives, friends, and even people we didn't know came to say good-bye. Many of them had requests or favors to ask which I either listed in my notebook, codified in secret code, or tried to commit to memory.

I had bidden farewell to the synagogue on my last *Shabbat* in Riga. *Kiddush* that day took several hours. The congregants parted from me with a heartfelt warmth which I shall never forget: trembling palms gripped in warm embrace; eyes pouring out benevolence and yearning, joy and hope and everlasting sorrow. The usual *Shabbat* singing, which somehow always sounded new, this time contained a special prayer, *Hoshia es amecha* . . . ("Save Thy people and bless Thy heritage . . ."—not just simply an abstract "save" but "save *us*, O ever-present and near God, our Protector, our own.") The beseeching words and melody soared upward to reverberate off the vaulted ceiling. Outside, all around, bustled the noise and exhaust fumes of the Soviet street. There, inside, under the arches of the cellar that housed the chasidic synagogue, *Shabbat* tranquillity reigned over Jews who, with overflowing hearts, were drinking *l'chayim* to their brother on his way to the Promised Land and wishing each other a speedy departure on the same path.

37

The Train Crosses the Border of the Soviet Union

T hus, the train made its way to Brest, getting closer and closer to the border that I had so often envisioned and dreamed about. Before crossing the border, we still had one final confrontation with the Soviet regime—a baggage check. Before leaving Riga, I had burned most of my published and all unpublished manuscripts, notes, and card files, so as not to waste time on making arrangements for mere papers in light of the more important and joyful occasion of our *aliyah* to *Eretz Hakodesh*. So we thought that we held nothing seditious in our bags. It goes without saying that we also had neither gold nor diamonds on us. Nevertheless, they found forbidden objects in the search: bundles of old letters dear to me and a box of family movies and tapes. They ordered all this to be returned to the Soviet Union by our relatives who were accompanying us to the border.

Finally, we were back on the train. Ever so slowly, it moved toward the border. We were exhausted from the prolonged excitement, and so the longed-for moment of our dreams slipped by drably.

And then we were in Poland. In Warsaw the train stopped for more than an hour at a suburban platform. I was eager to finally step on non-Soviet soil. Moreover this was the Poland which I had unsuccessfully tried to reach fifteen years before. Taking Geka, I walked out onto the dark platform. We walked around a station warehouse. Everything within me was singing and rejoicing, but my thoughts were racing forward to that still distant, but now attainable, Mediterranean shore.

The next day we arrived in Vienna. There we were taken beyond the city to the Schönau Castle, where the Jewish Agency ran a transit camp for Russian Jews. We were accompanied there by Austrian policemen, armed with automatic rifles to protect us against Arab terrorists. Entering the castle, we heard people speaking Hebrew and saw large photographs of Israeli landscapes hanging on the walls. And we were choked with tears. An incomparable feeling of being among our own, among brothers, filled us with indescribable happiness.

We stayed at Schönau for a day and a half. There were group singing and song-teaching, lectures, films. There were Hebrew- and Russian-language books, journals and newspapers printed in Israel. It was an unpleasant surprise to see how mediocre and grammatically incorrect the Israel Russian-language publications were. But I had neither the time nor the inclination then to worry about such things. The holiday feeling at meeting my homeland prevailed over everything. And it was only just beginning.

The Jewish Agency workers—those indefatigable angels—put us aboard an El Al plane. We departed from Vienna after midnight, but I kept my eyes glued to the portholes, straining to discern something in the heavy darkness beyond. At last the Israeli coastline appeared beneath us. The lights of Tel Aviv shot through the darkness, and in a few minutes the plane was rushing along the runway. I would have liked to go back and relive those minutes, like going over slow-motion film, lingering upon and savoring every detail.

38

I Kiss the Land of Israel

B ut it was already time to alight. Dawn was beginning to brighten the eastern sky. We stepped outside onto the stair-platform. The warm humid air of the Mediterranean night blew in my face. I looked down and stopped. Anxiety and confusion seized me. Twenty steps below me lay the Land of Israel—the land eternally promised to Abraham, Isaac, and Jacob; the land to which Moses led the Jews; the land upon which had stood the First and Second Temples; the land to which generation after generation had turned in prayer and tears. Was I ready to meet this land? Did I have the moral right to tread on it, to soil it with my coarse shoes? Someone pushed me in irritation. I was blocking all movement out of the plane. I had no choice but to go down. Reaching the bottom of the stairs, I fell on my knees, bent over and kissed the ground. But, sensing the astonished stares of the passengers around me, I immediately got up.

Everyone was in a frightful hurry. Upon entering the airport building, they rushed to the tables where representatives of the Ministry of Absorption sat. Everyone was afraid of missing out on the best housing offers.

I was still trying to comprehend the magnitude of the occasion. Therefore, being reminded about mundane arrangements seemed to me to be disgraceful and blasphemous. Circumstances did not allow me, however, to concentrate on my thoughts. Not only my brother and Notke had come to meet me, but also Knesset member Avraham Verdiger (of the Poalei Agudat Yisrael religious party) and a number of newspaper and radio correspondents. Avraham Verdiger was the first person with whom I spoke in Israel. My throat was so parched from the excitement that I could not talk. Verdiger brought me some juice to drink, and gradually my voice returned.

Leaving the airport building I was met by a large group of *Chabadniks* from Riga and elsewhere, a representative of the religious university of Bar-Ilan, and several people whom I didn't know. After kissing and embracing, the *Chabadniks* immediately broke into *chasidic* dancing on the sidewalk, and we sang and danced for a long time. Then all my family got together at my sister's house in *Rishon Letzion*. It was Friday, *Cheshvan* 19, 5733. Before evening set in, we went to Notke's house at Lod to spend the first *Shabbat* in *Eretz Hakodesh* with him.

Exhaustion and a torrent of impressions and feelings of unimaginably great magnitude slightly subdued my euphoria. But, just the same, it was a holiday— an endless and unending holiday where human warmth, friendliness, and benevolence prevailed. Dancing *Chabadniks* carried my son and me into the old synagogue in the *Chabad* section of Lod, overflowing with friends and acquaintances from Russia and with strangers, apparently people from the streets who recognized us from the photos and write-ups about our arrival in the newspapers. These people were all so genuinely happy about our *aliyah;* they so sincerely wanted to help us and smiled in such a kind way.

39

First Trip to Jerusalem

W ithin a very short time I began to be literally torn to pieces by invitations to every possible kind of meeting, soirée, and discussion. I had to learn how not to quail before large, strange audiences and to address them in Hebrew, English, or Yiddish. I had never formally studied either Hebrew or Yiddish, except for one year of Hebrew in elementary school and a brief effort at independent study during my student years in Leningrad. However, learning Torah and the prayers with the *Chabadniks* in Riga had given me—among other things—the gift of two Jewish languages. It turned out that I could express myself in both of them quite adequately.

Two types of audiences intimidated me—religious Jews and children. The former intimidated me because of their immeasurable superiority in Torah. How could I—trying to compensate for what I had missed in my childhood—measure up to people who from early childhood on had systematically studied in *yeshivot?* I remember how difficult it was for me to speak when they brought me for the first time to Kfar Chabad for a national conference of Lubavitch *Chasidim* in Israel. They wanted to hear about Jewish life in Russia. I stood in front of the microphone, looking at the enormous hall filled with gray-bearded Jews in black frock-coats. Alongside tremendous joy, fear overcame me. Who was I to appear before such people steeped in Torah wisdom? Finally, I got hold of myself and began to speak. Seeing hundreds of smiles and eyes radiating friendship, I calmed down.

I was always afraid to address an audience of children. Being aware of the tremendous responsibility involved, I would fear that I would not succeed in convincing them or in establishing genuine contact.

Among my impressions of that time, I remember my first visit to Jerusalem. Avraham Verdiger invited Fania, Geka, and me to the Knesset. All four of us went there, together with my brother and his wife. On the way from Tel Aviv, I was afraid of missing the smallest detail of the landscape. After the littered eyesores and rusted wrecked car dumps of the outskirts of Tel Aviv, there followed cultivated fields and kitchen-gardens, irrigated by water sprayers, and tidy little houses of agricultural settlements. Finally the eucalyptus-tree-lined road brought us to the Valley of Ayalon. At the other end of the valley, the Judean hills floated in the haze. Ten minutes later we were already traveling through these hills.

My excitement was growing by the minute. It seemed that we were approaching far too fast, at a pace that did not allow me to collect my thoughts and prepare myself spiritually to meet the Holy City. And indeed Jerusalem caught me by surprise. The indifferent car engine sped us uphill at eighty kilometers per hour, and suddenly I found myself in Jerusalem. I did not notice then the unique Jerusalem sunlight, multiplied by the reflection of the golden Jerusalem stone. I did not notice the quaint, alluring side streets climbing up the hill slopes. I was distressed that here I was, standing in Jerusalem, *Ir Hakodesh,* but I had not yet managed to prepare anything to offer. Tears of happiness and gratitude welled in my eyes.

On that first visit to Jerusalem, my chief worry was to make sure that I wouldn't find myself by chance at the Western Wall. This meeting demanded more thorough preparation. Only days later—on *Rosh Chodesh Kislev*—did I finally resolve to go to the Wall.

At first I kept count of my visits to Jerusalem, as each one was an event in itself. I counted up to twelve and then lost track. However, for a long time I was unable to get used to the fact that it was possible to say simply, "I'm going to Jerusalem"—and actually do it.

After a few months we went to America to see the Rebbe. I also had to give the seminars in several universities that had been postponed for so many years. I wasn't earning a living yet, but *Chabadnik* friends lent me the money for the trip.

40

First Personal Meeting with the Rebbe

S ince leaving the Soviet Union, I have met and talked with many famous people—prime ministers, presidents of states, city mayors, ministers, writers, Jewish and non-Jewish leaders and public figures. Many interesting things could be written about every one of these meetings. Here, however, I wish to describe only my most important and impressive meeting, with the man of unsurpassed exaltedness and stature—the Lubavitcher Rebbe, the great man and the great Jew and mentor of our generation.

We arrived in New York—Fania, Geka, and I—in the beginning of the month of *Shvat,* a little over two months since the day we first trod upon the soil of *Eretz Yisrael.* At the New York airport we were met by two *Chasidim,* themselves recent arrivals from Russia. One of them was Mendel Gorelik, an old friend of ours, Notke's "in-law," whom we had already met in Israel. The other, a young man by the name of Hershel Okunev, was one of the few people who, while still in Russia, had managed completely to escape school studies and to acquire their entire education at the underground *yeshivot.* Now Hershel had come to New York in order to study at the Rebbe's *yeshivah,* and in the meantime he had founded a society whose aim was to help Russian Jews.

The two went out of their way to give us a warm and hospitable welcome and to make our stay as convenient as possible. They arranged a place for us at the home of a young couple—Michael and Leah Slavin. At that time the couple were expecting their first child (today, ten years later, praise God, they have nine), and so they devoted all their warmth and time to guests. The home of this wonderful couple, who could serve as the model example to be emulated by all young couples, became a permanent refuge for me whenever I visited New York. The Slavins resided on the same street—Eastern Parkway—where, at number 770, the World Headquarters of the Lubavitcher Movement and the Rebbe's office were situated. The distance between their apartment and Seven-Seventy was only a two-minute walk. It was only natural that the first place we were shown by our hosts was the *Chabad* World Headquarters, where we were given an opportunity to see the Rebbe—from afar.

Once again I had the same feeling that had seized me upon my first arrival in Israel, and later in Jerusalem. Am I ready? Am I worthy? Has the hour finally come? Or do I still have to complete something, to learn some more from the Torah? To do a good deed? Yet my hosts left me no time for misgivings. However, I still insisted on first cleansing myself in the *mikveh.* It was already evening; most of the *mikva'ot* had closed. After a lengthy search, we managed to find a *mikveh,* dark and neglected. The water was ice-cold; yet I immersed myself a number of times. And then I was being escorted to Seven-Seventy, my heart faint with excitement and tense expectation. In my head, heavy after the long and exhausting journey, the present intermingled with memories and images from the wonderful chasidic world. Over the years since the time I had met Notke, the Rebbe had been invisibly present in all our actions and thoughts. The chasidic world had opened before us concealed depths, filled with warmth and light, that stem from the personalities of the Baal Shem Tov and the Alter Rebbe.

There I was, then, heading for the Rebbe's house, the place where he works, prays, and studies the Torah: me—a *baal teshuvah,* unlearned in Torah, unversed in God's works.

During prayers I beheld the Rebbe for the first time. Surrounded by a tight ring of people waiting for him to arrive, I was shivering with emotion, feverishly trying to recall the little I could recall from the Book of Psalms. I did not know how to thank God for the favor He had granted me by finally bringing me here, to this fabulous place where everything spiritual and abstract became tangible and real, while everything tangible and plain to see became a fantasy. Unstoppable tears of gratitude were pouring down my face, as I vainly tried to come to grips with the idea of someone like me, who until recently did not even know the alphabet, being granted the privilege of standing here as an equal, and accepted by all the "newly born" brothers who shared my views. How could I absorb this unbelievable reality of standing there, with all the rest, waiting with bated breath for the entrance of the *tzaddik,* as people must have once antici- pated the appearance of the high priest in Jerusalem.

Suddenly everything stirred into motion. The circle of people grew even tighter. There was total silence. The Rebbe had come. With rapid steps, he approached his seat, scanning the faces of the audience on his way. For an instance his gaze fell on me. And what a gaze it was! I felt that in that moment he was taking instant X-ray photos of my entire life, all my thoughts and feelings. Yet how strange: his piercing look, far from being disconcerting, radiated a warmth and genuine concern that gave me a sense of well-being and exhilaration. In a split second the Rebbe shifted his eyes to other people, while I remained riveted to my spot, awe-struck. Then I noticed that the others were praying, and tried to join in, to catch up with what I had missed.

That was my first encounter with the Rebbe. Yet the most important meeting was still to come: the *yechidut* – a private interview with the Rebbe. I waited for this first personal meeting with the Rebbe with a degree of excitement and impatience that I never experienced before. However, I cannot deny that these feelings were mixed with some fear of disappointment. The unbounded devo- tion, admiration, and adoration of *Chasidim* for the Lubavitcher Rebbe some- times bothered me. Although, by then, I was already quite steeped in the ideas of *Chabad,* this particular aspect of it disturbed me. It awakened echoes of skepticism, which I had long since overcome.

I prepared myself for this meeting just as a *Chasid* ought to prepare for a meeting with his spiritual teacher, *tzaddik,* and intermediary between himself and God. I fasted all day (the meeting took place after midnight; the Rebbe had already held about fifty such private meetings that night), cleansed myself in the *mikveh,* and girded myself in a prayer belt.

We stood in a room adjoining the Rebbe's office, and awaited our turn. The room was small, most of it taken up by the stairway leading up to the second floor. A few other people were there with us. Earlier, we had waited outside, in the small lobby of Seven-Seventy. When it was close to our turn, we were shown inside by Laibl Groner, one of the Rebbe's secretaries.

In the lobby a minor mishap had taken place involving Fania's hairdo. Quite a while back, she had assumed, willingly or not, all the main obligations imposed on a woman by the Torah. Yet the duty to cover one's head was among the few requirements she still rebelled against. However, as she prepared to meet the Rebbe, it would never have occurred to her to enter with her head uncovered. Preferring to wear a wig rather than a kerchief, she had succeeded in combing and arranging it in such a way that no one could have told it from real hair.

One of our *Chasid* friends, passing us as we stood in the lobby, approached me somewhat hesitantly and called me aside. Baffled, he asked me if my wife was going to see the Rebbe with her head uncovered. He knew that Fania was having difficulties resigning herself to kerchiefs and wigs. . . . I calmed him down, explaining that she was wearing a wig, and he went off in relief. Some of the people waiting in the reception room wore black clothes and prayer belts; others were dressed in colorful clothing, with *kipot* showing through manes of hair.

I had heard that here one could meet world-famous writers, scientists, army officers, and government ministers. I tried to guess the identities of these people waiting in the small hours of the night to be received by the Lubavitcher Rebbe. Some of them did not even look Jewish. Yet I was much too agitated, and quickly gave up my attempts to identify the people around me. All the *Chasidim* present were holding pamphlets containing articles and discourses by the Rebbe. I, too, had one with me, but I confess that my eyes had skimmed over its many lines without my being able to grasp the meaning behind them. My heart was pounding; my thoughts were a jumble, and all my attempts to get hold of myself were of no avail. Again and again, I found myself assailed by thoughts, trying to imagine the approaching meeting, frantically rehearsing all the questions I had prepared for the Rebbe. It was already past midnight, as people continued to enter and leave the Rebbe's office. The reception room was gradually emptying. Geka, who had slept a lot during the day, was now wide awake and behaving with the seriousness of a grown man. Groner came to tell us that our waiting was almost over. Since we had just come from Russia, the Rebbe wished to see us last, so as to have enough time to give us his undivided attention.

Presently, the last visitor came in. By then it was nearly two A.M. Laibl Groner, looking as excited as ourselves, opened the door to the Rebbe's office and ushered us in.

In my dismay, I was afraid to stir, feeling that every bodily movement, every mental reaction, was sending ripples and reverberations through this incomprehensible atmosphere charged with holiness.

Am I worthy of the honor?

Groner noticed my confusion and impatiently waved his hand. And then the three of us—Fania, Geka, and I—stood facing the Rebbe's desk. His eyes were so warm, his smile radiated such fatherly concern, that I quickly regained my composure and offered the blessing of *Shehecheyanu.*

"*Shalom Aleichem,*" said the Rebbe, sounding as if we had last met a few days ago, his eyes sparkling and beaming, lighting up the room, making us feel warm, comfortable, completely at ease. The Rebbe pointed to the chairs and asked us to sit down. However, remembering the instruction I had received even in Riga—namely, that sitting or shaking the Rebbe's hand during the *yechidut* meant lowering the meeting from its exalted sacred level to that of a mundane meeting between two Jews—I hurriedly declined. Then the Rebbe turned to Fania and suggested that she, at least, might sit down; yet she too insisted on standing. And so we remained on our feet throughout the two hours of the first *yechidut* in our lives.

The Rebbe was interested in knowing all the minute details of the situation in Russia and our first days in Israel. He called each of us by name and mentioned the names of dozens of other people; he knew everyone's age, occupation, interests, problems, and needs. He discussed anti-Semitism, assimilation, politics, economics, literature, science, medicine, technology. And into every problem he inserted the problem of all problems—Jewish education.

He addressed Fania in Russian, Geka in Hebrew, and myself in Yiddish.

Even though I had heard a great deal about the Rebbe's phenomenal memory, I was astonished. What amazed me even more was his ability to listen. My agitation gradually subsided, and I regained my concentration. I even noticed the modest and old-fashioned way the room was furnished. However, I could not focus on smaller details, since immense concentration was needed to follow the kaleidoscopic outpouring of issues discussed by the Rebbe, to answer his questions, to absorb his message, and to try to memorize every word. Although I did my best to concentrate on the contents of the conversation, occasionally my mind was diverted by external details, and my attention disrupted. I was deeply affected by the Rebbe's face. Even though I had thought I knew him from dozens of photos, his splendor amazed me. I thought that if a man who has never seen the Rebbe were shown a thousand people with refined Jewish features and a thick beard, he would unmistakably recognize among them the Rebbe. The Rebbe's image was further enhanced by his frugal gestures and intonations; these were underscored by unwavering self-control, the embodiment of the "chasidic criterion"—"The brain is ruler of the heart." At the same time, the countenance of a man of iron will did not suit the Rebbe at all, for the unflinching voice was melted by the warmth he radiated as he spoke about Jewish children, education, or simply a Jew in need of help. In this room, the abstract idea of *Ahavat Israel*—love for your fellow Jew—took on such a concrete reality that it seemed one could physically sense it.

Needless to say, even the tiniest residues of my skepticism and fear of disappointment were melted by this warmth and vanished. Now I felt that even the most exalted descriptions of the Rebbe by *Chasidim* are just a pale shadow of what the Rebbe really is.

And finally—his wonderful blue eyes. Sky-blue and pure, sometimes they penetrate through and through, making the interlocutor actually feel the omnipresence of his attention and involvement. And sometimes they sparkle with a thousand smiles. And between these extreme expressions there are countless others that never seem to be repeated but are all alike in their infinite dedication to the person with whom he is talking.

As I have already mentioned, in the months that lapsed between my arrival in Israel and my meeting with the Rebbe, I met dozens of public and government figures, each of them a prominent and special person in his own right. Yet I have never met anyone who could listen as the Rebbe can, with total involvement, cutting off any distracting thought. When speaking with those other people, I have always felt that most of their attention is engrossed in what happened before the conversation or in what is going to happen after it, or simply in their own private concerns. The overwhelming majority of human beings are able to understand you at all only if you talk to them from their position, in their own mental code. If you analyze a problem from a standpoint unknown or unacceptable to them, they simply shut you off, like a radio suddenly switched to another station. Moreover, it always feels that they weigh their words only from the point of view of personal or party interests, or of their own prestige. As to giving advice or making a decision, they always try to avoid answering or to procrastinate.

With the Rebbe, it is a completely different matter. Whatever your topic, whatever your position or point of view, the Rebbe is totally there with you, feeling your problem or story more strongly than you do, and with a decision or advice coming immediately. He does not have to confer with anyone, and you always feel that his advice or decision is made solely with the good of the Jews in general and of yourself in particular in mind—both in the spiritual and in the worldly sense.

During this first meeting, when I had the occasion to see and hear the Rebbe make instantaneous decisions, it occurred to me how different he was from all the other people I had seen in moments requiring a decision. On the one hand, I recalled the Soviet functionaries constantly looking over their shoulders at their superiors; on the other hand, I saw in my mind's eye the Israeli politicians, whose resolution usually suffices, in any complex situation, to establish another committee which "just might get to the bottom of the matter."

Later I found out that the Rebbe's advice is sometimes hard to accept. At times it even seems illogical at first, and you rack your brain trying to figure out its rational basis. But if you have the integrity and willpower to follow the advice, even without having found its logic, you invariably come to realize—

sometimes months or years later—the wisdom of the advice, as well as the consequences of your disregarding it.

More than once, the Rebbe has given advice to Israeli statesmen on life-and-death matters. Unfortunately, being driven by preconceived notions or party discipline, they have not heeded the Rebbe's advice. I was personally present at a *hitva'adut* (a chasidic gathering) a few days before the outbreak of the Yom Kippur War, where I heard the Rebbe warn us of the impending war and even explain in detail what Israel's reaction should be. Alas, even at that terrible hour his advice went unheeded.

Later I wondered more than once what it was that gave the Rebbe this wonderful gift of foresight. Was it genius? His phenomenal memory and analytical insight? Tireless study of the Torah and the lack of any personal, worldly ambitions—the attributes that define the Jewish concept of a *tzaddik,* a holy man? Or an unknown divine revelation at work? Or perhaps it is the boundless faith of the mass of *Chasidim* that confers on the Rebbe the unique status of an intermediary between God and man? I shall not try to answer. Perhaps all of these factors play a role. . . . What is clear is that something is at work here far greater than all the exceptional human talents put together. As to myself, I had already decided, during that first *yechidut,* that the Rebbe was the only person in the world in whose hands I would unhesitatingly entrust my own fate and that of my loved ones.

After a half-hour of the *yechidut,* the Rebbe suggested that Geka be sent off to sleep. Geka left the room, after receiving a blessing from the Rebbe. Afterward he told me that as soon as he left the room he stumbled into a group of *Chasidim* crowding the lobby of Seven-Seventy. They were patiently waiting for the people at the *yechidut* to come out—and what is more, for the Rebbe himself to appear. They showered Geka with hugs and kisses, as well as countless questions, entreating him to repeat over and over again every word uttered by the Rebbe.

After the first hour of the *yechidut* had gone by, the office door opened a crack as Laibl Groner peeked inside and immediately disappeared, shutting the door behind him. A quarter of an hour later he reemerged; after that he kept opening the door at shorter intervals. I understood the hint: it was time to conclude. Yet the Rebbe continued talking, showering us with questions, and his face showed no signs of fatigue. I did not know what to do. I knew that Groner was concerned for the Rebbe's health. Stealing a glance at the watch, I realized that it was past three A.M. Yet I obviously could not cut the Rebbe short, telling him it was time for us to leave. Besides, there were so many questions left unasked—questions about our new life, requests from friends left back in Russia, philosophical issues. And on top of it all—it was such a pity to leave! The Rebbe went on talking; we went on asking questions, and Rabbi Groner went on opening the office door, wordlessly appealing to our conscience. After two hours had elapsed, the Rebbe rose to his feet, and we knew that now it was really time to go. The Rebbe gave an especially broad smile, gave us his blessing, and said that before we went back to Israel he hoped to see us again, with God's help.

The *Chasidim* in the lobby almost broke my ribs with hugs, crying "*Shalom Aleichem*" as though greeting a man returning from a long journey, and asking numerous questions. Then someone hoisted me on his shoulders, and everyone started dancing. When we returned to the Slavins', it was past four A.M. The snow-covered sidewalks were deserted, but from the road, as though in the middle of the day, came the rustling sound of streaming limousines. The nippy winter air helped us recover and clear our heads. Clearly we had just gone through the peak experience of our lives; it would require a great effort and distance in space and time in order to appreciate fully all that had happened.

41

A Little about the Worldwide Work of the Rebbe

During that same visit to the States, we had another meeting with the Rebbe, just as he had told us. In the following years I had the great fortune of having many more private meetings with the Rebbe; some of them lasted hours, and the "record" *yechidut* went on for three hours and fifty minutes. During that first visit I learned a great deal more about the *Chabad,* the Rebbe's activities, and the boundless devotion of his aides and followers.

One of the true miracles of our age, of contemporary Jewish history, is the world-wide network of *Chabad* educational institutions, founded and constantly strengthened and developed by the Rebbe. Schools, *yeshivot, Chabad* Houses, *Chabad* representatives in university towns—these are the present outposts and bastions in the war against assimilation and for the return of Jews to the faith of their fathers. These fortresses are scattered throughout the globe, wherever the Jews are living: in Israel, in Australia, in London, in Miami Beach, in Johannesburg and Milan, in Paris and Philadelphia. . . . In some places the staff of these institutions is quite large; in others a sole representative fearlessly mans his post alone, on behalf of the Rebbe, in the name of the Jewish faith and the future of Jewish children. These selfless people, most of them graduates of Lubavitch *yeshivot,* without any secular education, move about in the thick of society, knowing everybody and everything, well-versed in politics, philosophy, literature, and business (all this, of course, in addition to their knowledge of the Torah). They are equally at ease when carrying out a living room conversation, delivering a lecture on Jewish philosophy, or conducting a Talmud lesson. Heroically, they bear the burden of the enormous expenses needed to build and maintain the institutions they are running. Up to their necks in debt, sometimes they are forced to spend most of their time raising money from all kinds of businessmen. However, they never stoop to begging, never demean themselves before people of far less education, intelligence, and integrity. Ultimately those who make donations appreciate that they have been given a great privilege and do not feel that they did a favor to somebody.

Through these envoys, as through all of his *Chasidim,* the Rebbe brings order and harmony into the Jewish world, which is prey to thousands of alien influences and prone to chaos and deterioration. To borrow an analogy from physics, he miraculously reduces entropy, reversing the natural course of events. The Rebbe's envoys—each of them an outstanding personality who has confined his personal ambition to the service of an ideal—deserve our respect and admiration. Perhaps their families deserve even more praise, for they know neither vacations, nor days off, nor family privacy, nor simply a moment of rest. May the Almighty grant you health and strength, my newly found but true friends.

Since the Six-Day War, the Rebbe has been conducting a world-wide campaign to encourage Jews to fulfil some of the major *mitzvot:* putting on *tefillin,* having a kosher *mezuzah* on every Jewish door, lighting *Shabbat* candles, teaching children Torah, and universally observing the laws of *kashrut,* family purity, and so on. And now, in this ambiguous and ominous time for our people, with the entire world against us, thousands upon thousands of Jews in every corner of the world have been picking up tiny sparks of the Jewish spirit and the Jewish way of life, thanks to the indomitable efforts of the Rebbe and his *Chasidim.* And if we consider all this from the point of view of the interrelationship of all Jews with the Almighty—Who constantly creates anew all matter and life and elevates our world in proportion to the vitality and holiness that we, His creations, attain here on earth—then it is very easy to understand why the Rebbe closes nearly all his *sichot* on Jewish education and *mitzvah* campaigns by mentioning the coming of the *Moshiach.*

Everything I would have liked to tell about *Chabad* and the Rebbe would be enough to fill a separate book. Therefore, I will content myself with a brief description of the *Chabad* World Headquarters—Seven-Seventy—and of a festive gathering of *Chasidim, hitva'adut (farbrengen* in Yiddish) in the following two chapters. And finally, I will attempt in one of the next chapters to describe in more detail the Rebbe's unique approach to some scientific and philosophical issues.

42

"Seven-Seventy"

T he *Chasidim* have the habit of saying: "I am going to Seven-Seventy"; "I've just come from Seven-Seventy"; "I will be all evening at Seven-Seventy."

"Seven-Seventy" — 770 Eastern Parkway — is a three-story red-brick house with a sharp-edged roof in the style of an English mansion, heavy oak doors with brass handles, and lattice windows. The house and the sidewalk are separated by small lawns with single trees. The house was built in the early 1930s by a Jewish physician of means. He "put his heart" into the building, using authentic and natural materials imported from afar, with no expenses spared, as if he had a premonition of its future destiny. In 1940 the house was purchased by the previous Lubavitcher rebbe, Rabbi Yosef Yitzhak, who came to America from a Europe torn asunder by Stalin's Russia and Fascist Germany. Crown Heights, the Brooklyn neighborhood where "Seven-Seventy" is located, was at the time a prestigious area of New York Jews who had been swept in by the tidal wave of immigrants pursuing the unlimited possibilities of the American dream. In their firm belief that "in America everything is different," they gradually lost the spiritual and moral luggage they had managed to preserve through generations of poverty and hardship in Russia and Poland. Into this world of comfort and indulgence the Rebbe arrived as a prophet, a mentor, and a guide. Since that time the *Chabad* World Center has been based here, ready to wage tireless battle against assimilation and oblivion.

The second floor houses the living quarters of the former Rebbe, and on the floor above it lives Rabbi Shmariyahu Gurari with his wife Hannah, the former Rebbe's daughter. Rabbi Gurari serves as head of the Lubavitch *yeshivah* network. Residing in the same building is Rabbi Chaim Lieberman, a world-class expert on Jewish literature and the guardian of the unique library.

The rest of the rooms serve as the *Chabad* World Headquarters. The Rebbe's office, a modest-sized room with antique furniture, is used by the Rebbe fifteen to twenty hours daily; there he works, writes, studies Torah, and receives visitors.

The reception room, about 150 square feet in size, is jam-packed with mail, incoming and outgoing, and a few old-fashioned telephones. In a competition for the busiest telephones, these would undoubtedly win all the top prizes: they ring nonstop from eight A.M. until three A.M., except for *Shabbat*.

The space that is not occupied by mail, telephones, and piles of books is constantly filled by various visitors, locals as well as guests. Threading their way among all these are the secretaries and aides — Laibl Groner, Benyamin

Klein, Yehuda Krinsky. Their typical posture is to have a telephone receiver pressed to the ear with a shoulder, a stack of letters in one hand, and a pencil in the other. Another possibility: the right hand striking the keys of a typewriter, the left hand roaming through a pile of reply letters from the Rebbe in search for the right one; the face turned toward a visitor (or two or three at a time), while the ear is steadily glued to the telephone receiver, and sometimes both ears to two receivers.

These people see their families only once a week, at the end of *Shabbat,* when the office is closed. During the rest of the week none of them comes home before the wee hours of the morning, when the rest of the family are fast asleep. There is a story of one of the little daughters of Rabbi Benyamin Klein once coming to the reception room, only to be pushed into a far corner. "What are you doing here, little girl?" someone asked her. "Nothing," she replied. "I am only here to see my daddy."

Here, on the first floor, is also the tiny twenty-square-feet room that serves as the office of Rabbi Chodakov, the Rebbe's personal secretary, and the manager of the Education Center responsible for *Chabad* envoys throughout the globe. Another small room houses the communications center, from which the Rebbe's *hitva'adut* discourses are broadcast by radio and television to the entire world. Also situated on the first floor is the small synagogue where the Rebbe comes to pray on weekdays.

A set of stairs leads up to the hall of the large synagogue. It is a vast area that has undergone a number of expansions at the expense of the adjoining buildings. This is a place for prayer, Torah study, *hitva'aduyot,* children's gatherings, and women's meetings. In this hall, only the elderly members sit, on narrow benches made of plain wooden planks, with the rest standing in a dense crowd. It is said that on holidays the place is packed, counting the women in the gallery, with up to ten thousand people. On weekdays the prayers are conducted in many separate *minyanim* (groups of ten or more people). From six in the morning until midday one can join one of the groups, beginning with the morning prayer. Here you can also find numerous Torah lessons in progress. A suitable group can be chosen according to age or subject matter, including Talmud, *Mishnah, Shulchan Aruch, Chasidut,* and many others. One could even pick a group according to the language—Yiddish, English, Hebrew, French, Russian. Among those present in the hall, some may be talking, others eating, and some even taking a nap.

The adjoining buildings are drawn into the life cycles of Seven-Seventy. There is the youth *yeshivah,* the "*Kollel*" for young married scholars, and further on the girls' school and the seminar. Affiliated *Chabad* organizations are supervised from here. Thousands of books, pamphlets, and articles are written, edited, and published here. The place also houses the library and the periodicals archives. Here is conducted the meticulous work of editing ancient manuscripts on *Kabbalah, Chasidut,* and Jewish philosophy. Not far from here stands the *yeshivah* building for *baalei teshuvah,* those who returned to the bosom of Judaism from assimilated families. To a newcomer, the bustling activity of the place may seem like a madhouse that settles down only when the Rebbe enters or leaves the building, when everyone rises and falls silent out of respect. It takes time and considerable effort to understand the meaning and order of what takes place here.

43

"Hitva'adut"– the Chasidic Gathering

I will try to describe a *hitva'adut* with the Rebbe, as this unique occasion appears to me in retrospect, after I have attended dozens of such events.

A *hitva'adut (farbrengen)* is a gathering of *Chasidim* that takes place on *Shabbat,* holidays, and festive days on the Chasidic calendar. Thousands of people gather to hear the Rebbe, to receive his Torah teachings and instruction for righteous living.

The first time, I was taken aback at the sight of the crowd squeezed into the large hall at Seven-Seventy, waiting for the Rebbe to appear. I have said "crowd," but this crowd was a unique one. The Talmud says, "Whoever has not seen the joy of *Bet Hasho'evah*[1] has not seen joy in all his days." To paraphrase this, whoever has not seen a *hitva'adut* with the Lubavitcher Rebbe, has not seen how beautiful a human crowd can be. Usually the word "crowd" connotes something threatening and repulsive. The image goes all the way back to ancient Rome. "Bread and excitement!" the crowd demanded as it hungrily devoured the gruesome spectacle of gladiators and slaves. For thousands of years the crowd roared, throbbed, demanded blood, and ran amok. Thus the word came to represent a mob of bloodthirsty animals, pogroms, hacked bodies, pillage, and plunder.

Or take, for example, a modern stadium. The crowd of fans may seem to be different–but no, it is essentially the same, with the same animal instincts, apelike shrieks, and eventually the same mangled bodies. A similar sight are the crowds at wild disco parties teeming with punks and the like.

In contrast, let us peek into the large hall with the Rebbe's *hitva'adut* in progress–and what we will see is, at first glance, a crowd. For in a sense it is indeed a crowd–of five thousand, and sometimes up to seven thousand people.

---

1. Joy of *Beth Hasho'evah* is the highlight of joy during the holiday of Sukkot (Tabernacles).

They come from the surrounding neighborhoods, as well as from all corners of the world: rabbis, *yeshivah* students, salesmen and office clerks, millionaires and journalists, politicians, and hippies still sporting their shabby clothes and long hair. There are even some who only today became newly aware of their Jewish identity.

For the most part there are many *Chasidim*—New Yorkers, as well as those who had to save for an entire year for a plane ticket—thousands of men in the hall itself, and thousands of women in the gallery. In the center, on a plain wooden stage, behind a table covered with a white cloth, sits the Rebbe. Seated in rows at a small distance behind him are older *Chasidim* and the guests of honor.

The Rebbe is speaking—speaking in a voice that has a certain melody to it, quiet and calm. And yet the crowd of thousands is so quiet you can hear a pin drop. Even on *Shabbat,* when the Rebbe speaks without a microphone, his voice can be heard. Truly, then, in its size and diversity the audience is a crowd. Yet let us look closer, and see what has brought all these people here. In this place they will not be given bread or a tantalizing spectacle. Nor is there any need to prove oneself or rise to the occasion. Here everyone, be he ever so famous in the outside world, is but a listener and a student, on the same footing with everyone else. And certainly there is no one here with whom to flirt or fight for control.

Perched in precarious positions on tightly packed wooden benches are the older members of the congregation, while the young are standing on their feet, out of humility and respect as well as the shortage of seats. If everyone were to sit, the place would accommodate no more than one-third of those present.

What is it, then, that draws all these people here?

The Rebbe's speech lasts from four to five hours, sometimes even longer. He talks about the unity and harmony, both spiritual and material, between Torah and the people of Israel; about the observance of *mitzvot,* self-discipline, and Jewish education for the children of Israel; provides analysis and detailed elucidations on the Talmud, the commentaries, and *Kabbalah.*

Attending these speeches means work, hard work, a painstaking concentrated effort not to lose the golden thread of the Rebbe's thoughts: five uninterrupted hours of intensive philosophical analysis and instructions on self-improvement, occasionally standing on one foot because of the lack of space, and struggling to keep your balance while the thick ring of people tightens around you.

Listening to the Rebbe is an unmatched intellectual feast. However, it is far from easy to reach the level at which you can begin to appreciate this delightful experience. Prominent among the lessons taught by the Rebbe is the one dealing with interpretations of the classical commentary of Rashi on the *Chumash.* In this commentary, which every Jewish boy was taught for centuries and which has become a milestone of elementary Jewish learning, the Rebbe discovers completely new and hitherto undiscovered depths and insights. He demonstrates the profundity of this terse commentary, the importance and preciseness of each word and letter, and their relevance in everyday life. The Rebbe scrupulously analyzes each tiniest detail, citing many dozens of quotations drawn from the ocean of Talmud and *Kabbalah* in his memory, attacking the problem from every angle, with a jeweler's precision threading the intermediate secondary results onto the core of the evidence. For a while he dwells on one line of thought, leaves it for another, to return to the first. And suddenly the final conclusion is reached: clear, brilliant, irrefutable and . . . unexpected.

But let us return to the external process of the *hitva'adut*. From time to time the Rebbe makes brief intermissions, during which the entire audience bursts into a mighty rendition of a *chasidic* melody. The Rebbe joins in the singing, while exchanging *l'chayim* with the participants, with a smile and a warm glance for practically every one in the huge audience. Whoever meets the Rebbe's eyes feels not only that the Rebbe knows him personally but that he hurts with his hurt and rejoices in his joy, wishing him luck and giving him his blessing. The people sing on, united in the heart-rending melody just as they were united, a few minutes earlier, in the wisdom and warmth of learning. As it says in the Book of Psalms, "Behold, how good and how pleasant it is for brethren to dwell together in unity!" This "unity" means the unity of souls; it means the feeling of brotherhood; it means to communion with the Almighty. Therefore it is here, in the house at 770 Eastern Parkway, that one can behold the miraculous beauty and greatness of a "crowd." You feel here as if you were at the *Bet Hamikdash* (the Holy Temple of Jerusalem) itself. This miracle is brought about by the Rebbe, the greatest Jew, who has no control or influence over these people, except for his wisdom, righteousness, and love for every one of them.

I recall a *hitva'adut* attended by one of the leading New York public figures, a gentile. He stood next to me, unable to understand a word from the Rebbe's speech which was delivered in Yiddish. Yet his excitement and amazement at the over-all mood reigning here caused him to stand riveted to his spot for hours. During one of the intermissions, as the audience was singing, he leaned over to me and whispered, "I am enchanted! What emotion! Never in my life have I seen so many people united in such a spiritual elevation."

44

The Rebbe's Guidance Enables Me to Build a Laboratory

Our so-called absorption into Israel was unusually smooth and happy. While still at Lod airport I received an invitation to work at Bar-Ilan

University. A little later, the universities of Tel Aviv and Beer Sheva invited me, as did the Technion in Haifa. As I didn't have to spend time learning Hebrew first, the question of work had to be decided immediately. It was hard to choose. Beer Sheva especially attracted me because its university was very young and rapidly developing and because life in the Negev, in the heart of the desert, held a slight sense of pioneering. But even more than that, the ancient-modern town of Beer Sheva was deeply associated in my mind with Avraham Avinu, with his years in the Negev desert. However, as heavy pressure was being exerted by Tel Aviv University, I decided to combine working at both places.

And indeed, for more than a year I was full professor at both the Tel Aviv and Beer Sheva universities. A little later, the U.S. Department of the Navy signed a contract with me for research work in magnetohydrodynamics, and I had to decide where to build my laboratory. Although until then we had been intending to settle in Jerusalem, where I spend much time involved with my public work (which I shall describe later), in the end I chose Beer Sheva, and we moved there.

How I got the U.S. Navy contract, how the Rebbe "engineered" me into it, is an interesting story.

As I have already said, my first visit to the Rebbe was part of a four-week trip to America scheduled shortly after I arrived to settle in Israel. A number of professional colleagues throughout America had also invited me to come visit their laboratories and lecture on my work. I was planning on resuming my teaching and research career (interrupted by my departure from the Soviet Union) as soon as I returned to Israel.

Near the end of my four-week stay in the United States, a well-known *Chabad* activist, Rabbi Avraham Shem-Tov, invited me to come to Philadelphia to talk with Jewish students there. Before traveling to Philadelphia, I was received again by the Rebbe. Among other things, I mentioned this upcoming trip. The Rebbe was very interested in the details of my schedule in Philadelphia and afterward added, as if incidentally, "When you're in Philadelphia, don't forget to meet with the scientist in your field at the university." This astounded me. I knew the names of all the American scientists working in magnetohydrodynamics of liquid metals as well as the universities where they worked, and I was absolutely certain that there was no one in Philadelphia of significant professional interest to me.

After greeting me at the Philadelphia railway station, Avraham Shem-Tov asked me what the Rebbe had talked about with me in *yechidut*. Among other things I told him about the Rebbe's incomprehensible instruction to see a professional colleague in Philadelphia. "Apparently it's a misunderstanding."

"With the Rebbe there are no misunderstandings," imparted Shem-Tov. "Let's go straight to Temple University and the University of Pennsylvania and find this person."

I was bewildered. How could we look for him? And why go searching when I knew for certain that there was no laboratory, there was no specialist in my field at any university in that town. But it was impossible to withstand Shem-Tov's pressure. We went from building to building, from department to department, for many hours. We questioned dozens of strangers. They were surprised by our personal appearance and even more so by the questions we asked. And then, just before sunset, when the University of Pennsylvania was emptying out, someone in a dark corridor scratched his forehead and said, "Magnetohydrodynamics? . . . Just a minute . . . Professor Hsuan Yeh must be connected with that."

He explained how to find Professor Yeh, and in a few minutes we were sitting in his office. It turned out that Yeh, Chinese in origin, had been working many years in America on a number of magnetohydrodynamics projects conducted outside the auspices of the university. We spent several hours together. He described some of his findings but was even more interested in mine. On parting, he said, "The American Symposium on Magnetohydrodynamics is being held in five weeks, at Stanford. You must come and deliver a lecture. It's way past the deadline for submitting lectures, but I'm a member of the organizing committee and can arrange it, especially considering that you've just come from the Soviet Union."

I thanked him but refused, as I had to return to Israel that week.

Back in New York, I wrote the Rebbe a note about everything that had happened in Philadelphia, mentioning also Professor Yeh. The Rebbe answered immediately that the invitation to Stanford was of major importance and that I had to do everything possible to attend the conference. I didn't understand at all why this conference warranted ruining all my plans of starting work at Beer Sheva. But by then there was one thing I had learned: the advice of the Rebbe must be followed without argument, whether it makes sense to me or not.

Five weeks later I was at Stanford University in California. An hour after my arrival, even before I delivered my lecture, two representatives from the U.S. Office of Naval Research introduced themselves to me. They told me that they were well acquainted with my name and my work and that they wanted to offer me the opportunity to continue my research on magnetohydrodynamic turbulence in liquid metals under contract with the American Navy. They understood that I intended to work in Israel and were prepared to finance my work there.

Since then, this agreement has been renewed six times and has lasted six full years. During these six years I have set up and equipped my laboratory, where I have managed to develop a new way of converting solar energy into electrical energy, which has become the chief focus of my work. This would not have happened in this way had not the Rebbe given me his strange, incomprehensible advice . . . not unlike a mysterious instruction of the Baal Shem Tov sending a *Chasid* to a remote village, telling him only that he must go visit the home of the local water carrier. . . .

45

I Take on Responsibility for SHAMIR

And so we settled in Beer Sheva. Fania began to work as a doctor at the local hospital, and Geka went to a *yeshivah* in Beer Sheva. Since early childhood he had been so imbued with thoughts about Israel that his transplantation to Israeli soil was a natural process, part of a continuum. As for myself, it seemed that after a forced interruption I was returning to my normal place. I felt linked with this land through all the past generations and through the Torah, far more than many Israelis whose only link to it is the circumstance of their birth here. I have never regretted choosing Beer Sheva in the Negev. On the contrary, only here am I able to understand and to see how my homeland is being built and beautified from day to day and to take my small part in it.

Only my poor mother couldn't adjust to our new living conditions. I had dreamed that Israel would bring her the happiness and satisfaction which she so much deserved after all her suffering. But, alas, she was almost seventy-five years old when she arrived. Learning Hebrew seemed impossible to her. All the familiar things to which she was accustomed had been left far behind. And she, poor woman, became very, very weak.

Right away I was faced with an old dilemma. Should I take advantage of the opportunity to enjoy a quiet, settled, orderly life or should I seek something greater? Indeed, I could conscientiously work at the university, teaching and doing research, publishing articles and books. And with all this, I would still have many hours for relaxation, reading, contemplating the spurs of the Judean hills seen from our window, or even cultivating roses or a vineyard on my native land (about which I had dreamed so much in Riga!).

I didn't take advantage of most of these possibilities. To do so would have meant to sit by and allow my fellow Jews to sacrifice their Jewishness to modern and ultramodern idols of so-called civilization and progress. Although I was not a *Chabadnik* by birth, I had some right to call myself an adherent of *Chabad.* According to my understanding of it, the concept of "*Chabadnik*" and the state of satiated well-being were incompatible. Finally, there is another reason why I voluntarily condemned myself to a life of chronic lack of sleep, of constantly feeling a catastrophic lack of time.

And this is why. When I arrived at Lod, a young *Chabadnik* named Betzallel Shif, whom I had known in Russia, told me about an association of religious Jewish intelligentsia from the Soviet Union in Israel. This association had been founded upon the advice of the Lubavitcher Rebbe, who thought that people who had struggled to create Jewish homes and Torah education in Russia were duty-bound to continue their efforts after settling in Israel. Rabbi Israel Leibov, Director of Tzeirei Agudat Chabad ("Tzach") in Israel, took on the responsibility for creating this association. He entrusted Betzallel to direct it temporarily. Betzallel told me that he had exhausted himself trying to do this, but he lacked sufficient experience and therefore wanted me to head it. A considerable time later, I consented – after long deliberations and consultations with Israel Leibov and his associate, Avroam Godin. I knew the latter from Riga, where for a whole winter in the mid-1960s he had taught me *Chumash* with Rashi's commentaries.

It was clear that this organization was necessary not only for the realization of the fundamental *Chabad* ideal of Jewish family life and education, but also for the success and continuation of Russian Jewish immigration to Israel. After all, what was it that induced Jews to cut themselves off from their familiar habitats, friends, and life routine, if not Jewish consciousness? However, as I have explained earlier, the extent to which this consciousness flowed was so minute among so many Russian Jews that it was enough only to produce an occasional protest or emotional outburst.

Deeper feeling and more substantial knowledge are needed for the long process of absorption into the Land of Israel. Thus, the purpose of this association was to develop Jewish feeling and to give Jewish knowledge to Russian Jews in Israel. To do this, teachers and lecturers had to be found to create serious, academic-level literature on Jewish subjects in good Russian and to deal with all possible psychological and sociological aspects of acclimatizing Russian Jews to their homeland. All this (and more) was to become the range of activities of this association, later to be known as "SHAMIR" ("*Shomrei Mitzvot Yotzei* Russia" – The Association of Jewish Religious Professionals from the Soviet Union and Eastern Europe in Israel).

SHAMIR had incredible difficulties to overcome. There was a shortage of suitable personnel, a catastrophic lack of funds, and an absurd necessity to prove over and over again to the powers-that-be the vital necessity of their supporting SHAMIR's activities. Now, however, both the Israeli government and the Jewish Agency recognize its importance. SHAMIR has been undertaking difficult and indeed historic tasks, such as the publication of a Russian translation of the Five Books of Moses with the commentaries of Rashi, Ramban, Ibn-Ezra, and others (the first such annotated Russian-Hebrew *Chumash* ever to be printed). It is also preparing new Russian translations of the *Shulchan Aruch* and the *Kuzari*. Gradually, a Russian-language Basic

Jewish Library of the classics of Judaism is being created to serve as the cornerstone of Jewish revival and self-education among Russian Jews, on both sides of the Iron Curtain.

46

Peter Kalms and SHAMIR

H undreds of people turn to SHAMIR and to me as its chairman. Many come requesting literature or consultation on religious-philosophic subjects, as well as seeking help in finding work, appropriate schools for their children, loans, or even better apartments. Sometimes fathers come looking for a match for their daughters.

The degree of my activity in SHAMIR grows greater and greater. To my great fortune, a wonderful person who has now become my close friend, Peter Kalms, has entered the SHAMIR orbit to help me. The Rebbe brought Peter to SHAMIR. Peter's grandfather emigrated to England three-quarters of a century ago from Russia. For this and for other reasons, Peter became interested in the problems of Russian Jews and began to empathize with them. He made a deep impression on me from our very first encounter. I was still very "green" then in the free world, but I had already managed to form an impression of the typical Jewish businessman-philanthropist. In many cases, the charity of such a philanthropist seemed to be primarily for self-"publicity." His ignorance and lack of desire to understand the cause for which he sometimes gave and sometimes didn't give money was simply appalling.

By that time, I had already attended a few meetings on behalf of Soviet Jewry, which had been conducted according to the unwritten laws of cocktail party games. Everyone made the rounds, exchanging intoxicating compliments, getting carried away with themselves, and gustily eating and drinking, radiating charming smiles, and delivering an uninterrupted flow of sheer nonsense.

Peter appeared to be the exact opposite of this stereotype. He genuinely lives through everything he does, feeling its excitement and trying to penetrate into every detail and understand all. He is always ready to perform the most menial task, to take upon himself every possible obligation. His intelligence, competency, quick-wittedness, and intuition, combined with unusual accuracy and feeling of responsibility, have, to a great extent, secured SHAMIR's success. He has been an invaluable help to me, and I have tried to follow his example many times.

The course of events has confirmed more and more the importance of the concerns with which SHAMIR deals. As the miraculous exodus of Soviet Jewry dries up and withers, turning into a far-from-idealistic emigration settling on five continents, it becomes evident that without real Jewish education, any Jewish undertaking—even the most grand and historic—is doomed to fail. Alas, our ignorance of our roots and the habit of thinking only in materialistic terms hide this simple truth from most of those who consider themselves to be today's captains and helmsmen of the long-suffering Jewish ship.

47

First Worries about Events in Israel

D id Israel live up to my expectations? During the first few months or even the entire first year after I arrived, this frequently asked question seemed outlandish to me. Drunk with happiness, experiencing unbelievable events, walking in a dream—all these are expressions far too weak to describe the state I was in.

It often happened, though, during that time, that I heard people say that the party leaders and "functionaries" were ready to betray and sell out everybody and everything for the advantage of their careers, party interests, and political gain. I heard allegations that a considerable part of the population related hostilely to all that is traditionally, eternally Jewish. Finally, I heard stories of disgusting examples of corruption. However, all these reports evoked in me only irritation and sheer distrust toward the people who told them to me. For me there existed only the holy and unique quality of this cherished and longed-for land. Therefore, even the most sincere criticism sounded slanderous to me. This happy intoxication was so strong that even now, years after our *aliyah,* it still makes itself felt.

However, for quite a while now, I have begun to see and realize what is going on and to become aware of the difference between the State of Israel and the Land of Israel, and my heart has begun to bleed. Most difficult of all was to see how secularism and socialism were considered the highest social values. I do not mean the socialism of the prophet Amos but the socialism of (as they say in Hebrew—"May they be separated by a thousand separations") Karl Marx.

The intoxication with socialism in certain circles is so strong that it is considered possible heedlessly to sacrifice anything to fulfill its dogmas. And if it should happen that the demands of socialist principles should conflict with an internal Jewish voice, then it is simply improper to allow the latter to have its say. From my recently accumulated experience I know that what I have just written would probably arouse a storm of indignation from members of the labor parties and applause from associates of the "Herut" party. Therefore, I hasten to explain that I do not belong to Herut, just as I do not belong to the labor parties, since I am convinced that the very division of Jews into parties is wrong. (I do not have in mind here the people belonging to the parties. As individuals, as Jews, they are frequently sympathetic and reasonable.)

Moreover, I must express my complete appreciation and respect for the socialists of the founding generation for their heroism and self-sacrifice and for their amazing achievements in building and defending the country. This, however, does not change the fact that they were tragically mistaken in their ideology and probably could not even guess the disastrous consequences that their world outlook would wreak within a few decades.

More than once I have had occasion to be convinced of the tragedy of the very existence of political parties and, even worse, that part of them—guided by their party ideology and mentality—are in a position of authority to decide questions critical to our people. I also saw that there are neither moral barriers nor logical limits to the endless animosity and strife among the various parties. It is significant that the Hebrew word for party, *miflagah,* comes from the root *pilug* (meaning separation, division). What could be more tragic for our small, persecuted people than internal division and discord?

By the way, before each election to the Knesset, several parties persisted in offering me a place on their list of candidates. In a number of cases a "sure seat" was offered. But it seemed preposterous to align myself with one group of Jews, thus automatically pitting myself in opposition to all other Jews. So naturally I declined.

Far more disturbing to me is the catastrophic national loss of a Jewish frame of mind, of a Jewish world outlook, of our age-old principles and ideas, of feeling the kinship and interdependence of all Jews, and of the formerly well-known Jewish fineness of spirit and mind. For many Israeli Jews, their link with the past, the continuity of the generations, has been lost. The machine of secular-socialist-atheist-cosmopolitan education ruthlessly grinds down the inner core of Jewishness, which miraculously is still reproduced in the souls of Jewish children. This system of education grew out of the views of German and Western European Jewish leaders of the "Enlightenment"—*Maskilim*—who, 150 to 200 years ago, started their monstrous experiment to substitute "universal humanism" for the treasures of the Jewish soul. After absorbing elements of Russian socialism, this system "enriched" itself with pearls of American didactic thought and the spirit of total permissiveness and unlimited personal freedom. Mastering all this eclectic broth, it then turned into the most banal anti-Semitism, hostile not against Jewish flesh and blood but against the Jewish soul and the Jewish heart.

It is hard to imagine anything stranger than seeing the heirs of the Chosen People—who for more than three thousand years were the bearers and guardians of holiness, justice, and human wisdom—turned into such a philistine race, whose heathen cult of the body, pleasure, and success is not very modestly covered by the fig leaf of "progress" and "service to the ideals of all mankind."

Unbearable pain is evoked in me when I think of the crowds on Allenby or Dizengoff streets in Tel Aviv, where among the half-naked girls, daubed-up old women, and long-haired males it is hard to detect a Jewish face or Jewish expression in the eyes. It is impossible for me to watch young men and women on television shamelessly declare that they are Israelis, Canaanites, but in no way Jews. It is terrifying to see newspaper kiosks and movie billboards in the Holy Land promoting blown-up pictures of the female body distorted, despiritualized, and degraded to arouse carnal appetites. It is unbearable to realize that all this is happening in *Eretz Hakodesh*. It is even more unbearable to realize that assimilation here is much more dangerous than in other countries where Jews live. In the Diaspora, assimilation ultimately causes the complete separation of an individual Jew or a Jewish family from the body of the Jewish people. Here, in Israel, however, a spiritually degraded Jew is still considered a Jew for the simple reason that he lives in a "Jewish state." Thus, assimilation here becomes not only a personal tragedy. It is devaluating the basic concept of a "Jew" and the "Jewish people."

48

Loss of Jewish Values

T he most valuable quality which has been lost in Israel is not even Jewish intellectual refinement or eternal thirst for knowledge. The most valuable Jewish quality which is decreasing in Israel is the sense of the limits of what is allowed, the feeling of the borders of sin. Traditionally, a Jew always strived to stay away from the forbidden, the immoral, and the shameful. Throughout the ages, the Jew tried to preserve the purity of all his actions and thoughts and the holiness of his family and community. "You are a Jew!" "We are Jews!" More than any explanation or moralizing lecture, these words always brought one of our people who was being led astray back to his heritage. It is agonizing to see how this priceless inheritance is vanishing. Although, to be fair, I must note that often I do have the occasion to see the strength of the *mitzvot* continuing to live in the souls of many whose intellects have tried to disavow them.

How agonizing it is to hear and read in the papers about murder committed by Jews, about Jewish prostitutes, about rape, about cases of robbery and theft, and about strikes sabotaging a war-time economy. However, all this can be attributed to a minority, the dregs of society. Therefore, it is even more terrible to hear of or to see incidents that at first seem much less scandalous. For example, in September of 1975, at the central bus station in Tel Aviv, a teenager attacked a man carrying a briefcase containing eighteen thousand *lirot* worth of bank notes. The boy was caught right away, but the briefcase popped open, allowing the bank notes to scatter. When they were collected, it turned out that ten thousand *lirot* had disappeared into the pockets of passers-by. In other words, dozens of chance passers-by turned out to be thieves. A hundred years ago in a remote *shtetl* in the Pale of Settlement, this never could have happened.

Endless sorrow floods the soul when a student, returning from fighting in the Yom Kippur War, says: "I've read in books about Jewish happiness and joy and the beauty of *Shabbat,* but although I grew up in Israel, I've never had the chance to experience it. I'm not the type who goes to discotheques, and all my entertainment consists of television on weekdays, and on *Shabbat*—more television."

Or take a very different example. When a cinema shows a film consisting of two entire hours of detailed depiction of nude bodies indulging in sexual acts and refined perversions, the seats are filled up. But when a film about Yanush Korchak comes, then the maximum number of tickets sold for a show is twenty.

It makes you suffocate from helplessness and despair to hear that, upon the advice of foreign didactic-schizophrenics, a course on sex education is being introduced into the schools, where the technique of the sex act is explained to boys and girls through films which demonstrate accordingly. And what can be said about seeing a fourteen-year-old girl taking a contraceptive pill, preparing to go out on a date, while her parents look on with condescension. And it never even occurs to them that there is anything reprehensible in this! What can we expect from our enemies when we ourselves—in the name of alien and depraved theories and in order to gratify our own dissoluteness—mutilate the purity and holiness of our children's souls, uprooting them from the Jewish spirituality, modesty, and self-restraint which our forefathers struggled to preserve for centuries? This, O God, is probably the lowest level to which Your will sentenced us to fall for our sins.

49

Dangers of Wrong Education

In Russia I had read about various reform movements in Judaism, but this information remained completely abstract for me. I recollect, however, that one *Shabbat* during the hardest period of our struggle to get out of the Soviet

Union, a young foreigner barged into our apartment. He said he was an American rabbi. Loaded with baggage and cameras, he had come to us by bus. His bald, bare head shone with sweat. All this made us very suspicious. Needless to say, the "rabbi" did not inspire us with the slightest desire to seek his advice or help.

By now I have had the occasion to meet face to face with more of these "experimenters" and "innovators." I have become acquainted with shaven, bare-headed men who devour pork sausage and drive around on Saturday in their Cadillacs, shamelessly calling themselves "rabbis." I have even had the opportunity to see—not in real life, but in a documentary film—a wedding ceremony performed by a "rabbi" and a priest together.

When I think about all these Reform, Conservative, progressive and heaven-knows-what-else movements, countless arguments rooted in the Torah, in historical experience, in philosophy, in logic and common sense come to mind, proving the absurdity of all these sorry innovations. First of all, there is no logical basis for calling these trends religion. As the reformers consider it possible for human beings to change *halachah* (the God-given Jewish law) at will, then there is no place for God in their "doctrine." How can something in which there is no place for God be called religion? It should be called, at most, a cultural movement or social club.

But the simplest and most convincing argument is possibly one which I heard recently from an engineer—a modest and reasonable man. When asked why he doesn't go to the Conservative "temple" near his home, the engineer answered without hesitation: "Once I read Rambam's *Book of Knowledge*. He says that *halachah* can't be changed. You know, the Rambam is good enough an authority for me. . . . " Actually, this man hadn't said anything special, but what immense, unsophisticated truth there was in his words! Oh, if only all of us could feel that "the Rambam is good enough an authority for me."

I must also mention here the compromising Orthodox Jews. With a heavy heart I force myself to do this. Far be it from me to equate the more liberal elements of Orthodox Jewry with Reformism. But I have become convinced (neither quickly nor easily!) that although this tendency toward liberalism does not eliminate any of the tradition, by changing the priorities of certain *mitzvot* and by relaxing certain restrictions on conduct it has also often allowed people to fall away from Judaism.

I am definitely not referring here to the disgraceful political intrigues that have unfortunately been exposed in the religious parties. I have in mind now only their founding ideology which presumed that young freethinkers would be attracted to Judaism through a lenient attitude. But, alas, life has proven that too many people are crossing the bridge in the wrong direction!

And to my friends of the religious parties (just think what a paradox it is to juxtapose "religion" with "party" when we are actually all one party, the party of Moshe Rabbeinu!) I wish to cry out: "How can you call the present fallen state of our land, this tragedy of the degradation of everything Jewish, the beginning of Messianic redemption? We must love and protect our land and our people with all our heart and all our might and try to bring the coming of the *Moshiach* nearer. But let's not stupefy ourselves by calling darkness light!"

Possibly the greatest tragedy of the modern age is not that the vast majority of Jews, including the most vainglorious intelligentsia, are totally immersed in atheism and skepticism, but that among those who consider themselves to be believers and *shomrei mitzvot,* there are so few truly possessing simple faith, trusting in God. Rationalism and skepticism are infiltrating more and more into circles considering themselves Orthodox. There are "religious people" who believe in an abstract God, the God of Creation or of History, but who have lost their personal connection with *Hashem* Who directs the most minute activities in the world. This "half faith" or even "quarter faith" has various manifestations. The believer in such a fractured faith sees the *mezuzah* as a beautiful tradition, but neither realizes nor feels that the *mezuzah* guards the Jewish home not only figuratively but also literally. Such a person, when talking about his future plans, does not add *"im yirtzeh Hashem"* (if God wills it) because it seems indecorous to him to display his faith so "primitively." Moreover, he simply does not feel that the realization of his plans depends upon the Almighty. If this person is a political leader dealing, for example, with the inadmissibility of returning territory liberated by Israel during the Six-Day War, then it doesn't enter his head to substantiate his position, whether arguing with Jews or non-Jews, by referring foremost to the fact that this land was given to us by the will of God and that it cannot but be ours.

When a young person doesn't constantly feel the presence of God and doesn't sense a Higher Power is observing his behavior; when he is told that not every *mitzvah* and, even more so, not every custom is equally binding and that the words of the Torah can always be taken allegorically—then very soon this youngster starts coming to *shul* in shorts and his *yarmulke* diminishes to the size of a coin, lost in his shoulder-length hair. His *tallit katan* turns into something resembling a baby's bib and then disappears altogether. Soon he starts dancing with girls, and after a while it's not unusual for him to go even further. Alas, what is written here is not theory, but simple observations of life. The Torah neither tolerates nor forgives compromises! The most dangerous innovation of all, though, is to change the Torah from being the basis of life into becoming an isolated part of it.

I must emphasize and stipulate again and again that all the painful examples of alienating and self-deceiving departures from Judaism given here are not meant in any way to slander or harm any individual or group. I have met many admirable people in every aspect of Jewish life who are immeasurably dedicated to the Jewish people. My intention here is strictly to warn my fellow Jews of the dangers incurred by trying to change, compromise, or eliminate any of the laws of the Torah. Because the quality of Jewish physical survival depends upon how well each individual Jew daily carries out true Jewish values and precepts, I am just trying to point out inconsistencies and contradictions demanding immediate correction.

50

Grandeur of the People and Grandeur of the Land

E very day I meet people here in Israel who are fully prepared to give of themselves, although sometimes they are too shy to openly display this old-fashioned virtue. Often during crisis or times of joy, Jewish light suddenly bursts forth, emerging from our common historical experience of thousands of years, binding the people around me in a precious intimacy. The Jewish soul is indestructible. Sometimes a seemingly insignificant event fills my heart with a happy surprise, when by chance a passenger on the bus turns around smiling and says *"Shalom,"* or a group of first-graders troops by, weighed down by back satchels far too heavy for them—schoolchildren like all other schoolchildren, but with large Jewish eyes. Sometimes a bunch of long-haired, gum-chewing teenagers in bell-bottoms come at me on the street, just like the most devil-may-care Russian hooligans. Out of habit I cringe, preparing to defend myself, but, instead, suddenly one of them turns to me and politely asks directions how to get somewhere. And the superman arrogance in his eyes fades, and in its place I see the look of my own son.

At such moments everything within me cries out and exults. Wonder and triumph beat on a kettledrum. You are all mine, my own, for better or for worse. You are not always as I wish you to be—may God set you on the right path. But I am part of you, and no one looks at me like a stranger. Do you hear? The officials here can be the rudest bureaucrats (although, to tell the truth, I have not often found them so), but they never, never think about me, "Look at what a kike he is."

And the land is ours, belonging to all of us, eternally so, commanded to all of us and linked to us through the great secrets of the Torah, even though many of us neither understand nor feel this.

In traveling across this land—and hardly a workday goes by that I do not travel at least one hundred kilometers—I feel a tremendous joy. If by some miracle I could suddenly be freed of all my endless obligations, I would prefer not to drive but to walk through this land, feeling her stones beneath my feet, breathing in the scents of her mountains, gardens, and deserts, talking with her people, grasping her soul.

But even shuttling along her exhaust-fume-filled highways, I feel connected with my, our, land. Every day newer beauty and additional depths of spirituality are revealed through the modesty of her external appearance, and I love her more and more.

I love her even in the unbearably hot summer days when the air in the valleys is thick and sticky, when the scents of broiling patches of green are dominated by a strong smell of parched dust. Only on the hills and in the mountains during twilight does the slightly weakening sun allow an invasion of cooling wind that somehow manages to hide and survive.

I love her in the lightning-blazed days of winter rain, when the streets of the cities turn into impassable streams, and even the southernmost stubborn, lifeless "wadis" swell with raging muddy waters.

I love her even more in the blessed weeks of spring when ripening grain of all shades of green play beneath the wind on broad expanses of plowed hills; when the almond trees are dressed in their floral pink and white wedding gowns; when pines modestly flower in the mountains, in every crevice of which, among stones washed by the subsiding rains, shy pink cyclamens blush with downcast eyes into their heart-shaped leaves, while glowing red anemones and majestic blue irises are drawn toward the sun.

Nothing disturbs the cool solemn splendor of the wooded slopes. Only now and then a stone zips down, dislodged by the sure hooves of a gazelle. A lizard rustles. A hoopoe bird, competing with the brightness of the flowers, announces itself. And at the same time, along the roadsides and in littered yards, grasses vie in their wildness, flecked with yellow calendulas and ubiquitous, cheerful daisylike blooms.

I love the cities of my land—disorderly and featureless, but mine. When I approach them at night beneath the unfathomable heaven, under the moon set at an angle strange to northern eyes, the twinkling, flickering lights of the city appear. And it seems to me that the place calls to me, "I am yours, truly yours, enter me."

The very word "desert" is supposedly depressing. I can't say anything about other deserts, but the Judean Desert, the Negev, and the Sinai for me are a focus of joy and unspeakable beauty.

It is possible to write without end about the tamarisks undaunted by the dry winds, about the fabulous magnificence of the cliffs and hills of these deserts with their charming play of color cast in beautiful profusions— from light gold to dark violet, in shades forever changing with the movement of the sun. Songs of praise should be sung to the Negev when its hills,

sown with wheat and barley, are dressed in all shades of green. And it makes
you marvel how boundless is this land, considered so small in terms of land
surveying.

But even more exciting is the fact that all these scenes are perceived—so to
speak—in four dimensions. To the three dimensions perceived by the eyes is
added a perspective of history unfolding in time. The eye searches for the tent
of Avraham Avinu in the Negev hills. A mental image is formed of this great
man, whose greatness lay in the full submission of his will to the word of
the Creator.

In the damp caves of Ein Gedi or on the slopes of the Hebron hills, among the
terraced vineyards and ancient olive trees, I hardly dare to breathe as I wait,
entranced, to encounter King David—young, fearless, and passionate, enrap-
tured with his love for God, which he expressed in the Psalms.

And it seems that the *kohanim* are walking the Temple Mount in their
priestly robes. And it appears that Ruth, the Moabitess who accepted the Torah
with all her heart, is carefully treading the golden sun-burnt field of stubble,
gathering sheaves.

And where shall I find the words to write about you, Jerusalem! Every time I
excitedly realize that I am turning the last bend on the road approaching the
Holy City, suddenly the sunlit brightness of the Jerusalem stone blinds my eyes.
I long to slow down and examine myself again: am I ready to meet the center of
the universe, the time axis of world history?

51

"Let Us Choose Life!"

My attitude toward this land and my yearning for it are just as reverential as
they were five or ten years ago, in spite of the unfortunate superficialities
about which I wrote previously. And my appreciation for this land is heightened
when I find myself in other countries. In recent years I have traveled a lot,
covering five continents. Whenever I am abroad, I miss my homeland even
more—her people and landscape, her charm and tension, all created precisely
to serve as background for events of cosmic significance.

It is not surprising, then, that I am torn apart when I read in the papers
or actually see with my own eyes cases of monstrous moral degradation.
And our national economic and political degeneration, which at first seems to
be an independent phenomenon, is actually a deep result of this fundamental
moral degradation.

The attitudes, values, and education absorbed from childhood first and foremost mold the character of a human being, whether he is a simple craftsman or a government minister. Thus, when people complain about the helplessness of their government, the only advice to give them is, "Look at yourselves. The ministers of the government are exact reflections of yourselves. Even if they were all Solomons, they would not be able to transcend the limits of your miserable, all-is-allowed, nihilistic beliefs. In reward for having fastidiously learned what you were taught and having preserved democracy, you get a government that resembles yourselves."

I want to run out into the street, grab the first people I see and shout:

Brothers! Brothers! Wake up! Aren't you convinced that your experiment of an atheistic Israel has failed? Can it be that you don't yet sufficiently realize that it is possible for Jews to live on this land only by keeping the laws of the Torah—because otherwise the land will spew us forth? Maybe you haven't had enough wars and suffering? Maybe you still imagine that Marx is going to bring you prosperity? Or that skillful diplomacy can convince the world to moderate its anti-Semitism? If you don't accept the Holy Torah, then how can you firmly believe that this land is ours, from time immemorial and forever, categorically ours? You must finally understand that peace will not be brought to the Holy Land by strength of arms alone, because the real question is: does our behavior make us deserve a peaceful life in our land? Are we worthy of it? For the sake of our children, let us finally put an end to the pitiful game of "sophistication," covering up our submission to alien paganism. He Who more than three thousand years ago gave us the choice between a blessing and a curse is still waiting patiently with fatherly love, urging us to "Choose life!"

So let us choose life. Let us entrust our fate to the Almighty. Let us cleanse our homes from all that is alien and borrowed imitation, hostile and crude. Let us make way for goodness and holiness in the souls of our children! Bearing the weight of war, our youth have been robbed and deprived too long of the simple and wise human joys of a Jewish Sabbath, of Jewish holidays, of the Jewish cycle of life.

Just remember what it is like here during the one day of the year when no one yet dares to separate the Jews from God—Yom Kippur. (I don't mean the Yom Kippur when the terrible war broke out on us.) People become attentive and sensitive, more patient, kinder. Strangers greet each other quietly on the street. Something invisible, long forgotten, descends upon us all. Suddenly Jews sense their commitment to one another, their commitment to the Jewish people and to the Almighty Who chose them from all other peoples. Cars don't rush around, driven by people intoxicated by feeling their own power increased by mechanical engines. The air—ordinarily suffocating with dust and fumes—is quiet, clean and fragrant with the aroma of the earth.

Oh, if only we could learn to behave like that every *Shabbat!* What a gift it would be for our children, who now at best are provided with immoral television programs and movies and at worst with discotheques and night clubs! How rightly did our sages say that redemption will come when all of Israel observes the Sabbath two times in a row as it is commanded to be kept. Just two Sabbaths!

52

A Wandering Jew

T hus do I want to cry out to my brothers, to entreat and implore them. And thus do I try to cry out, entreat, and implore at the countless meetings, lectures, and discussions which for the past three years have occupied almost all of my evenings and many of my days, too.

My time is as tight as a drawn bowstring. The smallest unforeseen delay, half an hour not spent as planned, can ruin my schedule for a whole week. Unexpected guests, even the most welcome ones, throw me into a panic. Alas, the people around me often cannot understand the tension of my timetable and are thus offended when I am not in a position to devote enough time to them. I steal time from my research and from my family to rush to Tel Aviv, Ashdod, Haifa, Jerusalem, Dimona. I almost catastrophically fall asleep behind the wheel on the way to meet with students, schoolchildren, professors, soldiers, officers, *kibbutzniks.* Sometimes it happens that I appear in three different cities in one day, while still spending a few hours in between at my magnetohydrodynamics laboratory at Beer Sheva University, delivering a lecture to students on turbulence, and fulfilling every possibly imaginable kind of duty connected with my dozens of academic and social responsibilities.

It weighs heavily on my heart that Beer Sheva, the capital of the Negev and a well-organized, rapidly developing city, is spiritually a desert. And thus, in addition to all my other activities, I have taken it upon myself to establish *Chabad* educational institutions for the children and the general public of Beer Sheva, and especially for its university students. With God's help and the blessings of the Rebbe, gardens are being cultivated to make the desert bloom.

And invitations and letters keep coming in. And the telephone keeps ringing. From students, schoolchildren, women's organizations, parents' committees, new immigrants . . .

Every time I decide to decline the next request, but every next time I don't have the heart to refuse. How can I not give way to the temptation to try one more time to change these people—my brothers who have thoughtlessly deprived themselves and their children, living as if there had never been a Baal Shem Tov or an Ari Hakadosh; as if the Rambam had never written his books or as if Rashi's commentaries had never been published; as if the great *Tana'im* Rabbi Akiva and Rabbi Shimon bar Yochai had never devoted their lives for us, or as if Moshe Rabbeinu had never led us through the desert and HaKadosh Baruch Hu had never given us the Torah on Mount Sinai? If five or ten years ago in Russia I had been asked to lecture on the significance of Judaism in the twentieth century, I would have dropped everything to go, no matter what the distance or what the cost. . . . So, I go.

I go because I know that Notke or any real *Chasid* would go. I go because I must tell my brothers that something inadmissible is happening: the People of the Book is turning into a people of television. I go despite the fact that I know that in an audience of one or two hundred people, possibly— with much luck—my talk will influence one soul. Everyone will listen attentively, many will even agree, possibly even applaud and ask questions. But only one sole person is likely to truly think about what he heard, consider it as affecting himself personally, and arrive at some practical conclusions and decisions. And if I don't have any luck, then not even that one lone individual will be there.

Yet, our sages teach us that to save one soul is the same as saving the whole world. And who knows—a drop of water eats the stone away. . . . Therefore they say in *Chabad:* "Man's job is to create. But for him to succeed in creating— that's God's job."

There is a parable that on the eve of Yom Kippur an eminent old rabbi met an elderly nonobservant Jew. The rabbi talked with the man about the approaching Day of Judgment. They argued and debated for two hours. Before parting, the rabbi asked: "So you will fast tomorrow?" His counterpart replied, "No. I've never done this before in my life, and I'm too old to change my habits." The rabbi's students, who had been waiting, irritated and impatient, for the end of what seemed to them to be a meaningless argument, asked: "Teacher, what is the sense of spending so much time on the eve of the most awesome day of the year in uselessly admonishing an old fool instead of devoting yourself to higher matters and *teshuvah?*"

"You are mistaken, my children," the rabbi answered. "I have no doubt that before this man departs from this world, he will remember our discussion and say in his heart: 'It's too bad that I didn't listen and fast.' And you should know that the repentance of a Jew deserves two hours of the time of even the busiest person."

53

*The Guidance of the Rebbe —
in Science and Life*

In delivering my talks I have been invaluably helped by the knowledge gained from my concentrated "private appointments" or *yechidut* with the Rebbe. Most especially has he enriched my understanding of science and Torah and their interrelationship.

The unavoidable discussion of science with the Rebbe at first distressed me because in *yechidut,* more than in any other situation, I wanted to be cut off from routine, to be raised up to touch, even though only slightly, the true heights of the spirit. But no, every time that I came to the Rebbe, after a benevolent welcome he would put aside my last letter of questions requesting his opinions and advice. And with an apologetic smile of rebuke he would say, "Again you don't write anything about your work. Let's hear first what's new there." And thus would start a new discussion about secular university affairs, about new experiments in my laboratory, scientific articles, and the unfinished manuscript of my new textbook.

After several such meetings, I not only got used to discussing science with the Rebbe, but I also developed my own explanation as to why he chooses this topic of conversation with me. First of all, everyone lucky enough to have ever met with the Rebbe knows that he adjusts his language, vocabulary, and style to suit the background and level of his guest. The Rebbe can intersperse his Yiddish with Russian, German, French, English, or modern Hebrew idiom. From one guest to another, he can switch from journalistic jargon to refined philosophic debate, from the mundane concerns of a craftsman or merchant to the cosmic heights of Talmud and *Kabbalah.* With a writer the Rebbe discusses the latest books; with a military leader, the most advanced weapons; with a businessman, stock exchange news; with a doctor, breakthroughs in medicine; with an engineer, the efficiency of a new instrument he is designing. Everyone feels at home talking to the Rebbe in his own familiar language and of his own interests.

If anyone were to ever eavesdrop on my *yechidut,* he would be hard put to believe that from the office of the Rebbe, the *tzaddik,* the personification of Torah, leader of *Chasidim,* and teacher and advisor to thousands upon thousands of Jews, emanate expressions like "advantages of direct contact heat transfer in liquids . . . ," "suppression of turbulence in a magnetic field . . . ," "difficulties of separating phases while preserving the kinetic energy of a liquid . . . ," "the budget for buying a new thermoanemometric system . . . ," "the composition of the organizing committee of the Conference of Magnetohydrodynamics. . . ." And all this in Yiddish, with the scientific terms partly in English, partly in Russian. Even I myself sometimes forget that I am not participating in an actual university consultation. But the Rebbe's immediate, unfaltering evaluation of every situation and his conclusions instantly recall me to reality and remind me in whose presence I stand.

The attention which the Rebbe gives to people is so intensely focused and empathetic that it is as if he clothes himself in the personality of his guest. And since the guest and the circumstances of his life are changing between any two visits to the Rebbe, in every additional encounter the visitor discovers something uniquely new in the Rebbe.

Everyone is always amazed at how expert the Rebbe is in any specialized field, but how many people marvel at the fact that the Rebbe is talking with each distinguished specialist about one and the same thing? For the truth is that the Rebbe discusses only one thing with his endlessly diverse guests: the indivisible unity of Israel, the Torah, and the Almighty. He talks of illimitable love for fellow Jews—especially for Jewish children—the chosen dwelling place for the Divine spark here in the lowest of worlds. Focusing on the individual interests of his guests, the Rebbe is then able to explain fundamental concepts of Judaism and to awaken people to realizing them in their own daily lives.

This is why the Rebbe has chosen in my own case natural science as the basis upon which to teach the refined and exact structure of Jewish thought and to map out instructions for action. Although the publication of new scientific articles, the start of new research or a fundamental change in existing experiments may result from a *yechidut,* the Rebbe's every word clearly hints that these were not his intentions. There is only one motive for the Rebbe's involvement in secular matters: "In all your ways know the Lord."

Furthermore, the Torah teaches that action is what counts. This means carrying out the *mitzvot.* Thus, everything that can help to disseminate and to fulfill observance of *mitzvot* is good. If my career, my place in the scientific world, my status in the eyes of young people, and my contact with them help to enable more Jewish children to receive a Jewish education, more Jewish families to discover the harmony and meaning of living by the Torah, then the success of an experiment in magnetohydrodynamics acquires real value in accord with the Jewish scale of values. Putting it plainly—the Rebbe wants the Jewish youngster to start putting on *tefillin* after hearing the university professor talk about science and Torah. And then all the professor's activities will acquire meaning. The inroads that the demands of his profession make on his Torah study then become justified.

In addition to this practical approach, there is a deeper plane on which the Rebbe talks with me about science. Often in the small hours of the morning after several intense hours of exchange, the Rebbe suddenly prompts, "Certainly this time, too, you have questions about science and Chasidism that are bothering you. Ask!" And so I feverishly hunt among the questions that have been assailing me or that my lecture audiences ask me. The Rebbe answers every question in detail, with numerous digressions into Chasidism: *Kabbalah,* on the one hand, and the most exotic problems of modern science, on the other.

I would never dare bring a tape recorder to *yechidut* or take notes in the Rebbe's presence. Therefore I must make a tremendous effort to remember. Alas, my memory is not capable of retaining all the details of the wisdom and knowledge which spring forth. I shall mention here only a few of the subjects upon which the Rebbe has expounded to me in private. He has given me a general evaluation of the natural sciences from the Torah point of view. He has probed the absolute truth of the scientific type of knowledge found in the Torah. He has weighed the advantages versus the detrimental factors found in examining the so-called contradictions between Torah and science. He has judged the authenticity of scientific speculations, particularly those which are extrapolated into the distant past. He has deliberated on the informative value of the sciences to Torah study and has discussed the meaning of miracles. He has discussed the connection between nerve impulses and consciousness and will; the structure of time and space vis à vis the Theory of Relativity; free will and Providence; proof of the Revelation at Mount Sinai; the usefulness of scientific examples and analogies to bring young people to identify with Torah. . . .

I shall try to convey here only a few of the most characteristic examples of the Rebbe's amazingly unique approach to the problems of science and Torah. As I am relying solely on my memory, unaided by exact notes, inevitably there will be mistakes in the details recounted here from the Rebbe's vast range of learning.

54

The Rebbe's Philosophy of Science

Perhaps I should begin with the Rebbe's opinion that it is intolerable for a Jew whose profession is in the sciences to be praised as "a great scientist and, by the way, a believing Jew who lives by the *mitzvot* of the Torah." This is a terrible recommendation. Judaism cannot be "by the way." It must be the source, the basis. Everything else should be a result of this source of life. A Jewish scientist must strive to be described as "a God-fearing Jew, observing the strict as well as the easy *mitzvot,* who, by the way, is a great scientist."

In this clear and constant consciousness of the essential versus the nonessential and of the fine line between them lies the very basis of the Rebbe's perception and outlook. Living by the Torah does not mean learning and comprehending it abstractly. Moreover, it does not mean merely adjusting decisions and actions to fit into the instructions of the Torah. The meaning of living by the Torah is that the purpose and content of one's day is literally derived first of all from the meaning which each day has in Torah. Only after actualizing the concrete instructions of the Torah in one's daily life can political events and practical world considerations be taken into account, as they must be.

From his unified, comprehensive view of the world, the Rebbe also formulates his attitude to the natural sciences and their value. Like all other of God's creations, science was created to serve holiness. Whether something actually serves holiness depends on who uses it and under which conditions. For example, explosives can help obtain natural treasures from the earth or they can kill people. Even atomic energy can be a boon. But it also has the potential to exterminate humanity, God forbid. This depends on how man, exercising his freedom of choice, decides to use it.

Science per se is neutral. Potentially it can and ultimately it must lead toward a deeper comprehension of Creation and the Creator. Thus, if properly understood, it can bring a Jew to a more complete life based on *mitzvot.*

The same can be said about technological progress. For example, radio and television in themselves are neither good nor bad. If these media are used for disseminating lies and encouraging animalistic inclinations, introducing concepts alien to Judaism into the minds of children, or simply "killing time" at the expense of Torah study and good deeds—then both radio and television are absolutely evil. But when these instruments are used to teach Torah, to bring back errant Jews—then radio and TV are absolutely good. Moreover, radio waves broadcasting a Torah lesson literally "fill" material space with the spirit of God's Torah.

Likewise the Rebbe does not criticize the study and advancement of the sciences per se. But criticism is evoked the moment that these studies replace or impair Torah study or *mitzvah* observance, the moment they swell a Jew's head so that he forgets his place and purpose. This is why the Rebbe does not encourage a young man to enter the university. Furthermore, the universities—especially the student dormitories—are dens of physical and spiritual degeneration.

Although the Rebbe has no criticism against science as a pursuit in itself, he rejects any apologizing for or compromising of Torah in order to resolve questions about so-called contradictions between Torah and science. Often the supposed contradiction lies in the distant past, for example, in connection with the age of the universe, the theory of evolution, and so on. Here, as the Rebbe demonstrates, science has nothing to contribute. All the so-called scientific data in connection with the above-mentioned problems are in reality results of scientifically invalid extrapolations over huge periods of time, that is, they are simply speculations.

But there are also cases in which the phenomena under question relate to the contemporary world. I asked the Rebbe about a number of such cases where it seems at first glance that contemporary science denies the possibility of some phenomenon mentioned in the Torah or gives an explanation in contradiction to the Torah view. In every one of the cases that I brought to his attention, the Rebbe demonstrated that confusion is caused either by a lack of understanding of how to evaluate and interpret indirect observations (which are very far from being objective knowledge) or because some individuals cannot comprehend that the fact that something has never been observed does not constitute proof of its nonexistence. Assumptions based on such "proofs" actually block the progress of science. And such perverted logic, the Rebbe says, is as "valid" as the distorted logic of the once-popular joke in which a boy convinces his friend that the wireless has existed in their village for centuries. How does he know? He's dug and dug in the yards and gardens and still hasn't found any telegraph wire.

The Rebbe stresses the point that the simple, literal meaning of the words of the Torah is always binding. Grave damage has been caused by attempts past and present to "smooth out" people's inner confusion by claiming that the words of the Torah do not have to be understood in their simple, literal meaning. This is an especially dangerous claim when the matters under discussion pertain to practical *halachah*.

It is unacceptable, for instance, to doubt the imperatively literal meaning of the six days of Creation. Days—not ages! Because the six days are the basis for keeping the seventh as the Sabbath—the basis for the entire concept of *Shabbat*.

A person of strong faith is not bothered by seeming contradictions between the Torah view and what is called the scientific view, because the basic assumption of his faith is that the Torah is absolutely and eternally true. But if other people are bothered by what seems to them to be a contradiction, there is no need to evade such questions, and it actually becomes necessary to examine the problem in a detailed and serious way to avoid confusion.

When confronted with any such seeming contradictions one should keep in mind that experimental science is not able in principle to prove the *impossibility* of any event. Science can only discuss something that has actually been observed and the *probability* of other occurrences. But from this one cannot deduce the impossibility of something that has not yet been successfully observed.

Incidentally, today the probability approach to phenomena prevails in science, particularly in thermodynamics, molecular physics, quantum mechanics, and so on. This approach has replaced the concept of an "impossible phenomenon" with the concept of "phenomena of low probability." It does not mean, though, that we should take this idea to the extreme and claim that the miracles mentioned in the Torah weren't supernatural miracles at all, but rather natural phenomena of low probability. The basis of our Torah is that *Hakadosh Baruch Hu* directly supervises the world and determines the course of every event and phenomenon. Upon this is based, among other things, our understanding of the *mitzvah* of prayer. The prayer of a Jew is not only an expression of feelings of gratitude to God and admiration of His greatness, but it can actually influence the course of events in the world according to the requests and desires expressed in it, to the degree that this is the will of God.

It is impossible therefore for a Torah Jew to agree with Laplace, who claimed that if given the knowledge of the precise position of all the atoms in the universe and all the forces acting on them, he would be able in principle to calculate mathematically the future of the entire world. This kind of determinism is unacceptable to twentieth-century science, which is based in great part on statistics and probability. For completely different reasons Laplace's determinism is also unacceptable to the Jew who knows that God creates the world every moment, sustaining and directing its entirety, down to the smallest details. The Jew knows that whether extrapolation of laws deduced from observations made yesterday and today will be correct tomorrow depends upon the will of the Creator.

The Torah perception of the universe excludes any fortuity since every event happens only with the knowledge and will of the Creator. Although it is true that modern science can no longer consider miracles described in the Torah as impossible, it is wrong to view extraordinary events or miracles as natural events of extremely low probability. The Torah unequivocally explains that miracles are *supernatural* events, which occurred only because God willed that the natural order of things be violated.

When I asked the Rebbe once what the Torah says about the possibility of extraterrestrial life, his response was especially characteristic. The possibility of life existing on other planets, replied the Rebbe, is not denied by the Torah. The Talmud mentions such a possibility, but not the possibility of other civilizations of intelligent creatures. According to the Torah, only creatures possessing free will can be categorized as intelligent beings. And free choice is granted and realized only by the Torah. If there were intelligent beings somewhere else in the universe, then they would have to have a Torah. But if they did have a Torah, it could not be one other than ours since our Torah is the Torah of truth, and there is only one truth. However these hypothetical creatures could not have our Torah, because the giving of the Torah to the Jewish people is described in fine detail. Great attention is given to these details, which have the profoundest meaning and are necessary for the understanding of the Torah itself. Thus we must conclude that from a Jewish point of view the existence of extraterrestrial civilizations is impossible.

This answer is particularly characteristic of the Rebbe because the conclusion in the scientific realm is taken entirely from the Torah. The conclusion is based on absolute, unlimited belief in the Torah and also on the concept that the universe and all events therein are secondary to and actually derived from Torah.

55

The Literal Meaning of Words of Torah

O nce I asked the Rebbe whether he means to say that it is necessary to examine and judge scientific conclusions in the light of the Torah rather than simply ignoring the claims about contradictions between Torah and science. The Rebbe answered that it is necessary to explain how scientific data comes to terms with Torah knowledge, because there are people who need such an explanation. The correct explanation could remove confusion and worry from their hearts.

The Rebbe added that in this respect the approach of the Rambam represents an excellent example. The Rambam demonstrated the key to understanding the proper place of science with relation to Torah—namely, that "All the works of God are for His sake." Since in addition to his greatness in Torah the Rambam also had an encyclopedic knowledge of philosophy and the natural sciences, he found it necessary to also use these for serving God. His major work was the highly revered and authoritative *Mishneh Torah* (*Hayad Hachazakah*), but he also found it necessary to write *The Guide to the Perplexed,* dealing with philosophy and science. He discussed them in such a way that he made them serve the highest purposes.

It is characteristic that even the first part of Rambam's *Yad Hachazakah*— which is actually the earliest code of Jewish law—is called the "Book of Knowledge." In this introduction, the Rambam shows how and to what limits the human intellect is able to comprehend and cognize the Creator. In other words, it is possible to say that in the realm of knowledge of the physical universe, he prepares the ground for learning spiritual subjects—*mitzvot,* the detailed *halachot* discussed in the subsequent thirteen parts of his *Mishneh Torah*.

This progression, namely from physical to spiritual, can be observed in the fulfillment of many *mitzvot*. Although the *mitzvot* express the revealed will of God and their meaning and content are purely spiritual, their fulfillment demands preparation in the material realm. For example, if the Almighty had wanted to, He certainly could have created complete ready-made *tefillin* for us to place upon our arm and forehead every morning. But this is not the case. The craftsman must prepare the boxes, straps, and parchment, the *sofer* has to write the *parshiot,* and the Jew buying them must do so with hard-earned money. The same holds for the *etrog.* Instead of waking up on the first morning of Succoth to find an *etrog* in his hand, the Jew must expend time, effort, and considerable money before the holiday to seek out a good *etrog.* Similarly, for some Jews the clarification of natural sciences from the point of view of Torah can serve as a preparation in the sphere of the physical for their acceptance of the Torah and *mitzvot* upon themselves.

The Rebbe's uncompromising view on the need to follow the simple, literal, direct meaning of the Torah especially pertains to the halachic content of the Torah. If a certain book is recognized and accepted as a halachic work (the criteria for which are put forth in the Torah), then every word and letter in it must be respected as binding as the Law of Moses from Sinai. A classic example of such a halachic work is the Rambam's *Yad Hachazakah.* We are not bound, however, to accept absolutely the literal meaning of scientific-type information contained in nonhalachic books like the Rambam's *Guide to the Perplexed* or Yehuda Halevy's *Kuzari.* There is no contradiction in the fact that both the *Yad Hachazakah* and the *Guide to the Perplexed* were written by the Rambam, because the Rambam wasn't, so to say, exactly the same Rambam when he wrote the *Yad Hachazakah* and when he wrote the *Guide to the Perplexed.* Indeed, Moshe Rabbeinu wasn't the same Moshe Rabbeinu when he taught Torah as when he ate. (But of course the way that Moshe Rabbeinu ate only remotely resembled the way that a simple Jew eats.)

56

To Learn to Understand Torah from Everything around Us

In keeping with the chasidic principle that every object and phenomenon which we see and hear must be used to strengthen our worship of God, the Rebbe makes wide use of examples from science and technology to teach the essence of Judaism and the Torah and to explain what the purpose and behavior of a Jew ought to be.

The modern age of science and technology itself was predicted in the *Zohar.* The *Zohar* says that in the sixth century of the sixth millennium from the creation of the world (5500 in the Jewish calendar or 1740 in the non-Jewish calendar), the wellsprings of knowledge, including non-Jewish knowledge, will be opened. (Non-Jewish knowledge, that is, the natural sciences, is called

"external," as it is outside the "internal" knowledge of the Torah. This description applies even more if this type of knowledge is not used to worship God.)
The *Zohar*'s prediction refers to the outburst of scientific and technological
progress of the past few hundred years, progress which brings us toward the
state of "the world being full of the knowledge of God," as it will be in the
Messianic age. We mentioned above the example of radio waves carrying a
Torah lesson and thus filling material space with the words of God. Modern
physics supplies us with another example: in its conclusion about the equiva-
lency of mass and energy, it demonstrates the unity of the Creation, and this
gives man an indication of the absolute unity of the Creator.

Modern science and technology can also provide images or parables for a
better understanding of the Torah. For instance, the Rebbe uses computer
technology to make the following example:

The operating principle and structure of the computer are based upon the
sum total results of many years' work in mathematics, electronics, and other
branches of science and technology. The computer does not create new
knowledge—it only elaborates upon information conveyed to it according to
certain general principles, producing meaningful results ranging from specific
to general, the results of which can be applied to various areas of science and
technology. Theoretically, all the work produced by a computer could be done
by a human being armed with pencil and paper, but it would take months,
perhaps years to complete a single assignment. Moreover, if a mistake were to
slip into the handmade calculation—which is very likely—the entire calculation
would have to be done over again.

In today's computer society no intelligent human being would even consider
solving any concrete problem by first reinventing computer technology. On the
contrary, anyone can directly benefit from the tried and proven methods of
computer programming and data processing without re-proving the theories,
formulas, and algorithms and without rechecking the hardware structure and
internal operations of the particular computer being used. Computer users
place absolute trust in the scholars who developed computer theory and in the
engineers who constructed the computers.

In contrast to this, many Jews think that they must use their own heads to
clarify everything rationally—from the beginning. They hear about Torah, the
mitzvot, halachah, and Jewish life, but they don't want to rely upon the
authority, knowledge, experience, and work of the great Torah sages. They
don't want to benefit from the *Shulchan Aruch,* which was prepared for their
simple and easy use. "After we have become orientated in everything by
ourselves, after we've checked, proven and argued it out," they say, "then
maybe we'll start living by the Torah, putting on *tefillin* and keeping *Shabbat.*"
Isn't it clear that such people are putting themselves into a situation far more
ridiculous than the hypothetical fool who has access to a computer but who

spends years doing calculations because he refuses to use the computer until he himself has determined how the machine works and how each program in the machine was developed?

The Jewish principle "First we will do and then we will hear and understand" does not prohibit the *mitzvah* of study and achievement. On the contrary, it encourages learning. But study must be preceded by deeds based on the experience and knowledge of our forefathers and Sages of blessed memory — the "experts" of the Torah.

There is another lesson which the Rebbe finds in the example of the computer. As has already been mentioned, sometimes the results of electronic computations are so general that it is possible to use them in several different areas of science and technology. Sometimes a computer program designed to solve a differential equation describes simultaneously several phenomena of dissimilar physical natures. If an additional phenomenon is discovered which fits the same type of differential equation, then the same program can be used for calculations by simply changing the parameters and boundary conditions. Similarly, the *Shulchan Aruch* gives general rules, a general program, and general solutions which are applicable in all ages, regardless of changes in external conditions.

Another of the Rebbe's examples is taken from the interest in solar energy caused by the energy crisis. "What is the unique quality of the sun," asks the Rebbe, "which makes everyone consider it a blessing? It is, of course, its capacity to radiate ('to give light to the earth' — as the first chapter of Genesis says). What would happen if the sun had the same temperature, the same energy, but did not radiate or give heat? Indeed there are such stars, called black holes (their existence is, incidentally, mentioned in the Talmud), the force of attraction of which is so strong that not even one light ray can depart from them. If the sun were such a star, whom would it interest then? Of what use would the sun be if it were a black hole? So it is with the Jew whose primary function is to put forth light, to radiate, to better his fellow man through the *mitzvah* of *ahavat Yisrael*. Without this, he would turn into a black hole, when he was created to be a sun."

57

Advice in Philosophy and in Practical Scientific Work

T he Rebbe's Jewish philosophy of science may be (to the best of my knowledge and understanding) summed up as follows:

1. Objective scientific knowledge, if properly used, can strengthen faith. Thus, for instance, natural sciences demonstrate unequivocally the unity of the very diverse Creation which has its single source in One God.

2. Exaggerated admiration for anything labeled scientific is most dangerous and converts science into an object of idolatry.

3. Many of the conclusions in science are based on interpreting more or less direct observations and measurements. How adequate and objective these interpretations are usually remains an open question, especially when the subject of the scientific research lies beyond direct sensory perception. This can happen either because of the remoteness of the subject in space (and even more so in time!) or the smallness of its size, or because its nature makes it imperceptible in principle. In all these cases, the question of objectivity cannot be checked without making even more assumptions.

4. The conceptions, interpretations, and theories of science are constantly changing and alternating between divergent views, with no indication that they will ever arrive at significant agreement on the truth. Thus, often that which is called a theory has a cognitive value corresponding at best to a hypothesis.

5. The acceptance of the assertion that a phenomenon which has not yet been observed does not exist means freezing science to the level corresponding to the moment when this assertion was made.

6. Any judgment about events or objects in the distant past (beyond the time in which related research was carried out)—like any extrapolation extending far from the interval of research—has nothing in common with science and is in fact pure speculation. The classic example of this is "scientific" speculation on the age of the universe.

7. If any seeming contradiction between Torah and science cannot be satisfactorily resolved immediately, at this time there is no reason for panic, or for, God forbid, a Jew to be repelled by Torah and *mitzvot*. Nothing can be more dangerous than setting a deadline for finding an explanation, since this leads to self-deception out of haste and not to truth.

All of the above-mentioned show the absurdity of placing speculations (not objective scientific knowledge!) against the eternal, unchanging truth of the Torah. This pertains to Torah discussion of the natural consequence of things. As to the cases where the Torah describes the supernatural, the miraculous, it would be even more foolhardy to try to define the suprarational in rational categories or to discuss supernatural phenomena on the grounds of analyses of nature.

The Rebbe also shows how doubt and disbelief are often generated by subconscious attempts to attribute human logic, thought, and attitudes to God. This is why, for example, the Copernican conception of the solar system so triumphantly captured people's belief: it demanded fewer corrections for the description of planet movement than the Ptolemaic conception. But think about it: Is there any basis or justification to the assumption that God constructs the universe in a manner that will seem the most simple to human reason? Human concepts about economy, optimality, and simplicity have nothing in common with the Divine act of Creation because man is limited and finite whereas God is infinite and absolutely unrestricted. In the natural world created by God, extravagance (from a human point of view) is a universal phenomenon— extending from the energy radiated by the sun to the semination of plants and animals.

Continuing along this line, the Rebbe has an analogy which explains why so many people are attracted to Darwinism: Suppose that you had to create the world with its multitudinous life forms. Suppose also that you can choose between two ways of doing this. The first is to create each species, each individual separately. The second way is to create matter, then assign it laws of development, and from there on have everything go by itself. Which would you choose? Any normal human being would choose the second. He would be afraid to even contemplate "engineering" and constructing billions of organisms, each one separately. Thus, when considering the Divine Creation, people subconsciously thrust their own human criteria on God. But the Almighty has warned us that "My thoughts are not your thoughts."

All of the above relates to the Rebbe's Jewish interpretation of science. In addition to this, he has given much practical advice to scientists, helping them to develop specific aspects of science. There have been many cases where the Rebbe has found basic mistakes in the professional articles of physicists, microbiologists, mathematicians, and psychologists and has instructed them how to correct the error.

Several years ago, shortly after starting to develop a magnetohydrodynamic system to convert solar energy into electrical energy, I had the privilege to meet with the Rebbe again in *yechidut*. At once he started to interrogate me about my new invention, delving in depth into the technical details.

Upon hearing my replies to his questions, he immediately brought my attention to two circumstances. First, he said that if the velocity of the two-phase flow was really as I had indicated, then the efficiency factor received was too low. Secondly, he pointed out that through storing solar heat during the day and converting it into electricity during the cold Negev nights, it would be possible to take advantage of the special climatic properties of the Negev to increase by approximately a third the amount of electrical energy produced. It turned out that the Rebbe's two comments were absolutely correct. I found my mistake in calculating the efficiency factor only two years later. The second suggestion is to be applied in further stages of the project. Surprisingly, of all the many experts with whom I consulted at length about this project, nobody thought of the points which the Rebbe clarified instantaneously after hearing a five-minute briefing.

Such and much other advice which the Rebbe has given on scientific research work in the most diverse fields cannot be explained merely by the fact that he holds a diploma from the Sorbonne and a few other universities. The explanation to this phenomenon is more likely connected to a comprehensive spiritual vision of the world, a vision mirrored through the Torah and feeling the constant presence of the Creator, a vision wherein the material world is but a pale reflection of the spiritual worlds. This phenomenal insight is also greatly explained by the Rebbe's ability and desire to enter entirely into the problems bothering his guests, whoever they may be.

Much has been written about the Rebbe's advice on medical problems. His medical advice is usually based on a deep esteem for the opinions of doctors and experts. But sometimes the Rebbe's advice directly opposes these opinions. Against the consensus of doctors, for example, the Rebbe has prevented quite a number of abortions, and, in all cases known to me personally, healthy and perfect Jewish babies were born.

58

What I Tell My Listeners

There are so many things I want to tell my audiences—about everything that I went through searching for my world outlook and all the thinking I did during those years. Chasidism has taught me to see the deep interconnections of all phenomena. Finally freed from the wretched framework of rationalistic and deterministic thought, I can honestly say that not only do I understand but I also deeply feel the unity of this world in God. I can now realize that the countless distinctions between things and events are cancelled within the Infinite Light of *Hashem*. I understand the direct correlation of all the things and events in the universe with the letters and words of the Torah. Chasidism has taught me to see their total interrelationship with the will of the Creator.

And this is the key to understanding why fulfilling the *mitzvot* of the Torah—written in the same letters and words out of which the material world is created—is literally a stronger weapon than tanks and planes and missiles in defending ourselves from both the physical and spiritual threats of the non-Jewish world. As the Lubavitcher Rebbe said recently: our people always have been and still remain like a sheep surrounded by seventy wolves. However, the sheep can resist the wolves only so long as he trusts more in the Almighty than in any material means of defense (the importance of which no one can deny), and therefore God protects it. The current tragedy is that the sheep imagines himself a wolf, not needing Divine protection and not realizing that even if he succeeds in becoming a wolf, he will be still only one wolf against seventy.

It isn't easy to explain this to audiences saturated in materialism, but I try to convince them over and over again. I try first of all to make them stop thinking that "faith is impossible in our times." I attempt to get an answer to the question: "Why was your grandfather a believing Jew who practiced the *mitzvot* and studied Torah, but you aren't? Perhaps you have discovered something new that justifies your departure from the tradition of your grandfather and great-grandfathers that makes you better than they?"

I have never heard a reasonable answer to this question. People say things like: "My grandfather didn't have electricity." "He didn't watch television." They've even said: "My grandfather didn't have a modern toilet."

Then I attempt to clarify what – in their opinion – is the connection between an electric light and a television set on the one hand, and the ability to explain the essence and purpose of things, to understand the creation of the world, to find the meaning of life and to define a code of behavior for human inter-relationships on the other hand.

The replies are almost always unsubstantiated claims that man has changed, man has become more perfect, more refined. Life itself is different now, they say. The structure, ideals, and driving forces of society have changed, they say, as well as the motives of individual actions and the set of values which controls them.

And then I must show my audience the absurdity of its claims. No scientific progress or technology is capable of spiritually or morally perfecting a human being, of changing the essence or meaning of life, of influencing the factors which measure human happiness and satisfaction, of changing human passion, feeling, or motivations. In moral-ethical spheres, the life of man and society has not changed, not in hundreds of years nor in thousands of years.

It is enough to randomly open any book of the Bible, to leaf through any tractate of the *Mishnah,* in order to become convinced that two or three thousand years ago, just like today, people lived and died, raised children, loved and hated, rejoiced and suffered, envied and sympathized with one another. Man's fate was just as full of vicissitudes and chance and just as inscrutable. Just as now, there were then greedy people and generous people, egoists and altruists, those who valued friendship and confidence and those who suffered from treachery and suspicion. In theory they upheld righteous-ness, honesty, and uprightness, but in deed, they lied, cheated, and dissembled. There were the same temptations then as today. Just as now, the ambition and lust for gain harbored by a few individuals in ages past could throw an entire people into torment. Not in vain did King Solomon say, "There is nothing new under the sun." Man has not become more noble by switching from riding a donkey or a horse to driving a luxury automobile. Man's soul, his aspirations, his capacity for happiness have not been improved by replacing candles with electric lights and definitely not by replacing books with movies. On the contrary, all these technological innovations, as everyone knows now, destroy nature and maim the soul.

Concerning refinement and spiritual perfection, it is enough merely to recall that in the Pale of Settlement there was not a single Jew who did not know how to answer questions about the essence of the soul and the essence of matter, about the purpose of man, about the origin of the world—whereas today university professors contrive to exist without any world outlook at all to embrace these issues. And even the claim that modern man is more competent professionally is also a myth. For the ancient specialist in steel, it was enough to look at a sword or to touch it with his hand to detect defects in manufacture, whereas today's metallurgists, armed to the teeth with spectroscopy and ultrasonic fault detection devices, sometimes struggle for years to remove the reason of a defect. Modern doctors, with all their electronic and other special equipment, with their thousands of sophisticated tests, hardly remember that the object of their work is a human being. And in the end sometimes it turns out that they can do less than a doctor aided only by his own thought and intuition a hundred years ago.

The best illustration of the fact that scientific progress improves neither man nor mankind is space travel, particularly the flights to the moon. Thirty years ago, when we were children, we would devour science-fiction novels describing man's adventures in space. We were convinced, along with the authors, that this grandiose achievement was going to change everybody and everything on the face of the earth. This happy future simply took our breath away. And now man has visited the moon, more than once; but not only have injustice, bloodshed, and hunger not decreased, but the man on the streets has long since forgotten that there ever were lunar flights.

Thus, since scientific-technological progress bears no influence on that which is truly important to us—on our character, on our capacity to love and hate, on our consciousness, on our feeling of duty, or even on our understanding of ourselves and the world we live in—then why is it commonly thought that science negates faith?

Our generation imagines that its adopted atheism and nihilism are the natural world outlooks both for mankind in general and for Jews in particular. The souls of our secular youngsters are not conscious of the generation of the desert led by Moshe Rabbeinu to become a People through receiving the Torah. They have no conception of how hundreds of generations of Jews suffered in order to keep their faith pure and whole. They have no idea how the recent generations have been gradually losing their faith, how the German and French Emancipation, the Jewish "enlightenment" movement, the eminent German Bible critic Wellhausen, and the dazzling growth of the natural sciences tempted so many of our grandfathers to deviate from the upright path of Judaism.

My audiences further give me old, hackneyed arguments that the findings of science negate the Torah. So of course I tell them, explaining in great detail, that it is nonsense to assume that science, which deals with the mutual inter-relationships of phenomena in the material world, can be contrasted or com-pared with the Torah, which interprets the spiritual sphere of life, the sphere of morality and ethics, and provides comprehensive, all-embracing answers to questions about Creation and about the essence, interconnection, and purpose of all things in the universe and the universe itself.

Innumerable times I have had to answer questions about the six days of Creation. So many people dreadfully want to understand these days as periods of millions of years. If only they could realize that the very creation of the world by God *ex nihilo* is by far a greater miracle than the fact that it was completed in six days!

Once I tried to explain to my audience the essence of the concept of a *tzaddik*. I said that living strictly according to the Torah, subordinating personal and physical needs, constantly studying Torah and penetrating into its deepest se-crets, and uplifting himself through prayer elevate such a Jew and qualify him to mediate between God and Israel. Thus, a *tzaddik* can reveal otherwise unseen things to his fellow Jews. The people in the audience, who considered themselves to be terribly intelligent and modern, were greatly annoyed by all this. One man even came up to me after the lecture to express his surprise that I−a man of science, a natural scientist (that's how he characterized me)−should be trying to fool a sophisticated audience with naïve fairy tales.

The next time that I had occasion to lecture on a similar theme to a similar audience, I decided to carry out a psychological experiment. Again I spoke about the supernatural gifts of the *tzaddik,* but this time I masked my talk in scientific imagery. I not only used terminology like "parapsychology" and "telepathy," but I also expanded on "thought-energy fields," about spaces with more than three dimensions and, after writing a lengthy differential equation on the blackboard, I chattered about quantum mechanics. Everything that I said was sheer nonsense−scientific-sounding verbiage. But you should have seen the hypnotic effect it had upon the audience and how many questions they respectfully asked me. Curiously enough, no one in the audience stood up to inform me that I was speaking nonsense from the purely scientific point of view. And that was an audience composed entirely of university graduates!

It turns out that such people base their belief neither on the strength of ideological reasons, nor on the results of logical analysis, nor on the basis of a well thought-out investigation. They simply have gotten into the habit of rejecting everything that sounds like religion and automatically accepting everything that sounds like science.

It is curious and sad that, tormented by the pace and strain of modern life, there are people, lonely within their swarming human ant colonies and hounded by fears, who are easily taken in by merchants of every possible cheap merchandise like yoga, Indian transcendental meditation, and other forms of paganism and witchcraft. To join any of these modern cults of idolatry no intellectual deposit or effort is required, no self-restraint is needed. Everything is easy and accessible. Moreover, they spice their wares with pseudo-scientific references to physics, biology, psychology. This hypnotizes people into swallowing the bait, while it never occurs to them that their grandfathers, who rose before sunrise to study their daily lesson of Torah, put on *tefillin,* and pray, and then worked sixteen hours a day while raising ten children, didn't need either yoga or meditation and didn't worry about "stresses," even though their physical life was a series of pogroms, hunger, and other dangers.

59

Why Return to Torah Is a Must

I explain to my audiences why they must return to Torah and to the *mitzvot.* I explain to them that they are depriving themselves by remaining passive outsiders to the eternal values of Judaism.

This essential return can be carried out on at least three levels. The first level is purely personal and individual. A man of faith has strict order in his life. He has clear aims. He knows where to find the answers to disturbing questions. Having an integral world outlook, he therefore has a greater chance to achieve inner harmony and peace. He has upon Whom to rely and from whence to derive confidence for the future. To the extent that he succeeds in bringing up his children in this spirit, they will respect and honor him and be protected from vices raging in the modern world, such as drugs, perversion, and violence.

Religion, faith, and a sense of the constant presence of God overseeing every human step are the most secure means of self-defense that a young person can have. To use one of Notke's analogies: just as a car without brakes can't be driven, so a human being without a protective system of self-control inevitably becomes sacrificed to his own inherent source of evil, pulling him to lusts and passions.

And here is one final important point concerning personal happiness. No matter how hard a Jew tries to assimilate, no matter how much he disguises himself in alien attire, he is not free from belonging to Judaism (unless, of course, he crosses over the final border of physical assimilation—of inter-marrying and raising his children as non-Jews—against which many non-identifying Jews still retain an inner aversion). Sooner or later the moment comes when the enemy reminds him that he is a Jew. This is an empirical fact. And then, when this inevitably does happen, lacking the treasures of the Jewish soul, seeing no reason to be proud of belonging to the Jewish people and ignorant of its purpose in the world, he takes his Jewishness as an everlasting, inescapable curse. And then the life of this Jew running away from his own self becomes a real hell. It never occurs to him that his very own parents robbed him, deprived him of an ideal and a guiding thread in life. Out of a mistaken notion of love for their children, the parents of such a lost Jew struggled to integrate their sons and daughters into a "culture common to all mankind," to give them an "intellectual profession," and to take them out of the "world of the *shtetl*" into the "big world."

The Almighty said to the Jews in the Torah: "Here I give you a blessing and a curse, life and death. Choose life." Every Jew has to make this choice, and the tragedy is compounded when a person's children and grandchildren are deprived because of his mistaken decision.

The second of the three necessary levels of return is national. We became a nation in an entirely different way from all other nations. Usually groups of people become a nation as a result of having lived together for a long time, occupying the same territory, and having built an economy and a system of social attitudes. But we became a nation on the fiftieth day after the exodus from Egypt when, standing at the foot of Mount Sinai, we accepted the yoke of the Torah, saying: "*Na'aseh venishma.*" Torah and faith united us from the very onset. Everything else was secondary and resulting from this source. Ironically, our enemies consider us a most calculating people. But the truth is that we were born as a nation in an irrational way, and all our subsequent history has also been completely irrational. Our most noteworthy deeds demonstrate that in critical moments, free of all calculations and logic, we stand ready to sacrifice ourselves. Thus, it is not surprising that the Marxists do not recognize us as a nation. In their own way, they are being consistent. People who have forced human consciousness to fit into a narrow, rigid, cramped, primitive, Procrustean bed are not able to accept the Jewish people or even to recognize its existence. It is simply beyond their comprehension.

Since the Jewish people arose thanks to and for the sake of the Torah, naturally it can exist only in connection with the Torah. For those who accept and realize this simple truth, further explanation is unnecessary. However, insofar as most of us have been educated in scepticism and rationalism, I must also present here rational explanations based on history and national experience.

It is a fact that the Jewish people has lost more of its sons to assimilation during the entire course of its history than to the monstrous periods

of destruction of ancient Rome, the Inquisition, the pogroms, Bogdan Chmielnicki, and Hitler. Those who assimilated were those who abandoned the Torah.
Statistics show that families who abandon the Torah, the *mitzvot,* and tradition
can manage to avoid physical assimilation at the most for four generations or, in
rare cases, five generations. (This pertains to Israel just as much as to the
countries of the Diaspora.) Even the most extreme atheists agree that religion is
the main and even sole factor which preserved our people for thousands of
years. However, they are convinced that now things have changed and this
factor can be thrown away. In addition to their old argument that our modern
age is a special one, they refer to the fact of the existence of the State of Israel.
They forget that:

1. the danger of assimilation is possibly even greater for those Jews breaking away from tradition within Israel itself than for those in other countries
where the hostility of the environment impedes assimilation somewhat;

2. there is no more convincing proof of our right to our land than the fact
that it was commanded by God to Abraham, Isaac, and Jacob for eternity (a fact
well known by any Christian or Moslem);

3. were it not for the Torah and the *mitzvot,* even if we had physically
survived until today, we simply would not know that we once had a land in the
Middle East. And even if we did know about it from history and archeology,
without the practice of our religion we wouldn't think that this land still bears
any relation to us today.

If more empirical proof is needed to show the importance and inevitability
of returning to the Torah after the establishment of the State, then consider the
words of the Torah that we are "a people who dwells alone." Never has history
so convincingly confirmed this than just after the proclamation of the State
of Israel.

Here is one last analogy to conclude our discussion of the national level of
return to Judaism. Most people nowadays have life insurance. This doesn't
mean that they're getting ready to die. On the contrary, everyone hopes for a
long and happy life. Well then, isn't it time to start thinking about life insurance
on a national level? We all believe and hope that our new state will last forever.
However, as serious people, it is incumbent upon us to consider the worst
possibility. And if we do this, then we immediately discover that if the younger
generation raised in Israel were forced, God forbid, to go into exile, their
ability to resist assimilation would be a thousand times worse than was that of
the previous generations of the Diaspora. Alas, children of nontraditional
families would be simply defenseless against alien influences. It would probably take not even an entire generation, but only a number of years, to bring
about their absolute assimilation.

And, finally, let us discuss the third level upon which it is necessary to return to the Torah—the philosophical level. As my book *From the Depths* deals with this subject, I shall not elaborate here. I shall simply recall its major conclusion. And that is that the Torah contains the only possible irrefutable explanation of the essence of the universe, its origin and existence, and also of the essence and purpose of the Jewish people. It also reveals the essence, origin, and purpose of all things. The Torah contains truths which are tightly sealed and inaccessible to the rational mind, acquainted only with relationships and phenomena. These categories of the essence, origin, and purpose of Creation are conveyed to man in the Torah, revealing to those who perceive it the highest knowledge that a mortal being can possess. Whether you accept and recognize this knowledge or not depends on you. But even if you reject it, it doesn't cease being the truth.

A Jew can believe or not believe, accept the Torah or not accept it—this is actually the only degree of liberty that he has. Whatever choice the Jew makes, it will determine his fate, although nobody imposes a decision upon him. For everything else except this free choice, however, there operates a universal and inviolable predestination—the direct manifestation of the will of the all-penetrating presence of God.

Whether someone likes this truth or doesn't like it bears no influence upon the truth itself. A "revolt" against the truth of the Torah has even less significance than someone "revolting" against the laws of gravity by jumping out the window or protesting against the necessity of breathing by putting his head in a plastic bag.

And here I often have the opportunity to add one more argument to my case. The Torah cannot be penetrated by cold reasoning and analysis. It is impossible to feel the happiness and joy of a Torah life by looking in from the outside. Torah must be tasted. Torah cannot be understood only by the intellect. The heart, soul, and intuition must be involved. The world of Torah must be entered and lived through, not just for a day or two, but until the scab of many years peels off the soul, revealing secret sensitive receptors, and a long slumbering forgotten "I" rejoices, "Yes, this is my very own Jewish self—this is what I was meant to be."

60

I Believe . . .

I t yet remains for me to express my boundless gratitude to the Almighty for giving me the chance to return—to make my *teshuvah*—and for providing me with guidance. In my recollections I review the thirty years since I started to search for the blessing in being Jewish, stressing the last fifteen years since I put on my *tefillin* for the first time and thus became a Jew by deeds and not just be conviction. What would my life have been without the return? But that is an idle question. Instead of dealing with it I have tried to explain to myself and to others what I have found thanks to the *teshuvah*.

But, although I have tried to give the answer on the philosophical level, on the national level and on quite a number of other levels, one simple human aspect remains that I have probably still not put into words clearly enough on the preceding pages. And that is how good it is to be a Jew openly and proudly and to know clearly what it means to be a Jew. All the words in the world would not suffice to explain the joy of going to the synagogue in Russia, or to a Torah class, or to a chasidic gathering. To move through the hostile mob, to sense the eyes of the shadowers on your back and to remain proud and confident. How sorry I am for those still there who did not yet return and who still are—as I was years ago—continually ready to melt into their surroundings, to annihilate self, to imitate, to feign. . . .

But is it really just there, in Russia? Did I not meet hundreds and hundreds of American Jews who are doing exactly the same? Moreover, did I not see even observant American Jews, even members of an association of Orthodox scientists, who shamefacedly hide their *yarmulkes* in their pockets as soon as they reach the threshold of their university or laboratory? Yes, years ago I did the same. But now, thank God, I learned that the gentile colleague respects you more when you explain to him that you cannot have a "normal" dinner at his home. And there have been many cases when gentile professors, even without my reminder, prepared special kosher meals (ordered from the suppliers to airline companies) for me at scientific conferences, or invited me home for a meal of fresh, unpeeled fruit, served specially on new plastic dishes, or finally when a gentile colleague at a meeting Friday afternoon looked at his watch with worry and said, "You have to rush—it's almost your Sabbath."

These may seem to be mere trifles, but they make you feel at peace with yourself. And even more important, they make you be whom you are truly meant to be.

And finally I wish to add one more expression of my unending gratitude to the Almighty Who, in this world filled with lies and illusions, has let me taste the truth and delight in some small measure in knowing Him and His *mitzvot*. I am infinitely fortunate that, after having gone through many errors, now I can repeat the principles of faith of the great Rambam with a clear conscience and complete belief:

1. I believe with perfect faith that the Creator, blessed be His Name, creates and guides all the created beings, and that He alone has made, does make, and will make all things.

2. I believe with perfect faith that the Creator, blessed be His Name, is a unity, and that there is no oneness of any kind like His, and that He alone is our God, Who was, is, and will be.

3. I believe with perfect faith that the Creator, blessed be His Name, is not corporeal, and that He is free from all the properties of matter, and that He has not any likeness whatsoever.

4. I believe with perfect faith that the Creator, blessed be His Name, was the first and will be the last.

5. I believe with perfect faith that the Creator, blessed be His Name, is the only one to whom it is proper to pray, and that it is not proper to pray to any being besides Him.

6. I believe with perfect faith that all the words of the prophets are true.

7. I believe with perfect faith that the prophecy of Moshe Rabbeinu, peace be unto him, was true, and that he was the chief of the prophets, both to those who preceded and to those who followed.

8. I believe with perfect faith that the whole Torah now in our possession is the same that was given to Moshe Rabbeinu, peace be unto him.

9. I believe with perfect faith that this Torah will not be changed, and that there will be no other Torah from the Creator, blessed be His Name.

10. I believe with perfect faith that the Creator, blessed be His Name, knows every deed of human beings and all their thoughts, as it is said: "Who fashions the hearts of them all, Who comprehends all their deeds."

11. I believe with perfect faith that the Creator, blessed be His Name, rewards those who keep His commandments and punishes those who transgress His commandments.

12. I believe with perfect faith in the coming of the Messiah; and although he may tarry, I will wait daily for his coming.

13. I believe with perfect faith that there will be a revival of the dead at the time when it shall please the Creator, blessed be His Name, and exalted be His mention forever and ever.

Afterword

Thirty-two years have passed since I wrote *From the Depths* (Part II of the notes contained in this book). That was in Riga, under the Soviet regime. Since then, my life has undergone great changes. Most importantly, I have met the Lubavitcher *Chasidim,* started living by the laws of the Torah, and have had the honor of becoming a *Chasid* of the Lubavitcher Rebbe.

In 1972 I managed to escape the Bolshevik clutches and come to Israel. Here, in Beer Sheva in 1976, I wrote my philosophical autobiography, *Return* (Part I of the present book).

When the Jason Aronson editors came up with the idea of publishing a new edition of my notes, I reread everything I had written twenty and thirty years earlier. To my surprise, none of it had lost its relevance. In the interim, the world had gone through mind-boggling changes. The Soviet empire had collapsed, and communism had suffered global defeat. The State of Israel had fought a series of wars. The era of secular Zionism had yielded place to what the press and officials of sundry government and public bodies in Israel term the "post-Zionist" era. The result was a woeful situation whereby most of what I had written so many years earlier—on Jewish problems, the meaning of Jewish history, the sacred mission of the people of Israel and the Holy Land, on Jewish philosophy and Torah-based education, the harmony between Torah study and rational scientific learning—had become even more relevant and pressing.

Many things have become clear, many others even more complex and vague. In all honesty, I ought to have written a new book. Yet, caught up as I am in the daily whirl of endless affairs, the mad rush of major and minor problems suffering no delay, for the present I am forced to limit myself to this Afterword.

* * *

More than two decades of living in Israel have taught me a great deal. Alas, disappointments have been innumerable and vast. Yet before going into this subject, I must explain some things. Nothing, thank God, has shaken my boundless love for my people, for every Jew carrying within his soul a spark of the Almighty Himself, and for the land of Israel, where one feels the breath of nearly four millennia since our forefather Abraham acquired the right to it. Yet all the stronger is my repugnance upon seeing the purity and holiness of our mission consigned to oblivion, while witnessing the depravity, deception, immorality, and the masochism of blind hatred and envy—so unnatural in the Holy Land, yet so firmly rooted and cozily flourishing in it.

Twenty years ago, in the book *Return,* I deplored the alienation of Israelis, especially the younger generation, from Jewish philosophy, traditions, and moral values. I spoke about the fears instilled in me by the system of formal education (not *upbringing,* mind you, but *education,* since fighters for liberalism and democracy have proclaimed *upbringing* to be out-of-bounds—supposedly because it "violates individual freedom"). This system of formal education, devoid of all Jewish substance, decimates the holy and pure souls of Jewish children, processing them through the filter of "being like other nations," turning them into people without kith or kin, without the slightest idea of why they are here, in this land where it is much more difficult and dangerous to live than in Canada or the United States.

Back then, I had written about these tendencies in an attempt to sound the warning bell, to ward off evil. . . . I wrote, hoping and praying that my misgivings would prove ungrounded. To my infinite regret, they have not only come true but have exceeded by far my worst fears. The 1992 elections have brought an ultraleftist government to power. The tragic irony lies in the fact that as communism disintegrated throughout the world, Israel, of all places, swung in the opposite direction. The irony was further exacerbated by the substantial contribution made to the victory of the left and ultraleft by immigrants from the former Soviet Union, naive and bewildered by the pre-election campaign. In the Soviet Union under Stalin, a slogan called for "building communism in a single isolated country." Since 1992, it appears that Israel has adopted this motto precisely in the period of communism's demise. In contrast to the gentlemanly course taken by Mr. Menachem Begin upon coming to power in 1977, the leftist block began with a thorough "purge" of the bureaucratic establishment, the press, and television in 1992. Control of the media has become virtually absolute, both in the aftermath of this purging, and as a result of economic sanctions. The more recalcitrant opponents have been subjected to "preventive administrative detention." These events painfully remind me of Russia during the 1960s–1970s.

Everything came to a glaring and frightening climax in 1993 when, despite experts' warnings and contrary to plain common sense, the country rushed with suicidal madness into the arms of murderers who openly proclaimed their final goal: to destroy us, to cleanse the land of all Jewish presence. This is written in the covenant of the Palestine Liberation Organization. It is proclaimed at every possible occasion by Arafat, the head of this organization. However, we are told that he does not mean it and that we should not pay attention to his words. At the same time, we are urged to believe him when he signs a piece of paper, a "peace treaty," and we should be happy, in exchange for this piece of paper, to give him our land, slice by slice, and to release thousands of convicted murderers from our prisons. All he has to do is wait until we become so small and indefensible that he, together with several Arab countries, will be able to take by force whatever remains. This tragedy, daily claiming human lives and similar to human sacrifices made during Stalin's drive to build communism, goes by the absurdly ironic name of a "peace process." What makes this so awful is not so much the demented conduct of the politicians, or the brainwashing from the increasingly perverted media that learned the methods of the Soviet press all too well—and not even the witches' Sabbath of the left and ultraleft, who are trying to turn Israel into a last stronghold of decayed global communism. What is most horrible and threatening is that a large (perhaps an overwhelming) part of Israeli society acts in tacit or open support of all this. Hypnotized, plagued by an inferiority complex and a pathological sense of guilt concocted by someone, this society masochistically prefers the deaths of its soldiers and compatriots to efficient and unconditional extermination of terrorists and their bosses. Having lost the connection with previous generations, with Jewish history, with Torah—the foundation of continuity with everything Jewish—members of Israeli society lost confidence in our right to this land and therefore they are ready to parcel out, piece by piece, the land that their fathers and grandfathers have perished defending. Not only Hebron, but even Jerusalem, is seen by them as "a pile of stones only fanatics care about" (in the words of a popular scribbler from the *Maariv*). They delude themselves thinking that, after handing over everything, including Hebron and Jerusalem, they could take things easy in Tel Aviv and the remaining coastal strip—the very words of the above-mentioned pen pusher. What could have caused a people so "able and wise," as the Torah defines us, to reach such heights of inane absurdity? The point of the matter is that our nation's success and wisdom derive not from certain genetic traits but from our devotion to the Torah, our adherence to the path ordained by the Almighty. Alas, this is not the first time that departure from Torah's commandments has resulted in disaster both spiritual and physical. For it has all been foretold in the same Torah! The present generation of Israelis, raised in total isolation from the Torah, has suddenly felt itself the object of a paradox created by secular Zionism. Here is the nature of this paradox: On the one hand, according to Zionist tenets, every Jew must live in Israel. On the other hand, secular Zionism does not accept the Torah; hence, Israelis are expected to become "like all other nations." However, hostile Arab claims make life in Israel more trying and perilous than elsewhere. And so, Israelis ask themselves—whether openly or subconsciously—what makes this risk worth taking? Since they are no different from "all other nations," the sensible solution would be to blend in, merge with the surrounding world, assimilate (the way they have in other countries, through conversion or mixed marriage), or simply leave Israel. Therefore, it is obvious that the seed of self-destruction was planted in the concept of secular Zionism at the very moment of its birth.

In their many-thousand-year history, Jews have had to endure incomparably worse predicaments than the current one—Babylonian captivity, the Greek conquest, the destruction of the Temple by the Romans, Spanish Inquisition, the mass murders perpetrated by Bogdan Chmielnicki, and finally the recent Holocaust. During many of these calamities, Jews had neither a country, nor an army, nor means of self-defense. And yet the Jewish people have endured, have outlived all their enemies. This survival was due to a legacy mightier than any weapon: the power of the spirit, the knowledge of their mission in this world. It was clear to all that "the sons of Israel are responsible for each other," and individual misfortune was shared by the entire nation. They knew *in the name of what* they had to live, and turned to the Almighty for help. The modern-day Israeli, on the other hand, has squandered this treasure and is forced to confront his dangers face-to-face, naked, defenseless, apathetic. The memory of his ancestors had extended for thousands of years into the past, feeding the imagination that stretched into the future all the way to the coming of *Moshiach*. Our contemporary's memory, on the other hand, is meager and bare, with the days to come lost in the haze. Thus he can only live for the moment's pleasure and pain, with his private and fleeting interest his sole concern. During the early decades of Israel's existence, a terrorist act anywhere in the country sent waves of shock and sorrow throughout the nation. Today, people dying on the next street, let alone in another city, are regarded as a routine event, a matter for the police at most. However, the ups and downs of the stock exchange—that touches the heart-strings! Or the distress one feels when a neighbor or colleague buys a new car that is bigger or better than one's own.

Another terrifying development is the polarization of Israeli society, the antagonism and blind hostility of the secular majority towards the Torah-observing minority. For the sake of earning political credits and votes, various parties resort to the lowest populist methods, including the incitement of hatred for the "religious." What could be easier and handier? The religious wear different, outdated clothing—a perfect target for caricatures, à la Goebbels' *Sturmer* of the 1930s! The religious protest against the running of public transportation on *Shabbat* or the sale of pork—ergo, these "representatives of the dark ages" are infringing on the individual freedom of the "enlightened" neighbor wearing jeans and a ring in his ear. As a result, this "enlightened" neighbor's heart fills with malicious and irrational hatred that seems alarmingly similar to that nursed by anti-Semites of every creed and color. This hatred is aimed at people who, while relatively small in number, shoulder, for the sake of the entire nation, the indispensable duty of studying and observing the Torah day and night, a duty that assures the continual existence of the people of Israel. Another duty they have taken upon themselves is to maintain the country's demographic balance: the number of children in their families is two to four times larger than the country's average birthrate.

There is one more target for incitement and ridiculous accusations, fabricated by antinational forces and fueled by the media: the settlers in Judea and Samaria and the Gaza strip. These people, most of whom had moved there with the support or active encouragement of the government, put their lives at risk every minute of the day. With their bodies and the bodies of their families, they shield the residents of the more secure parts of the country. Nowadays, however, they are branded as instigators, "enemies of peace," "an obstacle to the implementation of the peace process." According to the accusations, the Arabs would simply adore us, were it not for these fanatical settlers. Our leaders, whose endless concessions encourage our deadly enemies and give them added impetus to escalate their terror, heap the blame for all our ills on . . . the settlers! Were it not for this lunatic fringe (they tell us) nothing would be simpler than to give Judea and Samaria to the Arabs, whereby they would immediately become our good neighbors. The resulting situation is painfully similar to what once took place in Germany and Russia, whose rulers, looking for an outlet for their citizens' frustration, played upon anti-Semitic tendencies by blaming the Yids for their every failure. The absurdity of the present situation is that the role of anti-Semites is taken over by Jews who have gone through the process of de-Judaization, while the role of the Yids has been assigned to Jews sacrificing themselves for the sake of the nation's security, who are especially hated for wearing *kippas* and beards.

The all-pervading anti-Jewishness has by now eroded not only the distinctive, unique spirit specific to the Jewish people, but also the normal national pride inherent in all nations capable of common sense and natural self-respect. While the French and the British jealously cherish even the purely external aspects of their tradition, many Israelis harbor a pathological hatred of Jewish customs and struggle to do away with them. The anti-Jewish bias at times crops up in seemingly innocuous settings. Thus, TV announcers, especially in children's programs, more and more often end the broadcast with an American "bye" instead of the Hebrew "*shalom*" and, if the program falls on a Friday, replace the traditional "*Shabbat Shalom*" with "Have a nice weekend." Passengers of Israel's El Al airline, which in the past had played Jewish songs before landing, are increasingly subjected to pop music.

The era that is labeled, in both the media and academic circles, "the era of post-Zionism," is also marked by a process of "deheroization." In the first decades of Israel's existence, even the secular schools and press devoted a good deal of attention to national Jewish heroes, at least those who could be portrayed in more than religious terms. Now, however, these figures too have become targets of attack, debunked, in virulent fits of masochistic abandon, by the press, the politicians, and the ultraleftist campus professors alike. The Massada fortress—the last refuge of Bar Kochba, leader of the Jewish revolt against the Roman invaders—had been, during the first decades of Israel's existence, a place of pilgrimage for teaching schoolchildren and soldiers the lesson of courage and national pride. The figure of Bar Kochba had served as a symbol of fortitude and independence, contrasting with the "servile mentality of the Diaspora Jew." Few could have envisioned a future wherein the press and academic publications would feature articles inveighing against the futility and harm of Bar Kochba's fanatical act of leading the nation on a suicidal course.

Hanah Senesh—the Israeli girl who, at the end of World War II, parachuted into Hungary to help save the Jews from Nazi slaughter and who was killed in the attempt—is suddenly branded a traitor who supposedly betrayed her comrades to the enemy.

This smear campaign reached its peak with the revolting slander directed by a certain top-ranking politician against King David himself. The fabled leader, warrior, and psalmist who, for countless generations, had been venerated as the symbol of saintliness, hope, and faith in the rebirth of the Jewish nation, has been turned into a subject of ridicule by this vulgar scandal-monger.

Abhorrence of all that is Jewish—heroes, patriots, rabbis, traditions . . . all that sets us apart from other nations—is so powerful and all-pervasive that the notion of Israelis as one people inhabiting their homeland is increasingly felt to be a fiction. It appears that this country contains two peoples: on the one hand, those Israelis who carry the torch of the Torah, of morality and wisdom, selflessly continuing the eternal Jewish mission in this holy land and caring about every Jew; on the other, the ones filled with vicious hatred of their brothers, ashamed of their kin, and falsely calling themselves Israelis. Instances illustrating this dismal situation are plentiful. Thus, one so-called professor from Hebrew University has stated that, in his eyes, the Jewish youngsters living in Hebron are no different from members of the Nazi Hitler Youth organization, while the *Tanach* they observe is equivalent to Hitler's *Mein Kampf!* The author of this pronouncement has not been committed to a mental hospital, and a group of professors from his university have confined themselves to a vapid statement deploring the "inexcusable inaccuracy" of his assertions, while in the same breath lambasting the "settlers' chauvinism." In another instance, a successful impostor of a sculptor (whose work one must wrack one's brain to decipher) announced that, when he looks at a religious Jew, he can sympathize with the feelings of Hitler and the Nazis.

Universal perversion is another disaster. What about the army of official prostitutes fighting for their "social rights," the homosexuals demanding financial benefits from the government and pensions for their "wives" and "husbands," and the lesbians accompanied by dubious Knesset members clamoring from TV screens to include lessons on the "lesbian view of the world" in school curricula? In the same context, we can mention the mud-slinging against the expert on Jewish religious law who had dared to declare that the Torah equates sodomy with bestiality. The homosexuals, wouldn't you know, had taken offense!

The above-cited examples could be multiplied manifold, but what we have is quite sufficient to realize the deadly peril to the people and the land of Israel lurking in these present trends. All of this causes me not only deep concern and apprehension, but unbearable loathing as well. It is difficult to foresee what will be the end of the current "peace process" and the process of de-Judaization that accompanies it (or that engendered it). From the rational standpoint, it is obvious that we are headed for either a devastating war or the extinction of the State of Israel. I pray to the Almighty that Divine intervention halt this headlong slide into the abyss before it is too late.

To avoid misunderstanding, let me repeat that all the abominations of which I have spoken have not shaken the love and devotion I feel toward my land and my people. I am disgusted by what is happening to a large part of the nation, to its mind and behavior; I grieve and fear for it; but, God forbid, I do not hate it. And, thank God, despite all the above, there are still so many wonderful people in Israel.

In view of my previous statements, I see it as my duty to intensify the efforts aimed at delivering Jews back to the bosom of Judaism, of Torah. After all, if each person among those born into an observant family or who found their own way to the Torah succeeded in influencing at least two or three others, all the problems I have mentioned would vanish.

* * *

During the years since the *Return* was written, I have managed to considerably expand and intensify the activities of my laboratory of magnetohydrodynamics in Beer Sheva University. The laboratory has been transformed into the Center for Magnetohydrodynamic Research, involved in a wide range of fundamental scientific studies and applied engineering projects. Making use of a contract I had signed many years ago with the U.S. Navy Research Department (which, as described in *Return*, was entirely the result of the Rebbe's instructions and advice), I was able to provide the center with unique experimental equipment. The most important result of the in-depth research conducted by the center was the discovery of a new type of turbulence with a nonconventional inner pattern, dominated by large-scale structures. These findings, on one hand, allow for a deeper understanding of the nature of the turbulence phenomenon itself, one of the most complex and widespread of physical phenomena. At the same time, the above-mentioned laboratory-produced nonconventional turbulence turned out to bear considerable similarity to conditions existing in the atmosphere and stratosphere. Thus, laboratory data can be used to predict atmospheric phenomena such as the spread of industrial pollution, the appearance of typhoons and hurricanes, and so on.

At the same time, the center is engaged in solving a number of important engineering problems, with the foremost priority being given to research and development of a fundamentally new method of producing electrical energy. Based on the flow of liquid metal in a magnetic field, this method is much more efficient, economical, and ecologically safe than the current methods used in existing power stations. This method is preferable in a wide range of specific applications – in factories, solar power stations, spaceships, and so on. In the context of space research, my center was invited to participate in President Reagan's American project known as "Star Wars." Yet another important engineering field is the development of magnetohydrodynamic methods of obtaining new alloys, as well as a wide variety of uses of electromagnetic forces in metallurgy and the smelting industry.

All of the above has resulted in Beer Sheva's becoming the host of an international conference on magnetohydrodynamics and turbulence, held every three years, and attended by scientists and engineers from every corner of the world. Beer Sheva has turned into one of the world's top centers for magnetohydrodynamics (MHD), while I have become known as "Mr. MHD" in the international scientific community.

Since 1989, in the wake of the radical changes occurring in the Soviet Union, there has been a growing avalanche of contacts and information exchanges with my former colleagues, with whom I had been unable to communicate for almost twenty years. In the summer of 1990 my wife and I, for the first time in all these years, visited Moscow, Leningrad, and Riga. Even prior to this trip, the collapse of the communist regime had impressed me as being something decidedly supernatural. However, actually being there made this miracle even more striking. My wife and I strolled along the familiar streets, the very same streets we had walked twenty years ago, seized with the fear of being trailed, dispirited by feelings of hopelessness and defenselessness, by a sense of the omnipotence and immutability of the Bolshevik regime. Now, however, it was all like a dream, an intoxicating joy at the ultimate triumph of justice, and boundless gratitude to the Almighty. The crowning point of this surrealistic situation was probably the strictly kosher dinner, arranged through the efforts of my old friend academician Sheindlin, during the ceremonial reception at one of the largest research institutes of the Soviet Academy of Sciences.

Soon afterwards, I was elected a member of the Moscow Energy Club, the Latvian Academy of Sciences, the Russian Academy of Natural Sciences, the Higher School Academy, and awarded honorary doctorates by the Russian Academy of Sciences and the St. Petersburg Technical University.

My MHD Center in Beer Sheva was literally showered with thousands of offers of joint research projects and exotic technological applications. These offers arrived in mail parcels weighing many pounds. They were brought in by visitors from the former Soviet Union and by innumerable new immigrants. Before long, not only every shelf and desk but even the floor of my study, my office, and my home were covered by a thick layer of files containing plans, projects, patents, and sketches. This turn of events gave me the idea of establishing some sort of an organization that would deal in a systematic way with the absorption and utilization of this windfall sent by the heavens, as it were, to Israel. The need for such an organization appeared even more urgent in view of the alarming indifference and even contempt that Israeli society and government officials, with relatively few exceptions, showed toward the enormous potential opening up. In part, this was due to psychological and language barriers, the inability to read the situation correctly, and frequently to feelings of envy and a false sense of superiority, with an unwillingness to be saddled with additional problems. Another probable cause was the totally misplaced instinct of self-preservation, the urge to protect the entrenched official position from an unexpected invasion of untold numbers of specialists in every field of human endeavor. And, of course, the primary reason for this ill-considered reaction was the very anti-Jewish sentiment discussed above, the loss of the sense of love and concern for one's fellow Jew. In 1991 I managed, within the framework of the treaty for scientific and technological cooperation signed by Israel and the Soviet Union, to found the first of its kind Joint Soviet-Israel Laboratory for Energy Research. I envisioned this laboratory serving as a model for an entire series of similar laboratories in the field of energy and various other areas. The economic benefits to be reaped by Israel from the implementation of this project were obvious. For Russia, these laboratories, utilizing the joint efforts of scientists—both Russian citizens and recent arrivals to Israel—would represent a natural "window" to the countries and markets of Europe and the United States. Alas, this idea has been realized only to a very limited extent—to wit, my laboratory, despite having lived up to all the expectations, has remained the only one. The government institutions, the universities, and industry have not only failed to create similar laboratories, but they have done nothing to help my own. I am forced to both supervise the projects being developed at my lab (on a voluntary basis, of course), and to raise the funds, from every possible source, required for its functioning. I am convinced that it is in Israel's vital interests—not only from the standpoint of scientific, technological, and economical advance, but in the geopolitical sense as well—to take advantage of Russia's offers of cooperation. After all, despite the present difficulties, Russia has not ceased to be a superpower in every sense of the term. Making the most of the Russian alternative would place Israel, with its current excessive dependence on the United States, in a much better position. These considerations have led me to support the initiative, introduced by Russia's public- and government-affiliated sources, to found in both countries an association for strengthening economic, scientific, and cultural ties between Israel and Russia. I have succeeded in persuading the heads of a number of major Israeli industrial companies—the Dead Sea Works, the Electric Company, the Aircraft Industry, and others—and the association has recently come into being as a result.

In the book *Return,* I have already discussed my tightly packed daily schedule and the feverish race against time. Since then I have taken on dozens of other undertakings, projects, and duties. Some of them have been discussed in preceding pages, others will be mentioned below; yet all this is but a fraction of the flurry of activity that rules my time, my life. This is no exaggeration, I am literally ruled by it. True, at some point I set these tasks into motion, but later they take on a life of their own, becoming interwoven with human destinies, and suddenly it becomes clear that I simply cannot interrupt this task or disengage from it without depriving someone of vital support, ruining someone's professional career, or simply breaking the commandment of helping one's neighbor. And so I must go on carrying this unbearable burden, disregarding the limitations of strength or time.

Unfortunately, the natural, so to say, routine difficulties are exacerbated by problems that are artificially created and thus are totally senseless and uncalled for. I am referring to the malicious feuds and intrigues that flourish with such plentiful ease among Israeli officials, public and party bureaucrats, and perhaps most of all within the academic university "elite." I talk about this with feelings of bitterness and deep regret, but keeping silent would amount to distorting and idealizing reality beyond recognition.

My life in the Soviet Union had been a good learning experience, teaching me to confront enemies and ill-wishers of all kinds. I had to face anti-Semites, opportunists groveling before the powers-that-be, those openly or tacitly employed by the KGB. These were natural enemies, people on the other side of the barrier dividing us, and thus the need to challenge and resist them formed a part of objective reality. Whereas here, in Israel, with our commonly shared origins and destiny that were supposed to inspire everyone with the feeling of brotherly love (even aside from the Torah commandment enjoining us to love our fellow Jews), the existence of senseless hatred and venomous hostility is a hundred times more unbearable. During these twenty years I have encountered and experienced firsthand the feverish "activity" of every sort of hate-monger and evil-wisher. Some of them cause harm in order to reap benefit for themselves. Sordid and vile as their acts may be, at least they are explainable, a result of malice and not pathological evil. In most cases, however, the mischief-maker derives no benefit; on the contrary, he must invest considerable effort and time to achieve his purpose. What motivates him is spite, the envy of another's success, at times morbid resentment of his own incompetence and hence the urge to trample upon the other so as to leave him behind, and thus get the upper hand, relatively speaking—since he is unable to do so absolutely. In short, sheer pathology!

The above phenomenon is common to every stratum of society, every type of organization—government, public, or party. In universities, whose denizens fancy themselves to be the cream of society, pluming themselves on their independence and liberalism, rivalry and internal friction flourish with special abundance, spewing out their stench far beyond the institutions' walls. Trying to distance myself from this filth, naturally I have never laid claims to any administrative university post, nor participated in the pre-election battles of those who did. And, still, I would almost constantly run up against unprovoked, senseless hatred, jealousy, and malice. Technological projects, successfully developed to the stage of industrial implementation and praised by renowned international experts, would inexplicably become stuck in the office of some bureaucrat because, as it turned out later, a university colleague had besmirched my project and myself with slanderous rumours—anonymous, cowardly, and blatantly illiterate from the scientific point of view. My worthy colleagues were especially incensed by my piety, my beard, and my headgear. I will abstain from quoting excerpts from their anonymous epistolary masterpieces. My ability to combine Torah observance with prolific activity in many areas enraged them with its incomprehensible nature. As a result, I have had to spend years in senseless battle for every inch of university space needed to install my unique equipment, obtained through inhuman efforts and costing millions, which made it possible to conduct the research that earned worldwide fame for the university. My membership in the *Chabad,* and my views on Israel's security and future were sufficient cause for government or Jewish Agency officials, who were supposed to encourage immigration and the immigrants, to stifle and undermine my voluntary projects—projects that would create employment opportunities for the newcomers and harness their creative potential for the benefit of the country.

It is noteworthy that the majority of those bent on harassing me were people who had received substantial help from me at one point or another—especially those I had helped out of charity, despite the fact that they did not deserve it. Thus, for instance, on frequent occasions I had been of great help in assisting university members up the ladder of academic success. The less they deserved my help, the more determined and persistent they would later be in "revenging themselves" upon me for that help.

In the beginning I had been deeply troubled by this. I had tried to fight back, and indeed had every chance to win in this senseless battle forced upon me. However, this type of war must be either waged wholeheartedly, with no holds barred, investing every minute of one's time, or not entered at all. Realizing that the time required for this war could be spent on so many important and useful matters, I quickly reached the conclusion that these wars were not suitable for me. I endeavored to develop a measure of immunity to all the plots and machinations and learned to pass them by, to ignore them. Still, this definitely does not eliminate the damage caused by these intrigues, and I must pay by doubling or tripling the time expended on virtually every undertaking and every project.

* * *

Over the past years, the activity of the SHAMIR organization has expanded enormously. The SHAMIR publishing house has become the world's largest publisher of Jewish literature in the Russian language. It has earned the reputation of being a highly respectable publishing house, combining strict adherence to the halachic precision and "kosher" approach to the text with academic accuracy and meticulous care for the literary merits of the language. This was not an easy achievement. We had to seek out, like sifting through sand for bits of gold, gifted translators and editors with a thorough knowledge of Torah and mastery of the Russian language, in other words, a combination of qualities that seemed impossible after the long Soviet rule that had rooted out everything Jewish. At the cost of enormous effort and time, I had managed to find such people and guarantee their further training and education. Another unexpected problem to overcome was that, as a result of decades of atheistic tyranny, the Russian language had become incapable of adequately expressing spiritual and religious concepts. Thus, words like God, soul, miracle, and so on, had undergone a deep transformation in the minds of people brainwashed by atheism, becoming divorced from the notions they were meant to signify. Hence, the SHAMIR staff had to keep a sharp watch to ensure not only the formal exactness of the translation, but also that the text is understood correctly by a person educated in a Soviet school and university. Frequently, there was a need to literally invent new terms and phrases. (In the recent years, since Russia's return to religion, this problem has naturally become less acute.)

During the twenty-four years of its existence, SHAMIR has published over 350 titles, with a total circulation of five million copies. These include the fundamental works of Judaism—the Pentateuch with classical commentary by Rashi, Rambam, Ibn Ezra, and of course the latest elucidations and interpretations by the Lubavitcher Rebbe; the Code of Jewish Laws (*Kitzur Shulchan Aruch*); the Prayer Book (*Sidur*); excerpts from Rambam; *Kuzari;* as well as books on Jewish holidays, *Shabbat,* kosher food, philosophical enquiries into Judaism and Chasidism, and books for children and the young.

During the 1970s, books had to be smuggled into the Soviet Union in single copies or inside suitcases with a double bottom. It was exciting to be told by returning tourists that our books were being copied by hand, with carbon paper, and that people were swapping separate chapters and even pages of those books. During the same years, the voices of "refusenik" authors and translators began to be increasingly heard, and SHAMIR started editing and printing their books. To be sure, in recent years the situation has changed drastically, and we are publishing more and more books in Russia—where it is cheaper, and the delivery is simpler and quicker. In today's Russia, there is not a synagogue, Jewish organization, or school that does not have SHAMIR books. Many families also have them. During my recent trip to Georgia, some Kutaisi Jews, not knowing my name and unaware of my relationship to SHAMIR, invited me to their homes especially in order to demonstrate the object of their pride—a collection of Jewish books in Russian. You can imagine my surprise and joy at discovering that the entire library—the Torah, the *Sidur,* the books for beginning students of Judaism—had been published by SHAMIR. Our books have been spotted by SHAMIR envoys in Kazakhstan, Krasnoyarsk, Ukhta . . . SHAMIR has been accumulating hundreds of letters thanking us for the books. Mothers write to tell us how one book or another has caused a complete change in the lives of their family, bringing them light, meaning, spirituality, and joy. We will never know precisely how many Jews have been saved by SHAMIR books from assimilation and how many have become observant. That they are very many is certain.

I must admit that the job of "pulling" SHAMIR, combined with the rest of my duties, is an uphill struggle. Alas, if only the tasks of organizing and supervising SHAMIR projects, of planning, coordinating, training people, and checking and editing texts were my sole responsibilities. Far from it! The most difficult, the most time- and energy-consuming, thankless, and repulsive work is that of raising money. This was the kind of activity I had never foreseen in my "refusenik" years in Russia. I had known that there could be circumstances forbidding the dissemination of Jewish learning, that there could be a shortage of people skilled in this type of activity. However, the realization that projects to help assimilated Jews find their roots could suffocate due to a lack of funds—that I could not have imagined in my wildest dreams. I was sure that Israel's government agencies, Jewish Agency officials, and simply wealthy Jews from around the world were all queuing up for the privilege of contributing their share to funds for the type of projects run by SHAMIR. Alas, here too the reality had proved different, to say the least. Consequently, instead of creating, instead of realizing the ideas for books simmering in my mind for twenty years, instead of devoting every minute free from university duties and other activities to revising and polishing the translation of the next volume of the Torah, I have been forced to roam around the world, begging and demeaning myself. Incidentally, the research I conduct in my science laboratories also forces me to spend a lion's share of my time on fundraising instead of on the work itself. This makes me remember with nostalgic longing my work at the

Latvian Academy of Sciences. There, my budgetary duties were simplified to submitting a couple of pages in December that listed the financial needs of my laboratory for the coming year. Still, where funds for scientific work are concerned, at least you are dealing with institutions and not private donors. Though I would not call this more pleasant or less exhausting, at least you can raise some fuss from time to time. During the 1970s and the early 1980s, the larger part of the SHAMIR budget had been underwritten by the government and the Jewish Agency. During one of my numerous meetings with Begin, I had told him about our effort to revive Jewish culture and tradition in the Russian language. Greatly taken by the idea, he immediately called up the finance minister and arranged for a special budget to be allocated from government funds for the publication of the "library of holy books in the Russian language." This project lasted for over ten years—until the present labor government came into power. Published in this way were the Russian-language edition of the Pentateuch and a number of other major works. SHAMIR's activity was also appreciated and supported by the former Jewish Agency chairman, Dulchin. In recent years, however, officials of today's government and the Jewish Agency have withdrawn all support from SHAMIR, and this at the very time of an unprecedented wave of immigration, when SHAMIR's efforts are more crucial than ever.

Naturally, SHAMIR books are circulated not only in Russia, but also in Israel, the United States, and anywhere else Russian Jews come to settle. Besides publishing, SHAMIR organizes countless lectures, classes, seminars, and radio programs. Often SHAMIR's educational activities go beyond the sphere of Russian speakers, with seminars conducted in Hebrew and English on the subjects of Torah and science and on problems of contemporary Jewish education. As it turns out, people who have endured the tempering force of Bolshevik atheistic propaganda have something to say to Jews from other countries. The crowning point of this activity was the publication of the *B'Or Ha'Torah* (In the Light of Torah) magazine in English and Hebrew. The idea for such a magazine, as well as its name, had come from the Lubavitcher Rebbe. This magazine was intended to adhere to the highest professional standards and to shed the light of Torah—without any apologetics and compromises—on the problems of today's natural sciences, philosophy, sociology, medicine, and art. The editorial board was joined by dozens of prominent Torah-practicing scientists from Israel, Europe, and the United States. Today, after nine issues of the magazine have been published, it can be safely be said that it fulfills its purpose.

With the onset of radical changes in the Soviet Union and the approaching wave of mass Jewish emigration, SHAMIR's program of actions underwent considerable adjustments. Later I will describe in more detail the Rebbe's prophetic prediction, as early as the spring of 1985, concerning the imminent collapse of communism, the impending mass emigration of Soviet Jews, and the revival of the Jewish spirit and life-style in Russia. At this point, I will only note that during 1985–87 we had received a number of instructions from the Rebbe stressing that SHAMIR must prepare for the mass influx of immigrants; moreover, that in order for immigrants to absorb spiritual nourishment, it is imperative to begin by taking care of the earthly aspects of their absorption— means of sustenance, housing, and, of course, work in one's field. The Rebbe had emphasized the crucial role of the latter since, for Soviet Jews, their professions—engineering, science, medicine—had provided their sole means of self-expression and moral satisfaction for many years. The Rebbe had also urged us to start advance preparations for wide-ranging expansion of SHAMIR's activities inside the Soviet Union.

With respect to immigrant absorption, SHAMIR launched a wide array of initiatives. Here I will briefly describe only the projects related to employment. One of the concepts following directly from the Rebbe's instructions was the establishment of business enterprises geared towards the research and development of ideas and designs brought by engineers and scientists from the Soviet Union, and their transformation into commercial technological products to be realized in international markets. The famous *Chabad Chasid* Joseph Gutnick from Australia, a successful businessman and world-renowned benefactor, upon hearing of the Rebbe's instructions, proposed that I establish the proto-type of such a company in Jerusalem, funded at his expense, used by immigrant scientists to develop their inventions. This led to the creation of SATEC (SHAMIR Advanced Technology Engineering Centre) in Jerusalem's Har Ha'Hotzvim industrial area. My son was appointed head of the company. Beginning with a handful of immigrants, the company has traversed a long road of searching for the right solutions. Today it employs close to a hundred people, about half of them scientists and engineers who had immigrated from Russia. The company has developed and is manufacturing unique electronic equipment for measuring electric energy, and is also implementing a new advanced technological process of extracting precious metals from ore and industrial waste. SATEC products are sold in over forty countries and the company, by achieving self-sufficiency and profitability, has proved that busi-ness based on the knowledge and expertise of Russian immigrants is not only possible but highly lucrative for Israel.

I succeeded in founding the second company—ONTEC (Olim Negev Tech-nologies)—modeled on the same prototype, in Beer Sheva. Following the path mapped out by SATEC, it has developed within a short time a number of exotic technologies and is presently emerging on the global market. The company is headed by a student of mine from Beer Sheva University, Dr. Arik El-Boher.

In 1989, on SHAMIR's initiative, the "Public Manpower Headquarters for New Immigrants" was set up in Beer Sheva as an experiment. It took enormous efforts to develop the work methods, the computerized database system of information on immigrants and potential jobs, et cetera. In the beginning, the project received a rather favorable reaction from the Jewish Agency, which allocated space and funds for paying the salaries of a few employees. One idea raised was to create similar headquarters in at least five cities in Israel, and to pool all the databases so that the country would realize the enormous intellectual wealth that has literally been showered upon them by the heavens. The Beer Sheva headquarters began working with considerable success, interviewing many thousands of engineers, scientists, and doctors, and processing their data. Hundreds of people found jobs in their fields through the services of the Beer Sheva headquarters. However, in this instance as well, the apparent blessing of Jewish Agency support ultimately turned out to be a curse. The endless internal feuding of Jewish Agency officials, the bitter rivalry, petty squabbling, and the fighting for funds waged between various departments finally swallowed up the Beer Sheva headquarters as well. The highly skilled employees I had picked (who, incidentally, were immigrants and knew Russian) were replaced by someone's illiterate proteges. Moreover, two Jewish Agency departments, who were constantly at war with the department supervising our headquarters, decided to open similar manpower headquarters themselves and to staff them with their own people. Thus, the Jewish Agency building in Beer Sheva was suddenly housing three identical manpower organizations, each more impotent than the next. The unfortunate unemployed immigrants registered in all three, but their chances of finding work were more remote than ever.

I searched for ways to improve the disastrous employment situation, which was causing untold harm to immigrants and to immigration as a whole and irreparable damage to the country, which was failing to avail itself of the miraculous and tangible opportunity to become a technological superpower and to strengthen the economy in reality instead of making noisy declarations. It was obvious that solutions to problems of this magnitude—creating tens of thousands of jobs for highly qualified professionals—could be provided only by the government, with the support of the entire society. Moreover, this should not mean jobs artificially created and funded by the state, such as road paving. In a small country, the only way to utilize the creative potential of tens of thousands of engineers entails the creation of numerous small high-tech enterprises geared for export. These enterprises must be economically viable, flexible, dynamic—in other words, small-scale, and owned not by the government but by private businessmen. Fortunately, there are existing models for such enterprises—SATEC and ONTEC—which have demonstrated that engineers and scientists whose education and work experience were acquired under the communist regime can be taught the principles of capitalist economy. The role of the government is to create favorable conditions for investors, to train managers, and to provide refresher courses for immigrants.

With these conclusions, I came to Prime Minister Itzhak Shamir, in 1991. He heard me out with polite approval, yet did not seem to display particular interest or enthusiasm over the subject. I would not let it rest and met with a few ministers. A number of times I discussed the matter with Arik Sharon, with whom I had long been on friendly terms. Nothing moved. I argued that we need a comprehensive immigrant employment policy, that the state must at least realize what human treasure had come into its possession. In my estimation, the education of those who immigrated from 1989 until 1992 was worth at least $15 billion. In addition, the immigrants had brought a total of about 100,000 inventions, patents, and copyrights. In my subsequent meeting with Shamir, I also pointed out that work in one's speciality is the key to the immigrant's heart, and that the current dismal employment picture could deal a disastrous blow to Likud's election campaign. Shamir replied that he was not concerned. True to my nature, I refused to give up, continuing my attempts to "deliver the goods." I appealed to dozens of ministers, Knesset members, and other Likud functionaries. Even though twenty years of living in Israel should have inured me to surprises, I was still invariably amazed that, despite the fact that not only the good of the country and the immigrants but also the personal good of the Likud party itself was at stake, virtually every meeting, not to mention subsequent actions, demanded efforts that resembled a military operation. Secretaries would feed me with excuses for weeks on end, promising to return my calls and never doing so. At times, just to get through to the head secretary would require days. Appointments I finally succeeded in obtaining were repeatedly postponed or canceled. I termed this the "Likud Syndrome"—the inability or unwillingness to organize and act, even when their own party interests are involved. In this respect, the Labor people are far more lively.

At long last, in February of 1992, I finally succeeded in persuading Shamir, and he appointed me chairman of the prime minister's committee for developing a master plan for immigrant absorption. My campaign was greatly facilitated by the help of the prime minister's economics adviser, Shmuel Slavin. Shamir entrusted me with selecting the other committee members. I managed to convince six top specialists in industry, economy, sociology, demography, medicine, and health-care to join the committee. Naturally, we all worked on a voluntary basis; and even though the committee members were incredibly busy people, everyone gladly sacrificed many hours of sleep to the task of solving the problem before us.

In two months we were able to come up with a detailed draft of the absorption master plan. Its pivotal element was to provide conditions for the creation of 500 small private technological companies over a five-year period. Among the conditions to be created by the government was the establishment of a number of industrial zones free from taxation and any sort of bureaucratic government intervention; improving the system of state loans for exporters; reducing the progressive rate of income tax in general, and specifically with respect to those working second and third shifts; a series of measures for expanding foreign markets for Israeli products; and so on. Among the beginning incentives for the creation of new industrial enterprises, it was proposed to conduct an "inventory" of the intellectual assets gained by Israel due to mass immigration—in other words, to create computer databases on immigrants' education, professions, and experience, combined with information on inventions, patents, and the projects they submit. Furthermore, it was proposed that the government conduct a search for young, gifted managers willing to set up the new companies, gather the inventory data, and head and supervise the companies in the future. No fewer than a hundred of such managers were to receive annual salaries, with budgets for travel and communication expenses, to enable them to fully devote themselves to the project.

Assuming that each enterprise would employ an average of fifty people, it followed that the establishment of 500 new businesses would create 25,000 jobs for scientists, engineers, technicians, and workers (mostly immigrants), as well as economists, accountants, marketing specialists, et cetera (mainly veteran Israelis). These enterprises would be of special importance to representatives of those fields of technology where the number of immigrant specialists exceeds the demand, and which are underdeveloped within the existing Israeli industry. Such, for instance, is the case with engineers in the fields of metallurgy, oil industry, and high-current electromechanics, among others.

Global experience shows that every job created in industry generates at least two jobs in the service sector—banks, transportation, communications, healthcare, the food industry, and so on. Therefore, we may add another 50,000 jobs to the initial 25,000 in industry.

Finally, our plan provided for a number of solutions for doctors, teachers, musicians, and artists. It turned out that doctors, too, could be employed not only through government subsidies but on a commercial basis. Thus, for instance, a number of underdeveloped countries in Eastern Europe, Asia, and Africa are very interested in inviting groups of doctors and health specialists from Israel to set up hospitals, fight epidemics, and so on. They are willing to pay good salaries, especially since the World Bank allocates significant funds for these purposes. Concerning teachers, there was a proposal to put many of them to use as private tutors. A survey indicates that in Israel there is a demand for approximately 9,000 tutors. To be sure, immigrant teachers will have to complete an intensive Hebrew course and thoroughly familiarize themselves with the programs of examination requirements of the Israeli Ministry of Education. In addition, it was proposed that, following proper testing of the teacher's skills and Hebrew proficiency, teachers be issued certificates of their eligibility to work as private tutors. On the whole, our plan provided for a realistic total of 130,000 jobs to be created over a five-year period.

Itzhak Shamir received our committee, heard a detailed presentation of our preliminary plan, thanked us and said that, even though elections were only a month away, he would try to start putting the plan into effect. He expressed his confidence that the elections would bring victory to the Likud, and that either he himself or his successor would receive from us, after the elections, a completed general plan for immigrant employment. I told Shamir that in order to give his confidence in winning the elections a firm basis, he must enlist the support of Russian immigrants, whose numbers would yield enough votes to win more than ten seats in the Knesset. The key to their trust, meanwhile, is providing them with jobs suitable to their professions. Though one month is very little time, even a month-long implementation of some parts of our plan could be started. Unfortunately, Shamir did nothing. Nor were my appeals to leading Likud members—Beni Begin, Roni Milo, and others—of any avail.

In late June of 1992, the elections took place and the left-ultraleft coalition came into power. The immigrant employment situation continued to deteriorate. Our committee, due to the uncertain conditions, was biding its time. Unexpectedly, in August of 1992, two months after the elections, we were summoned by Rabin and asked to continue the work of completing the master plan for immigrant absorption. We described to him the already-prepared overall outline of the plan. I especially stressed the point that the scale of the task at hand was so vast that it would require the concerted efforts of all the ministries, as well as effective coordination of those efforts. Hence the crucial need to establish a supraministerial body to supervise the implementation of the employment project. Rabin did not display particular enthusiasm over the issue. We tried to draw his attention to the fact that the success of our plan would bring the country such major economic and strategic benefits that this could have a significant effect on the balance of power between Israel and its belligerent neighbors. Thus, it would be wrong to see our proposal merely as a plan to aid the immigrants and immigration. In the long-range view, it was above all a plan for taking advantage of the unique opportunity to raise the country to a totally new economic level, which would result in significant improvement for Israel in the sphere of security and politics.

Rabin did not wish to enter into a discussion of these arguments. Since our committee had been founded under the auspices of the head of the government, we pointed out the need for coordinating our further activity with the prime minister's office. Rabin delegated the coordinating task to some of his personal advisors, with the liaison to be maintained through his personal secretary, Eitan Haber, and one of his advisers, Shuki Zakkai.

That fall and winter were spent in intensive work. We meticulously collected and verified statistical data on the immigration and its professional indicators, analyzed the employment situation for each separate field, and heard and discussed surveys conducted by dozens of experts. We then drew up a detailed plan and its cost estimate, covering three main categories of immigrants: (1) engineers and scientists; (2) doctors; (3) teachers, professionals in the fields of the humanities, musicians, and artists. By April 1993 the plan was completed and submitted in the form of a two-volume report titled "Master Plan for Immigrant Employment and Advancement of National Economy." The plan, as I have already mentioned, spelled out practical ways of creating, within five years, 130,000 additional jobs for professionals in every field. The plan contained twenty-four specific practical recommendations, the overwhelming majority of which were based on economically profitable commercial options. The plan did not require the government to subsidize the wages. At the same time, the government was expected to undertake a major administrative effort and even to bring about a change in legislation, primarily in the area of taxation. The government's financial contribution to the implementation of the project would be limited to creating databases, financing training and refresher courses, and subsidizing managers for a stipulated period of time. Complete implementation of the project would cost the government $300 million, that is, about $2,300 for each job created; whereas, international statistics show that the creation of a new job requires an average expenditure of $50,000! It would also be advisable to compare the $300 million required to complete our project with the $10 billion in guarantees which the Israeli government had requested and received from the United States for the purpose of immigrant absorption.

The project was submitted to the Prime Minister's office and we began to wait for an invitation to discuss the project. The statistics we had collected and thoroughly checked formed an alarming picture of the employment situation. Thus, for example, it turned out that almost 60,000 engineers have arrived since 1989 – more than double the number of engineers employed in the country until 1989. The figure for scientists with doctor's degrees and higher was close to 10,000, that is, approximately equal to the number of scientists in the country until 1989. However, out of the total number of engineers only 12,000 have managed to find jobs in their field, with an additional 6,000 working in industry but outside of their field. As to the remaining 42,000, the situation is dismal in the extreme. A large part of the immigrants are sweeping sidewalks and washing dishes in hotels, while a significant number have left for other countries. The rest are living on unemployment benefits.

With respect to scientists, the situation was as follows. About 1,000 (that is, 10 percent of the total number) have joined the full-time staff of universities or state-run laboratories. Another 3,000 have obtained temporary positions in universities subsidized by the Absorption Ministry, or else they have been hired, once again on a temporary basis, by the so-called "incubators" –

institutions designed to create favorable conditions for scientists to research and develop their inventions, and to "sell off" the accumulated information and copyrights to private investors. The problem, however, was that the "incubators," while providing scientists with more or less adequate conditions for further scientific and technical work on their ideas, gave them virtually no help with the economic evaluation of their inventions, market analysis, or the search for investors—in other words, the vital stages of transforming ideas into finished products, with which the immigrants were the least experienced. From the very creation of these "incubators," officials from the Ministry of Industry who were responsible for determining their structure had catastrophically overlooked this crucial factor. I had heated arguments with them on the subject, to no avail. As a result, the "incubators," which were supposed to serve as a convenient and reliable way for the immigrant to enter the world of industry and commerce, have turned out to be a dead end. The majority of scientists, having spent two to three years in an "incubator" under rosy illusions, have once more found themselves on the sidelines.

The same fate awaited many of those who had been hired by universities to fill temporary positions subsidized by the Absorption Ministry.

Despite the acute immigrant unemployment situation, three months had passed before Rabin finally received our committee and was briefed about our project. We insisted that the implementation of our plan required the establishment of an Immigrant Manpower Department under the auspices of the Prime Minister's office. This idea was flatly rejected by Rabin, who placed Absorption Minister Yair Tzaban, head of the Ministerial Committee for Absorption, in charge of implementing the project. I asked Rabin what difference this would make—in light of the fact that this committee had been operating for some years, while the immigrant employment crisis was only worsening. He replied that the difference was that henceforth he will be personally involved in the committee's work, as well as ensure the participation of the minister of industry and trade and the finance minister.

Indeed, the first meeting convened by the ministerial committee to discuss the implementation of our project was attended by Rabin, as well as Minister of Industry and Trade Harish; Finance Minister Shochat; and a number of other ministers. I was asked to choose, as the subject of discussion, one out of the twenty-four recommendations included in our project. Suspecting that the matter would not progress beyond this first meeting, I proposed to talk about the project's pivotal idea: to stimulate large-scale creation of industrial enterprises modeled on SATEC and ONTEC. The committee met the idea with full approval and assigned Director General of the Ministry of Industry and Trade Nati Sharoni, together with members of his staff and myself, to draw up an operative plan for putting this recommendation into effect.

I would like to give due credit to Nati Sharoni, who realized the importance of our project and gave it his full attention. Within a reasonable time, the operative plan was ready. In January 1994 the Ministerial Absorption Committee gave its final approval and even allocated the first 12 million shekels to begin implementing the plan. Alas, the joy was premature. Absorption Minister Tzaban—who, as I have already said, was entrusted by Rabin to supervise the project—for eight months could not seem to appoint the project's administrative staff, which was to consist only of a project manager and his secretary. I hunted for Tzaban in the Knesset and called his home at midnight. He complained about bureaucratic red tape and promised to expedite the matter. Only in September of 1994 was the "Department" finally formed.

I am writing these lines in May of 1995—that is, eight months later—and so far not a single new enterprise in our plan has been created. What is more, not a single immigrant has found employment within the framework of our plan. The "Department," true enough, has expanded, with its officials situated in a number of cities. However, instead of limiting the role of bureaucratic government involvement to creating databases, supporting a selected group of talented managers, and promoting legislative measures to encourage investments, with the rest left to the unrestricted forces of market economy—in accordance with our plan—quite the opposite is taking place. The "Department" officials are the ones determining the projects' potential, whereas, areas such as market analysis are entrusted to Tel Aviv University students who do not know the first thing about the economy or the market!

The rest of the recommendations contained in our project remained in their virginal stage, ignored and unutilized. I continue to regularly petition and pursue everyone who is supposed to act on the matter. Meanwhile, the immigration is withering away, going from bad to worse with each passing day. Even though an average of 5,000 are still arriving each month, the majority of immigrants are composed of refugees fleeing from areas riven by conflicts and fighting—the Caucasus, Central Asia, and others. Over one half of all the new arrivals have reached, or are close to reaching, the retirement age, reconciled to the fact that they will not be able to work in Israel. The proportion of engineers, scientists, and doctors among the new immigrants has plummeted—for they know that their professional prospects in Israel are dim, and do everything in their power to reach the United States, Australia, and even, as paradoxical and sad as it is, Germany.

Thus, the exodus of Soviet Jewry is drawing to its lamentable conclusion. For more than thirty years, Jews and Gentiles throughout the world have been demonstrating and chanting "Let my people go" (incidentally, never stopping to recall that this quote is taken from the Torah, and its full version is "Let My people go, that it may serve Me"). And so, with the gates to the house of slavery miraculously thrown open, the world remains indifferent, and no one seems concerned by the slow but sure demise of immigration due to the lack of useful employment in Israel. What is even more tragic, almost no one in Israel realizes what a historical opportunity for the country's economy is being wasted. The press, with typical Israeli arrogance and conceit, ignores the skill and talent of new immigrants, while avidly devoting every inch of space to descriptions of penetration into Israel by Russian mafia and Russian prostitutes.

The only tangible result of my tireless efforts in the name of immigrant employment was that I have become the address for all those looking for work. The number of appeals—delivered in person, by letter, and by phone—reaches dozens each day. My laboratory staff is groaning under the weight of this burden. Many letters and calls come from people still in Russia. My wife is awakened by telephone calls beginning at 5 A.M. and continuing nonstop until well past midnight. Accumulating in my office are countless files with thousands of individual cases.

True, in 1989–90, when the wave of immigration was only starting, my assistants and I had managed to find jobs for over 1,000 people. However, our rate of success has been dwindling ever since.

The SHAMIR's manpower center, which has helped numerous immigrants, continues to function. The initiator and the driving spirit behind this center was a wonderful woman, who has recently passed away—Mira Krichevskaya. A mother of eleven, she treated immigrants as her own children and waged a tireless struggle to provide them with jobs. Her sheer enthusiasm knew no barriers, and she often succeeded where anyone else would fail.

There is one additional project I would like to speak of before concluding my account of SHAMIR. I am referring to the Encyclopedia of Russian Jewry.

Everything began with a proposal by the president of the Russian Academy of Natural Sciences, the late Professor Dmitri Mineyev. The time was August, 1991. I was staying not far from Moscow, in Zvenigorod, the site of the seminar for young Jewish public figures gathered from all over the Soviet Union. The seminar was sponsored by the New York Memorial Foundation for Jewish Culture, whose director, Dr. Jerry Hochbaum, and I share many years of cooperation and friendship. I was giving lectures on Jewish philosophy and the connection between Torah and science. I was informed that President of the Academy Mineyev wished to meet with me in Moscow to discuss the idea of publishing the Encyclopedia of Russian Jewry, which would reflect every aspect of the thousand years of Jewish presence in the former Russian empire and would highlight the Jewish contribution to Russia's economy, science, and arts. I was told that the proposal was brought to my notice as the editor-in-chief of the SHAMIR publishing house, and that I would be asked to head the project.

The proposal left me flabbergasted. Back in 1991 I still could not get used to the miracles happening all around me. Later I would witness even more amazing things. For instance, the visit to SHAMIR's Jerusalem office by a pair of senior KGB officers who, by way of a "compensation" and "apology" for everything done against the *Chabad* movement, have brought and handed over to me the entire set of archive records of the "case" against the father of the Lubavitcher Rebbe, the famous rabbi and sage, Levi Yitzhak Schneersohn. That was all arranged by SHAMIR director Bezalel Shiff. Later, we also received from the KGB archives previously unknown material from the "case" against the preceding Lubavitcher Rebbe and many *Chasidim,* as well as records concerning the founding father of the *Chabad* movement, the Alter Rebbe.

However, let us go back to the encyclopedia. The meeting was set for midday, August 19. That morning I was to deliver my final lecture to the seminar participants and leave for Moscow. During breakfast came the news of the anti-Gorbachev putsch. I called up the Israeli embassy and asked for instructions. They could not come up with anything coherent. My mood, I admit, was rather foul. I realized that the certainty of my return to Israel was far from self-evident. The likelihood of my ending up in Siberia was not easily dismissed. Only much later would I learn that someone had already checked with the Rebbe and received a clear answer: there is no cause for fear, everyone should go on with his regular activities. Still, I braced myself and went to the lecture. The sight of the unruffled seminar participants, displaying great interest in the lecture, helped me regain my composure. Barely managing to find a driver with a car, I left for Moscow. Making headway was increasingly difficult: the closer we got to Moscow, the more tanks were on the road. Eventually we found ourselves in the center of Moscow, not far from the "White House"—the building of the Supreme Soviet of the Russian Federation, transformed by Yeltsin into a citadel of resistance against the insurgents. All further movement was blocked. I went to a friend's apartment and from there telephoned Professor Mineyev, explaining that I was unable to make it through the wall of tanks. His suggestion was to discuss the encyclopedia project on the phone. I recall asking him whether he could focus on the subject, in view of everything that was happening. He replied that this was a historical project, which was far more important than the current events, no matter how frightening.

Thus the encyclopedia project was born. A few months later I returned to Moscow, accompanied by Dr. Hochbaum from the Memorial Foundation. We settled all the details, and the work began.

Today over 200 prominent experts from all fields are working in Moscow, conducting research in various institutes, archives, and libraries. They are supervised by a veteran SHAMIR member from Jerusalem, Zeev Wagner. Sir Isaiah Berlin, a world-famous Oxford historian and philosopher—who, incidentally, traces his origins to Riga and retains excellent mastery of the Russian language—has agreed to function as the chief consultant. The first Russian-language volume of the encyclopedia came out in 1994, with the English version in the offing. There are six more volumes ahead. The second volume is scheduled for the near future.

By working on the encyclopedia, we are doing more than preserving for posterity the names of hundreds of outstanding thinkers, rabbis, scientists, and musicians who perished in Stalin's camps. There have been dozens of cases in which the encyclopedia team experts discovered the Jewish origins of prominent individuals alive and well today, whose fathers and grandfathers were Russian, and who themselves are often unaware that, having Jewish grandmothers and mothers, they too are considered as Jews by the *halachah*—the Jewish law.

*   *   *

In the preceding pages of this Afterword, I have touched upon many crucial contemporary issues concerning my people and the whole of mankind. However, I have not yet written the main, the most essential part of the afterword—and that is what I shall attempt to do now. I am referring to the meetings and correspondence with the Lubavitcher Rebbe, which I have been vouchsafed since the time I wrote *Return*. I will attempt to briefly narrate certain facts, as well as at least a fraction of what I have learned during this time, about this incomparable, great Jew and his teaching.

In *Return* I described my phone call to the Rebbe when I was still in Riga, my first meetings with the Rebbe in New York, his limitless knowledge, his boundless love for all Jews, his wondrous gift of foresight, his advice and instructions, which shaped the lives of millions of people, including my own. Earlier, I have mentioned the Rebbe's directions concerning Jews from the Soviet Union and his instructions pertaining to other fields of my activities. However, having read all this, I can see how hopelessly lacking is the picture I have drawn, how remote from the original it was meant to portray. Previously, I had tried to depict the Rebbe through a mixture of descriptive categories— sage, genius, mentor, father, the embodiment of selflessness and self-denial. Now, after many additional hours spent with the Rebbe—whether at gatherings of thousands of *Chasidim* or alone—I realize how hopelessly futile this attempt has been. The point is that, according to the view of the world based on Torah, the ultimate goal of this God-made world is its transition into the highest state, the final transcendental condition marked by the coming of the *Moshiach* (Messiah) and the uplifting of mankind and the entire creation to the summit of light, wisdom, and total redemption—*geula shlema*—accompanying the messianic era. The Torah tells us that the coming of the *Moshiach* is to be the greatest miracle crowning the chain of miracles running through Jewish history. The details of this apocalyptic event are concealed, so that even the great codifier Rambam was able to describe the coming of the *Moshiach* only in the most general of terms. However, several centuries ago Baal Shem Tov, the founder of the contemporary chasidic movement, had a prophetic vision of the *Moshiach* and was told by him that he would come when Baal Shem's teaching had spread universally. Activities intended to speed up the coming of the *Moshiach* became the guiding thread of *Chabad* Chasidism from the early years of its existence. This was the main goal of the Alter Rebbe, *Chabad*'s founder; this was the golden rule of all the subsequent Rebbes heading the *Chabad* movement. Yet never had the efforts aimed at speeding up the coming of the *Moshiach* reached the scope and intensity they have reached under the present Rebbe. The concept of the coming of the *Moshiach* as the ultimate goal of the world's history was always the most fundamental concept in the teaching of the Torah. The Rambam included it in his Thirteen Principles of Jewish Faith. Nevertheless, many people perceived the idea of *Moshiach* as a symbol, as something remote, as a dream. The Rebbe converted this idea into a tangible part of contemporary history, into a goal achievable in the immediate future through proper action. Significantly, Chasidism emphasizes the connection between the coming of the *Moshiach* and the seventh generation, while the Rebbe is the seventh chasidic leader, counting from Baal Shem Tov. Rambam stresses that one of the first signs of the *Moshiach* is his bringing (or returning) multitudes of people to the Torah. No one can determine the exact number of people influenced by the Rebbe—in person, by letters and telephone, addressing them in speeches at thronged chasidic gatherings (also invariably attended by non-*Chasidim,* nonbelievers, even non-Jews), by means of his books, his envoys in every corner of the world, and in the so-called "common letters" published in the world's leading newspapers. By the most modest estimates, such people number in the millions. They include Ashkenazic and Sephardic Jews, believers and nonbelievers, *Chasidim* and *misnagdim* ("dissenters"), Jews and Gentiles.

If we were to simplify and condense the Rebbe's message to the utmost, his wish is for humans to lead normal lives, performing their human functions in accordance with the Creator's design. It seems that nothing could be simpler. Yet we are living in an age of depravity and decadence, an age inundated by pseudo-teachings glorifying all manner of filth and abomination, trampling on all that is decent and pure. What a refreshing contrast, then, to hear to the voice of the Rebbe, urging parents to be parents, children to be children, husbands to be husbands, wives to be wives, men to be not savage beasts but friends to fellowmen. The Rebbe's influence extends from heads of state to petty shopkeepers, from old men to children in kindergartens.

Summing up all that has been stated, it appears that saying that the Rebbe is an outstanding, unsurpassable person is saying nothing at all. Observing the

Rebbe under various circumstances, it occurs to me that since the six days of creation, the Almighty has not made a man as beautiful and perfect as the Rebbe who, if I may say so, is the model for an ideal human. He is indeed a man of unprecedented genius, boundless knowledge, and phenomenal memory. He has no personal interests, absolutely none, unlike the rest of us. He never does anything for his own benefit, the way we all do. Each minute of his twenty-hour working day is devoted to helping others, to giving advice to thousands of people throughout the world, easing their troubles and cares on matters of family, jobs, health, and inspiration. He addresses all Jews on the eve of approaching holidays. He delves into the depths of the Torah and Chasidism and withdraws prescriptions for the right Jewish reactions to the most burning topics of today. He exhorts non-Jews to observe the seven commandments of the sons of Noah ordained by Moshe Rabbeinu (Moses). He writes letters to government officials and to Jewish women. There is not a moment of respite in his unbroken chain of efforts aimed at the most important goal—to bring about the coming of the *Moshiach*. And at the same time—what self-possession! Not a single unnecessary movement or gesture! And finally, that remarkable face, those eyes that contain the entire world!

The more I learned about the Rebbe during these years, the more time I was privileged to spend in his presence, the more I became aware of an unfathomable contradiction. On one hand, no one is more removed from daily routine than the Rebbe. In more than forty years of being the leader, not once has he set foot outside of Brooklyn nor had a day of rest, not to mention entertainment (the very word sounds outlandish when applied to the Rebbe). On the other hand, his total knowledge and supernatural ability enable him to discuss every practical aspect of economy, business, schools, hospitals, universities, theaters, parliaments, and markets.

Starting from the mid-1980s, when the number of *Chasidim* increased manifold—children from large families had grown, and the *Chabad* family swelled from the influx of thousands upon thousands of devotees—the Rebbe could no longer receive everyone privately in his office, as had been his custom. At the same time, direct and immediate contact between the Rebbe and the *Chasid* is a crucial and integral part of Chasidism. Predictably, the Rebbe found a solution. On Sunday mornings, when people do not have to go to work, the Rebbe started to receive anyone interested but in the hallway, instead of a room, standing. A line forms a mile long, people approach the Rebbe one by one, and each receives his blessing together with a dollar bill which he must donate to the needy or some other worthy cause. In this manner, not only is the personal spiritual contact between the Rebbe and the *Chasid* preserved, but the Rebbe also makes the visitor his envoy for observing one of the main commandments—that of *tzedaka* (charity). Many linger for a few moments, a minute, or even longer, asking for advice and receiving it. An average of 5,000 to 6,000 people pass through daily. One time the crowd numbered 11,000, and they stayed for hours on end.

Once, picking a convenient spot not far from the Rebbe, I began to observe this ritual. It was hard to accept the reality of what was happening. In came respectable elderly *Chasidim* and *yeshivah* youngsters, old women and young girls (there are, of course, separate lines for men and women), clean-shaven businessmen, politicians from America and Israel, long-haired "hippies." The Rebbe addressed everyone in his own language—English, Hebrew, Yiddish, Russian, German, Italian, French, and many others. Each word he uttered was considered with meticulous care, to avoid confusion or misunderstanding on the visitor's part. Just try to imagine, reader, what you would feel were you to be asked for advice, not by 5,000 or 500 people, but, let us say, a mere twenty in the same day.

Perhaps the Rebbe could be most accurately defined as an unfathomable phenomenon, the heart and soul of our generation, his profound influence penetrating every aspect of existence. During the years that have elapsed since I wrote *Return,* I have amassed dozens of episodes, pertaining personally to me, that illustrate the Rebbe's wisdom, foresight, prophetic vision, and super-natural spiritual powers. Some of them I have described in the book *The Eye of the Heart,* published in Hebrew by the *Maariv* publishing house. Here I shall briefly recount only a handful of them.

A great deal of the instructions and directions I received from the Rebbe had to do with Torah and science. His categorical and uncompromising stand concerning literal interpretation of the Torah, including its comments related to the structure of our planetary system, bewildered even some of the believing and observant scientists. The Pentateuch and the Prophets, the Talmud, as well as Rambam's writings, depict the Earth standing still in the center, with the sun and planets revolving around it—in other words, the view held by the Ptolemaic system and not the currently accepted Copernican theory. The Rebbe has pointed out that, in the light of Einstein's general relativity theory, everything is reconciled, and no contradictions remain in this matter between Torah and science. However, the religious scientists, accustomed to apologetics and fear of public opinion, remained doubtful. I convened a special small seminar in New York, attended by experts on the relativity theory, in order to settle this issue. A few days of discussion left us totally confused. Soon afterwards I happened to have an audience with the Rebbe, and so I told him about our fruitless inquiries into the depths of relativity theory. Smiling, the Rebbe said that we were looking in the wrong place: the solution to our problem lies on the surface, on the level of the introduction to the relativity theory. Indeed, shortly afterwards one of us found a book by a German scientist, one of Einstein's closest followers, Hans Reichenbach, published as early as 1926, with many revised editions later printed in America. Entitled *The Philosophy of Time and*

Space, the book provides a clear and basic analysis of the problem, unequivocally demonstrating that today the theories of Ptolemy and Copernicus are equally sound, and that there are no scientific means to disprove the claim that the Earth is the fixed center of the universe.

Another issue in the same area concerned quantum mechanics. The Rebbe made frequent references to quantum mechanics and Heisenberg's uncertainty principle, in order to illustrate the indeterminism of contemporary science's map of the world and hence the absurdity of projecting backwards in time, which is common to all evolutionary theories. The Rebbe also stressed repeatedly that, according to Torah and the Talmud, the observer (or rather two observers whose testimony has been accepted by the rabbinical court) determines the behavior of animate and inanimate nature. In other words, the observer's testimony is primary, and the observed object is secondary, and not vice versa, just as the Torah is primary and the world secondary. In this respect, there is complete agreement with the conclusions of quantum mechanics regarding the role of the observer, his influence on the behavior of particles, and on the collapse of probability waves into a physical object. On the basis of all this, the Rebbe drew a general conclusion on the convergence of views held by modern science with the eternal and changeless truths contained in the Torah. This proved that the world, even its most "external," rational, and cool-headed elements, is ripe to welcome *Moshiach.* In this connection, it is interesting to note the publication, in the winter of 1994–95, of two books (there must be more, but these are the two that have fallen into my hands) that provide a most tangible illustration to the above. The first book came out in Moscow, the erstwhile citadel of communism and atheism. It is the brainchild of a physics professor at Moscow University, Yuri Vladimirov, and has the title *Fundamental Physics and Religion.* This book, shattering the myth of irreconcilable contradictions between religion and science, was published with the approval of the Russian Ministry of Education.

The other book was published in the United States, by the famous Doubleday & Company. The author is physics professor Frank Tipler. Its title is *The Physics of Immortality,* with the subtitle *Modern Cosmology, God, and Resurrection of the Dead.* The author describes how, despite being a confirmed atheist, he came to embrace the ideas of a supreme creator, divine providence, and free will, not through a revelation but by analyzing the latest physical discoveries.

In *Return,* I described the Rebbe's unique ability to see the hidden. I will describe here again one incident directly related to my scientific and engineering work. After my laboratory had filed another patent for a magnetohydrodynamic device for converting solar energy into electricity, I was in the United States and had the privilege of being received by the Rebbe. He immediately mentioned the newly patented device and asked me to tell him about it. I felt uncomfortable to be wasting the righteous man's time by describing a transitory tool and confined myself to a general and superficial outline. However, the Rebbe said that he would like to hear a report similar to the ones I deliver at university seminars (indeed, I had already lectured on our new device in many universities). This time, I cited all the technical data, figures, everything. No sooner had I finished than the Rebbe said that the efficiency of the conversion device could be significantly improved by utilizing the climatic conditions of a desert, specifically the wide temperature shifts between day and night. I was astounded. Neither myself, nor my assistants, nor the dozens of experts present at the seminars had considered this possibility.

The next remark was even more astonishing. Smiling, the Rebbe said that, though certainly trusting my expertise, he felt the figures I had quoted for the device's efficiency and the two-phase flow velocity within it did not match. All I could counter with was that we had used the most reasonable theory and that the highly complex and time-consuming data were processed on the university computer.

Aware of the importance of heeding the Rebbe's every word, upon returning to Beer Sheva I had my assistants double-check all the data. To my surprise, no mistake was found. We ran through the figures again, with the same result. Only two years later did a new doctorate student of mine discover the error made in recording one integer in the system of equations. We corrected the error and repeated the calculations. The results were drastically different.

How the Rebbe, without the use of a computer or even a pencil, had managed to locate the error during a fraction of a second—that is totally beyond my understanding.

And finally, the Rebbe's prophetic prediction, as early as the spring of 1985, of the impending collapse of the Soviet empire and global communism. Here is how it happened. At that time I was invited by New York University to give a course of lectures on magnetohydrodynamics for doctoral students, and thus I lived in Brooklyn for a few months. One day in the month of *Nisan,* close to the Pesach holidays, I was invited to see the Rebbe. The Rebbe met me at the door to his office, and our brief meeting was spent standing up. The Rebbe asked me to urgently telephone anyone I could find among the people who had returned to the bosom of Judaism in Moscow, Leningrad, and other cities; to encourage them in the Rebbe's name; and to tell them that from now on the situation would improve, until eventually the Soviet Union would change so much that anyone would be free to either leave or lead a full Jewish life in Russia. I was awestruck. I had been in constant contact with people in Russia, keeping careful track of all that was happening there, and yet had not spotted the least sign of any change for the better. True, there had been a recent change of the party's secretary-general, this time with Gorbachev replacing the dead Chernenko. Yet there had been similar shuffles before—Brezhnev, Andropov—with the situation remaining essentially the same. I still keep the newspapers I had bought that day – the *New York Times* and the *New York Post*. Both of them carry loud front-page headlines, announcing that the new Kremlin leader would be even more rigid than his predecessor and warning the world to expect the worst. Thus, even top Sovietologists could not help me find a rational backing for the Rebbe's prediction. On the contrary, what he had told me was diametrically opposed to the experts' opinions.

I spent the next few days practically glued to the telephone, trying to get through to the maximum number of people in Russia. At that time, getting a connection to Moscow or Leningrad was akin to a military campaign, demanding experience, patience, endurance, and hours of trying. Still, I managed to reach quite a few refuseniks and Jewish activists. They were astonished and overjoyed at once; however, some found the message hard to believe, even those who knew by then the worth of the Rebbe's word. One person told me that his wife had been summoned by the KGB three days ago and still had not come back. Another said that a KGB car was parked next to his building around the clock. In short, no changes or improvements in sight.

I wrote a note to the Rebbe to briefly report that his request had been fulfilled, also mentioning the reactions of the people I had talked to. That same day I received his reply, telling me that even though so far there had not been any changes in the natural flow of events, eventually everything was bound to turn out just as the Rebbe had predicted. I repeated my telephone campaign, doing my best to encourage and reassure.

What happened in reality is common knowledge today, and who proved to be right – the Rebbe or the Sovietologists – is equally clear.

However, the story did not stop there. In the summer of 1992, Gorbachev, by then relieved of all his posts, visited Israel. He spent one day touring our university, and specifically Sde Boker, the site of Ben Gurion's memorial. The university leadership asked me to head the official ceremony in honor of the guest. Thus I was given the opportunity to talk to Gorbachev and his wife in private. I told them that there is a great Jew living in New York who, as early as the spring of 1985, had already predicted the events that were soon to happen in the Soviet Union. Gorbachev was astonished, arguing that this was impossible, since in the spring of 1985 he had just come to power and he himself had no plan of action whatsoever. He added that a year later he did have a plan, but the actual turn of events, to his deepest regret, had been in total variance with his intentions. He therefore failed to understand how someone, back in 1985, could have foreseen the future developments. Gorbachev expressed a wish to learn more about this remarkable prophet and asked me to visit him the next time I was in Moscow.

The entire story makes it obvious that the prediction of the impending end of the communist era – the most important event of our time, not only for Jews but the entire world – was not a rational prognosis of a great analytical mind. It was a full-fledged prophecy, whose origins lie in the higher spiritual realms. Equally prophetic were the Rebbe's predictions of Israel's military victories, events related to the Gulf War, and many others described in the extensive literature published by *Chabad.*

However, the most important, all-embracing, what one should probably call "cosmic" prophecy made by the Rebbe is the prophecy foretelling the arrival of the *Moshiach.* For a number of years, the Rebbe had taught and instructed us that the world—the entire world, Jewish and non-Jewish, spiritual and earthly—was ready for the coming of the Messiah. All the preparations have been completed, all that remains is, in the picturesque phrase of the previous Rebbe, "to polish the uniform buttons for the parade."

A few years ago the Rebbe announced that this stage had ended as well, since now it is no longer a matter of waiting and wishing for the coming of *Moshiach* in the near future, for *Moshiach* is *here,* and all we have to do is learn to "open our eyes" and discover his presence. According to the Rebbe, this requires unity, "*ahavat* Israel," solidarity, and intensified observance of all the commandments. It is necessary for at least ten persons (a *minyan*) to devote themselves entirely to pondering upon *Moshiach,* acting in the name of *Moshiach,* praying for *Moshiach* to reveal himself. The Rebbe himself points out that his predictions concerning *Moshiach* are of a prophetic nature. How could we, then, having witnessed the fulfillment of so many predictions and prophecies, possibly doubt the fulfillment of the most important, most essential prophecy? By its very definition, a prophecy must of necessity be fulfilled. The sole question is when. And that depends upon us, every one of us. Rambam tells us that each Jew must realize that the world is suspended in a state of balance between virtues and transgressions, and that a single good deed, when placed on the scale of virtues, can tip the balance toward the world's *geulah,* the final redemption. The Rebbe teaches us that thoughts about *Moshiach,* longing for *Moshiach,* even the pronouncement "Long live our King—*Moshiach,*" have a great weight in the higher and the earthly realms, advancing the day and the hour when *Moshiach*'s presence will be made manifest.

In July of 1994, the unthinkable happened. We can no longer behold our mentor, cannot hear his voice. And yet he is here, in our midst. Every one of us senses his presence, continuing to observe the Rebbe's numerous personal injunctions and to follow his entire teaching. We can feel him guiding and protecting us, interceding for us before the higher powers. In a sense, this reminds me of our life in Russia during the 1960s. Then we had abided by the Rebbe's word, sensed his ever-present care, without being able to actually see or hear him—when even his written works had to reach us in infrequent, unimaginably devious ways.

It would be incorrect to say that the Rebbe is with us in the spiritual sense alone. The Talmud contains numerous passages arguing that, with respect to certain great Jews, the concept of "death" does not apply, not only in the spiritual but in the bodily sense as well. Thus, for example, referring to our forefather Jacob, the Talmud states (*Taanit* 5:2) that he did not die, and that means in the literal, physical sense — not only in the spiritual. It is explained that from the Egyptians' level of perception, Jacob did die, was mourned, and his body embalmed — however, that is the lowest level of perception. On the higher levels, the picture is quite different.

And what about the coming of the *Moshiach*? That the world has reached an impasse; that Israel is flooded with savage and self-destructive acts (which I described in the beginning of this Afterword); that morals are sliding downhill while perversions flourish; that the world is torn apart by local wars, destruction, and disasters, with no natural, rational way out of this situation in sight — all that is patently obvious to all. And from that perspective, the immediate coming of *Moshiach* is a must, is the only solution. Yet, what is more important, as I have already pointed out, is that we have the Rebbe's frequently reiterated firm prophecy assuring us that *Moshiach* is already here, and thus the era of *Moshiach* is essentially an accomplished fact.

In that case, who is *Moshiach*? As has already been said, the Torah states that *Moshiach* is certain to come, that our sacred duty is to hourly await and will his coming; yet it does not provide us with many details about the future kingdom of *Moshiach*. Rambam tells us that in all that concerns *Moshiach*, more is hidden than explicit, and that only when he comes will everything be revealed to us.

However, according to many authoritative Torah exponents, each generation contains at least one Jew with the potential of becoming *Moshiach*, provided the generation deserves it. The Rebbe tells us the *Moshiach* is here. Without laying claims to being a Torah expert, merely guided by sheer logic, I am forced to conclude that the Rebbe himself is *Moshiach*. He has brought millions of people (including many non-Jews) closer to Torah, and for Rambam that is the main yardstick of the initial stage of *Moshiach*'s deeds. He has created an atmosphere of approaching *geulah* in the world. He possesses all the unique, inimitable individual qualities I have described above. Finally, anyone who has ever stood face-to-face with the Rebbe has felt — as I have felt — with his heart, his soul, his entire being, that this was not a mere genius but a King. And besides, who else in this generation can possibly come even remotely close to the level that is required of *Moshiach*?

One encounters the claim that after what happened last year, we cannot possibly identify the Rebbe as *Moshiach*. Once again, this betrays a total lack of logic. After all, in any event, the coming of *Moshiach*, the total transformation of mankind and of the entire world is a miracle, the greatest of all miracles we can expect from the Almighty. The natural course of events has no relevance here. No attempts to grasp and explain this stupendous event by means of our human reason can ever succeed. All those who are in doubt do not realize that what they are doubting is the omnipotence of the Almighty. By definition, the Creator is above all limitations, and the notions of "easy" and "hard" are inapplicable to Him. How, then, can anyone claim that His ability to bring about the messianic era, to crown a certain person as *Moshiach,* depends, in the language of mathematics, on "contiguous or initial conditions"?

The problem is more psychological than anything else. I know this from my own experience. Like any observant Jew, three times a day I pronounce the *shmona esrei* (the eighteen blessings). It refers to the *yeshua* (the final redemption), the *tchiyat hametim* (resurrection of the dead), the *nisim* (miracles) and other supernatural events. When I utter these words, do I actually feel in my heart of hearts the reality and feasibility of the concepts and actions implied in these words? Or am I still a slave to skepticism, to the view of the world instilled in me in my youth by secular literature and education? Could I be trying to concoct some sort of an eclectic mixture of Jewish faith, Torah, and wretched rationality? I am aware that literal, unambiguous acceptance of the above ideas and others like them are a necessary condition of our faith. And if any one of us, including *yeshivah* graduates, has problems with the literal acceptance of miracles, of the presence of *Moshiach,* of the Rebbe as *Moshiach*—that is a result of the destructive influence of "enlightened" education. Our skeptical minds tend to reject ideas which have never yet been realized or have not yet been sensually perceived and registered as empirical facts. This means, however, that our faith is not complete, not perfect. There is no Jewish faith without full acceptance of creation, miracles, resurrection of the dead, final redemption and other fundamental concepts of this nature. The Rambam states this clearly in his Thirteen Principles. We simply have to work on ourselves a lot more. Especially since even the natural sciences, as I have written above, are not what they used to be a century ago, leading us nowadays *to* Torah and the life of the spirit rather than *away* from them. We have to overcome our trend to accept only ideas which we are able to visualize.

There is a passage in the Torah stating that *Moshiach* comes when the world is in a state of *hesech hadaat* (loosely translated as "distracted consciousness"). Perhaps that is what is required of us—less philosophizing, less reliance on our reason, a return to simple faith.

If only we could achieve the same confidence in the imminent coming of *Moshiach,* in his presence being here now, as we feel about the sun rising tomorrow morning! As a matter of fact, according to Torah philosophy, we should be much more confident of *Moshiach*'s presence than of the sunrise. Indeed, we learn about *Moshiach* from Torah, from the sages, from our Rebbe. Torah is the source and foundation of the world. Conversely, we know about sunrise only empirically. That knowledge is sensually derived only from the material world.

In addition to learning *what* the Rebbe says about *Moshiach,* we should listen more carefully to *how* the Rebbe speaks about *Moshiach.* He possesses the real, unlimited confidence! We should also pronounce, on any suitable occasion, "Live our master, our teacher, our Rebbe—King *Moshiach*—for ever and ever." This is a statement and a prayer. How do we expect God to help us if we do not ask Him to do so? Additionally, Torah in general and Chasidism in particular teach that a pronounced word has a tremendous impact on the course of events in the world.

The Rebbe often says (in Yiddish): *"Tracht gut—vet sein gut"* (Think well, and everything will be well). As has already been said, today even physics, so cold and rational, so remote from faith and spirit, contains a similar notion—man, possessing free will, becomes, as it were, the Creator's partner. If man's observation influences events in the physical world, this holds true even more in the spiritual reality. We need the Rebbe-*Moshiach.* The Rebbe-*Moshiach* is here. All we have to do is open our eyes and see. Learn to see! Our words make a world of difference. Our thoughts make a world of difference. *"Tracht gut—vet sein gut"*!

II

From the Depths

1

Instead of a Foreword

These notes are an output of various years. Not all of them meet with my current approval; however, I am leaving them unchanged. It seems to me that these notes may prove useful to those capable of seeking and finding their faith, capable of perceiving God yet prevented from doing so by their upbringing, education, environment, and the entire contemporary life-style. Needless to say, if I succeed in helping even one such person take one single step toward true faith, not only will my modest work thereby be justified but my whole life will acquire added meaning.

At present I envisage people as belonging to three basic categories. The first consists of the bearers of religion, those who inspire and sanctify the material world, giving it its *raison d'être*. This group, alas, is very small at this time. The second group contains honest and truly gifted scientists, philosophers, and writers. The superficial dazzle and headlong advance of natural sciences and technological progress have blinded these people to the real essence and potential of science, which has gradually become the object of their worship and unquestioning devotion.

This group, despite its small size, sets the tone for philosophical issues in the press and exerts decisive influence on the commonly accepted worldview. Between these two extremes lies the overwhelming majority of humans, from the lowly shoemaker to the self-seeker feeding off science and literature. This is a huge inert human mass humbly perusing the crumbs of official philosophy (a cozy and undemanding way indeed), or managing without a philosophy altogether, willingly relinquishing the privilege of possessing philosophical views to "science" and the "scientists."

The corporeal world has been unimaginably defiled by so-called civilization. Having deprived man of the natural means of existence, civilization is waging a pompous struggle to provide him with surrogates of natural goods. Yet more terrible by far are the ravages inflicted by civilization on the world of the spirit. Humanity can hardly be stopped from following the path that possibly stretches back directly to man's downfall at the Tree of Knowledge. Yet that leaves only one solution: to try to draw the people from what has been defined as the second group back into the first group, to teach them to differentiate between the craft of science and the true knowledge of religion. If this attempt succeeds, there may be hope that the human crowd will too shake loose from its mire of sloth and apathy. By finally finding their way back to God, people will attain the happiness they have sought for ages, not knowing— or rather, having forgotten—where to look.

It is beyond my power to accomplish this enormous task; but to try and contribute my modest share to this great endeavor is my duty.

With boundless joy I am embarking on this attempt. I know that people of deep faith have no need for these notes. Such people are infinitely above my reasoning. Yet to those still struggling in the dark, as well as those just beginning to glimpse the light, my writings may, I hope, be of some benefit.

2

About Myself

In the year 5723,[1] having shrugged off my timidity and sloth, I am daring to set down on paper the thoughts that have caused me untold torment, joy, and inspiration for over a decade—ever since the time when, still a child, I had suddenly felt dissatisfied and disturbed by the idea of the world as a geometrical receptacle containing myself and my kind, a receptacle as predictable, solid, and secure as the room where I grew up, as the city where, lost among the complex yet familiar and manageable maze of streets and alleys, stood the stone box in which I lived. Since then I have experienced many joyful insights and many disillusionments. I am not saying "bitter disillusionments," for shedding illusions, no matter how drawn out, is certainly a cause for joy, not sorrow. At times, I would sink in gloomy pessimism and despair; yet, more often than not, the radiant beauty of the world would infuse me with optimism—uplifting my spirits, brightening my hopes. And through it all I was filled with longing for a hidden, uncharted place—a sweet and delightful longing coupled with boundless grateful elation and admiration for the wisdom and sheer splendor of the world.

My views and notions of life and people were changing, and, I believed, maturing along with myself.

Being an outsider in a harsh and hostile environment, I shared none of my thoughts and doubts with anyone; my sole interlocutor was myself. For that

---

1. By the Jewish calendar.

same reason my erudition is rather one-sided and incomplete, so that I often wonder whether I am not struggling with issues settled long ago and coming to conclusions already reached by others. In fact, I have had occasions to realize that this was indeed the case.

I was constantly drawn to express myself on paper—paper as a mediator of sorts between me . . . and myself. Between me as a boy and as a teenager, between the teenager and the man.

I was sure that my daily, hourly analysis would move at a more efficient pace through the medium of paper, which would preserve my former, rapidly vanishing thoughts and meditations. I believed that the use of paper would help me to put in order all the years of my chaotic spiritual ferment.

Yet each attempt to resort to paper would
the enormousness of my task. Nor is this simply a matter of external circumstances. What is more important is that the moment I try to turn a pleasant, refreshing, heartwarming thought, grasped mutely or in two or three unassuming words, into rows of obedient, grammatically well-drilled phrases, I can no longer recognize my lovely thought; I lose heart. . . .

Perhaps this process of thought materialization could be made easier were I to write for others. Then all the suffering would be justified by its being the only means of sharing my conclusions. But I am writing for myself, and it is all the more annoying to need this unwieldy medium even for self-dialogue. Nevertheless, this time I am fully resolved to see my undertaking to the end. The trail of my ideas has recently come full circle. The result was something akin to what is termed a system. In order to extend and deepen my thought and analytical inquiry, it is essential that I fuse the matured yet still scattered limbs of my brainchild in order to look at it from the outside. That is the reason I am writing. This will not be a fundamental, exhaustive work—rather a set of sketches, of premises, every one of which I would be happy to elaborate at a later time.

It is obvious to me that I have not made any revolutionary discoveries, nor created a new philosophical system—though, in all honesty, I must say that most of the ideas and inferences described herein have been reached independently, through continuous and, I admit once again, delightful reflection and inner search. At first, whenever I encountered what I viewed as my ideas, my insights in books, I was dismayed. Yet as I grew older, I realized that the entire store of human knowledge is but a pale reflection of the wisdom contained in the Book of Books, and that if we have not been able—or rather, have lost the ability—to understand even a tiny fraction of its contents, then laying claims to discoveries of our own is quite premature.

So far I have been denied the ultimate happiness—that of reading the Book in the original. Yet even the scattered passages, the crumbs of knowledge vouchsafed to me, for which I am infinitely grateful, have provided the vantage point for glimpsing the structure of the world and my own place and boundaries within it, the roads of the past and the pathways of the future.

I do not know how well imagination and inquiry have filled the wide gaps in my knowledge; in any case, the reverent joy and the sense of well-being I have experienced give me hope that I have not been totally misguided in my search.

Let me repeat: I am not erecting a system of my own, but merely relating the things I have managed to discover and comprehend in the unsurpassed wisdom of the Book of Books. My path to this wisdom ran from the outside inward, a path of meandering through the dark. This long and thorny path is undoubtedly not the only or the best one there is. Yet what is also beyond doubt is that the experience of seeking and wondering has sharpened my perception, lending added power and depth to the joy of knowing.

3

The World as Perceived by a Child

A ny child brought into this world, from the earliest age, begins by learning to act so as to ensure his well-being. He has no use for the essence and meaning of objects and events. His objective is to add various skills to the instinctual ability to locate and consume milk.

To meet this objective, what is required is not the essence but the existence of varied objects, the different ways in which they interact with the child's body. Such a perception and notion of the world may be termed childish materialism. This philosophy, moreover, apparently continues to suffice at a later age, as a tool for feeding, acquiring food, protecting the body from pain, cold, and other hostile forces.

A few years go by, and the child begins literally to sizzle with all sorts of questions: "What is this?" "How?" "Why?" "Where?" The fact that the need to satisfy these questions springs spontaneously, both in parents who encourage these questions and in parents who consider them a terrible nuisance, shows that the philosophy of childish materialism is essentially unsatisfactory to man. The first tremors of the questioning volcano can probably be viewed as proof of the initial stirrings of the soul within the child. Skipping ahead, I should note that this period in human life furnishes the best evidence of thirst for knowledge as one of man's basic needs, one of his integral functions. The fact that this natural urge is often nipped in the bud by education, environment, social conditioning, and individual shortcomings does not alter its underlying reality.

Interestingly enough, a child's questions usually come in a cascading flow, with the answer to a previous question triggering the next one. Given the parents' patience and wisdom, the child is bound eventually to reach, in the course of some years, the bedrock of his quarry, the original source, the prime cause of all phenomena.

There and then comes the decisive moment in the spiritual path of the man in the making. The three possible situations are as follows.

In the first situation, the teacher or other mentor, peeved by his own inability to answer the questions, roughly cuts short the talk that fascinates the child, or chooses some ploy to avoid answering. A shout would probably be better, leaving the child dissatisfied; whereas slippery evasion stifles curiosity. In any case, eventually the child will either give up his inquiry and, relapsing into childish materialism, will be more or less content to live out his life without gaining his soul; or, if the child is persistent enough, he will sooner or later find the person or book that will provide the answer. This latter scenario, however, lies outside the boundaries of the case at hand.

In the second situation, the mentor will explain to the child that the questions at the extreme end of the chain lie beyond direct human understanding. Using this as the point of departure, he will turn the child's open, thirsting mind to thoughts of the invisible, boundless Creator, the world's supreme ruler, the ultimate source of all. The mentor's competence, the degree to which his own ideas have been perfected—those are separate issues. Meanwhile, the child's soul will have been sown with seeds of searching and reflection.

In the third situation, the mentor may turn out to be an adherent of contemporary philosophical materialism. Instead of answering the child's questions, he will subject him to vaporous ruminations woven around meaningless but ever-so-impressive and lofty-sounding terms: the law of moving matter, the infinity of matter in space and time, the cognizable nature of the world.

Arrogance and emptiness will be the fruits of this mentor's efforts. Arrogance—because the person will consider himself the salt of the earth, if not the only one then certainly among the chosen few, creative, omnipotent, comprehending and mastering blind nature. Emptiness—because one of the fundamental attributes of modern materialism is its rigid and absolute intolerance of any doubts, any searching outside and beyond this all-inclusive system pronounced to be the final and conclusive verdict in the field of philosophy.

Any research becomes the means of forcing, through casuistic cunning, any new fact or phenomenon into the tight frame of the materialistic system, so as to extol once again its flawless virtue and unshakeable superiority. It is only natural for mediocrity and sloth to cling to this system as a base of convenient support, a sturdy shield to hide behind, combining safety and security with a sense of being quite advanced and up to date. Anyone who is above the commonplace, whose mind is naturally active, will feel nauseated by the ceaseless gyration of hackneyed truisms. Then he will either dismiss them with a resigned smile and revert to the philosophy of childish materialism; or—a much less frequent outcome—he will find the strength to shake off the chains of self-evident truisms, breaking free into the vast expanse of doubts and questioning, the only atmosphere where spiritual evolution is possible.

Among the means of persuasion in his bag of tricks, our materialist mentor is almost certain to pull out, and more than once, the bogeyman of religion to intimidate his charge. The truth of the matter is that the modern mob (and therein, as we shall see further, lies Christianity's greatest fault) perceives religion as a mixed bag of every possible kind of superstition, mysticism, quackery, absurdity, and deceit. Given this common attitude, all our mentor has to do is hint at a link existing between religion and a given idea for the pupil to fearfully and quite sincerely renounce it.

Therefore, having traced the various routes the development of today's child might take, we come to the conclusion that the odds are heavily, not to say overwhelmingly, in favor of his becoming a materialist, and more likely than not a childish materialist.[1]

In our inquiry, we have made absolutely no mention of the various philosophies associated with idealism. These schools of thought are, for the most part, rather complex in both structure and adapted terminology, and become accessible only as a result of specialized education and systematic studies. That is the reason we have omitted this area in our review of the spontaneous formation of views and ideas.

The conclusion regarding the dominant role of materialistic views requires us to examine, if only in passing, their basic nature.

4

The World of Things and Conventions

L et us begin with childish materialism as the most prevalent kind. The person adhering to childish materialism is the average present-day man in the street. His mind is filled with worries about his daily bread—which he usually acquires not in the fields but through the enormous tangled network of

---

1. It should be noted that, besides the influence of parents and the environment per se, a no-less-crucial role is played by internal forces shaping the child's evolving soul, which sooner or later may prevail in spite of the stifling atmosphere.

social machinery, so that the quantity and quality of this bread depend not so much on natural and simple factors like hard work, sunlight, and moisture, as on the man's ability to fit in with the tens and hundreds of human cog-wheels spinning near him, as well as on the will and whim of powers-that-be that deliver jolts, now to the entire mechanism, now to some of its components. Man's needs are great, and only to a small extent natural. Besides shelter, food, basic clothing, he needs a great quantity of things for respectability, for protecting his place inside the human herd, for self-assertion. He needs fashionable items and perfumery, he needs ornaments, uniforms, badges of rank.

Things lead to things, things beget more things. Thus construction of new buildings increases the city area; the resulting increase in distances creates the need for cars. Cars demand roads and garages, gas stations and service stations. Things beget jobs and job-holders: managers, chairmen, directors, solicitors, conductors, ticket-collectors, cashiers, guards, traveling salesmen, clerks, doormen, traffic policemen, fashion models, and so on. Man hungers, craves, fears. He fears his boss, the police, his coworkers, a careless utterance; he fears authority, petty or supreme; he fears the impending war; he fears, and fears again, cowering, dreading, scheming. His life, his mood-swings are determined by loads of papers which he also fears, heeds, respects, and obeys. Receipts, checks, vouchers, contracts, petitions, bills, promissory notes, invoices, reports, summons, and pile upon pile of other papers, down to the most prized of all—money.

The weaker the traces of thought in a paper, the greater its influence and power, the more respect it commands. And added to this are the newspapers, the all-pervading, omnipresent newspapers whose domineering clichés make their steady, stealthy way into the brains of their perusers, blocking their thought, paralyzing the will, reverberating, amplified manyfold by the vociferous mouths of the crowd. The newspaper is a many-headed hydra; without changing its essence, it assumes various shapes: now the linen screen, now the flickering surface of a television set. The forces of nature are seen by man as infinitely remote from his immediate reality of a being fluttering amidst a sea of people and cars: infinitely remote, serving a decorative function at best in a world run and ruled by people. Naturally, there can be no question of penetrating into the core of existence, the nature of the outer and inner worlds. With the tempo rising, with no letup in the frantic pace, with rivals everywhere, it is a breathless rat race. Thoughts of competition, money, other people crowd the mind. The head is reeling.

The world, the universe—those are self-evident, their predictable reality determined by the frantic human bustle if nothing else. Religion is a bunch of fairy tales use to dupe our dim-witted grubby ancestors. Miracles are the domain of science, of the omnipotent modern technology.

Puffed up with the notion of his unquestionable superiority, the man can break into a mocking grin at the sight of a bearded oldtimer leaving a house of prayer. At the same time he can carry an issue of today's paper or a portable radio hanging from his shoulder, and treat with full seriousness the message being read or broadcast.

He may even express the view that "newspapers and the radio are all baloney"; and yet all the while he will continue to read newspapers and listen to the radio and consider himself a serious person. He will not be sickened by the flood of nonsense being spewed at him, by the inconceivable, all-consuming, hypocritical hogwash; nor will he tear up the paper, trample the voice-box, and flee with howls of horror.

And yet this modern, dignified, civilized man of the world will refuse to "fall for all that religious claptrap." While wasting nine-tenths of his time on observing rituals of social and state institutions, he will not allow anyone to take up five minutes of his precious time with "futile speculations" on reality and the essence of existence. He who regularly spends hours in the waiting room of one office or another smirks with smug contempt at a man who sets aside a half-hour each day for prayer. Holy and sacred are the things needed to eat; holy and sacred are the things needed to make ends meet; holy and sacred are the things required to succeed, to make it to the top.

Thinking and philosophizing are silly, useless, and often dangerous. Sunlight and fresh air are wholesome and conducive to health, and can be enjoyed at leisure whenever one is free from more pressing affairs. Not even at the end of his life will a person stop to ask himself where he came from and where he has been; he is still preoccupied with his vain unfinished business. His entire life appears to him as a prelude to something better, an *apéritif* before the lavish banquet that somehow never seems to materialize. That is the gist of the philosophy of childish materialism, which currently enjoys unprecedented recognition and success.

5

The Philosophy of Self-Assertion

Let us now examine the key features of philosophic materialism.
Its first and foremost concept is that of matter, which is understood as the medium of all physical phenomena. Matter is everything "objectively" existing in the world, everything that is not thought or sensation. A crucial attribute of matter is infinity in space and eternity in time. Major importance is attached to

the objective existence of matter, beyond and independent of the individual, of humans altogether. Consciousness, thought, ideas are proclaimed to be the functions, the product of matter; in other words, "matter is primary, consciousness secondary."

The very concept of consciousness is not given any clear definition, the assumption being that this concept is intuitively grasped by anyone. Consciousness is supposed to be an intrinsic property of all humans, as well as of any kind of sentient beings possibly inhabiting some remote corner of the galaxy.

The formulation of basic premises is followed by the question of gnoseology. Here the primary claim is the knowable nature of the world. It is presumed that the five human senses provide us with an immediate and accurate picture of the world, that "by means of our sensory organs we perceive the world as it really is." The mental process is assumed to be based on sensory data, on perception; next it involves the element of abstraction from the object; and its final stage is the verification of inferences through experimentation, observation, routine activity.

The main type of relationship between phenomena is acknowledged to be that of cause and effect. Also recognized is the factor of random coincidence, viewed as a complex and hitherto unexplored juxtaposition of cause-and-effect interrelations. The majority of inferences established by science are regarded as relative truths, in the sense that each object and phenomenon is infinitely multifaceted, and knowledge can never exhaust all the facets.

It is asserted, however, that as science progresses, relative truth approaches the absolute. At the same time, scientists admit the existence of certain absolute, final truths, such as the undeniable validity of past events. The main point, however, is that the basic premises of materialism themselves are considered absolute. While phenomena are assumed to be the objects of human observation, they supposedly guide us to the understanding of the nature of things.

Considerable importance is attached to laws operating in the universe, as well as in human society. Laws are considered to have objective existence. In the context of human society, the basic premise of matter being primary and mind secondary is taken to mean that material existence, work, the rate of consumption determine the state of mind, human aspirations, and actions.

That is the sum and substance of materialistic philosophy. Undoubtedly, the first reaction it evokes in a devotee is the sense of his unequaled personal and generic superiority. Indeed, man may be regarded as nothing more than randomly evolving matter with acquired mental functions; his ideas and social conduct may be viewed as largely determined by living conditions and the amount of food consumed; yet in spite of all this he still feels himself to be an exceptional and unique being endowed with intelligence that makes him, at least potentially, all-comprehending, all-knowing, all-foreseeing, all-powerful.

To substantiate their claims and persuade their students, materialists make generous and earnest use of data acquired by all natural sciences. The materialist school has developed a certain canon of criticism aimed at nonmaterialist philosophies and designed to demonstrate that the idea being challenged is tied to some theological concept. Once the link is successfully established, the refutation is thereby considered complete, for theology carries an irrefutable a priori stigma of deceitful and preposterous sham not even meriting discussion. Generation after generation is taught to regard religion as a scarecrow, as taboo; which naturally precludes any possibility of analytical criticism of religion, since none of the materialists has the slightest notion of what the term means.

He, our latter-day materialist, is fully content with his predecessors' categorical dismissal of religion as an object of derision and scorn. He shows no desire to decide the matter for himself, not only because such an attempt would bring him disapprobation at best, but mainly because he was brought up on unquestioning acceptance.

Some people may be prevented from independent thinking by their subconscious fear of losing the smug and comfortable belief in the invincibility of science, that flattering, soothing sense of self-importance afforded by materialist faith. Some are also held back by doubts about having sufficient stamina and strength of purpose needed to forge a different view of the world.

True, there are occasional attempts by materialists to examine and criticize religion. However, they are almost invariably based on three standard techniques: (1) the search for formal contradictions in claims and descriptions contained in religious texts; (2) the tendency to make use of the reader's penchant for anything smacking of sexuality and other intimate matters, so as to denounce, by twisting quotations culled from religious texts, all authoritative sources as immoral; and finally—the trump card applied as the ultimate weapon—(3) the appeal to the latest discoveries made by natural sciences.

Item one will be dealt with somewhat later. Item two hardly merits discussion: this device is much too transparent and shabby to be treated seriously. As to item three, the interaction between natural sciences, knowledge, and religion will be examined in more detail during the analysis of the basic premises of materialism.

It should be noted that materialism is worn by some as an impressive mask disguising their emptiness and general apathy; others simply use it to derive practical benefits; while the third group, made up of most intellectuals and artists who never rise above mediocrity, sincerely believe in materialism. The reservation in the last category applies to truly great artists who, like great natural scientists, are swept by the force of their imagination away from the dreary confines of materialism.

6

Some Contradictions and Some Conclusions

A s has already been said, materialists themselves do not even attempt to prove the accuracy of their system, which is erected entirely on the bedrock of premises held up as absolute truths. Where proof is absent,[1] we shall not bother with refutations. Instead let us observe the end result of the materialistic outlook when it is developed objectively and followed through to its logical conclusion. Our entire analysis will be straightforward and easy to understand, requiring no specialized background in logic or philosophy.

The cornerstone of any philosophy is gnoseology. Indeed, before launching into reflection or drawing inferences, we must clarify the essence of our views, the relationship between these views and the external world, the true validity and worth of our reflections about reality and ourselves. That is why we will begin with materialist statements on cognition and cognoscibility.

The fact that our notions of the world are founded on sensory perceptions seems to be agreed upon by everyone. On the basis of sensations perceived immediately or emerging as associations formed through hearing or reading, the soul (or let it be the mind—the name is unimportant) gives birth to man's inner world. For thousands of years debates have focused on the nature of our sensory-based concepts of objects and phenomena, the nature of sensory data itself—photographs, symbols; and finally whether objects and phenomena are actually no more than our perception of them. Leaving the last assertion unexamined, we shall address the view that objects and phenomena have an objective existence. In that case, however, by admitting that our sole connection to objects and external phenomena lies through sensations, we are forced to face the absolute impossibility of determining how remote or close, similar or opposed are our perceptions and their objects.

Allow me to demonstrate by citing this admittedly rather crude example. Suppose that we have a whole series of identical electrical instruments for measuring current intensity. The instruments are sealed, and we have no way of discovering their working principle. We have no other instruments at our disposal. Can we then, by manipulating our gadgets in any conceivable fashion, satisfy ourselves that their readings give us an accurate measurement of

---

1. In materialist philosophy, no attempts are made to verify anything. The entire system is erected by laying down key premises based on "common sense" and illustrated with instances of phenomena occurring in the physical world and human society.

current intensity in any electrical network? Certainly not! Or take another, equally crude illustration. Is it possible, by listening to a record without knowing when and how it was made, to form a reliable judgement as to the quality of the singer's voice? Once again, the answer is a definite no!

Those are only remote analogies, only illustrations not actually proving anything. All they do is merely support the following perfectly demonstrable premise: if the only way that humans can come into contact with the objective world is through sensory organs, then all that can be confidently stated about certain given material manifestations is that they constitute the objects of the given sensations.

It is inconceivable that even in a remote future people will be able to verify the truth or falsity of sensory data, to determine the correlation between their perception and some objective reality. This verification, this certainty are only possible as a result of comparison, which means that people must have data on given objects acquired by means other than sensations, and that contradicts the initial premise. In short, sensations cannot be verified by sensations themselves, and we have no other instruments to use instead.

Naturally, complex sensory functions possess no more objectivity than the initial sensations.

Any objects or phenomena that we try to view objectively still reach us through our perception, even if they existed outside the temporal span of our lifetime. Without at least some mental perception of the object being analyzed, no reasoning process is even conceivable. Thus, for us, the objective world can exist only in our perception, both the objective and the nonobjective nature of which are equally indemonstrable.

The only incontrovertible and fully comprehended phenomenon at our disposal is sensations—sensations combined, sensations recalled. By staging a simple experiment on oneself, anyone can test the truth of the earlier statement according to which, even when we discuss a rather hypothetical and hitherto unencountered object, subconsciously we still identify with this object, imagining it as a result of our perception—that is, as the sum total of experiences and sensations stored in our memory. Without this no thought is possible. None of us, for example, was present in ancient Rome. However, we do read about it in books; and it is easy to catch ourselves absorbing the information only after the words being read have been matched against concrete sensations, as if you were actually in ancient Rome, perceiving it with all the sensory organs.

Nor has anyone ever seen an electron; yet when discussing an electron we either picture it in visual, perceptual terms, or draw on the sensory impressions received by the instruments that trace its motion. The latter case is a wise course of action; to be entirely consistent, we would have to take an additional step. We would have to say that, to the same extent that the instrument's reading is merely a certain regularly recurring reaction to some object called an electron (which, strictly speaking, can only be said to cause these specific reactions in this specific instrument), our sensations too are but steadily recurring reactions to certain objects. The analogy, to be sure, is a rather loose one—but instructive nonetheless.

Indeed, sensations are directly understood by man, requiring no verbal clarification. The totality of all past and present sensations, the desire for some sensations and the fear of others, are what shape a large portion of the human "self." We do not know the objective causes of our sensations, nor the nature of the link between our physical body (for it too is perceived through no other means than the very same sensory organs) and sensations (later we will see that the link between soma and soul constitutes one of the ultimate unknowables). Yet we are well acquainted with sensory shifts, using them to evaluate the changes undergone by objects—that is, to evaluate external physical phenomena.

Therefore the essence of a physical object is a sealed book, since our only link to this object is through sensory organs, and we have no unbiased standard, no other point of reference. Phenomena, on the other hand, are open to our scrutiny, since they are accompanied by shifts in discernible sensations. We can analyze the interconnections between objects; we can examine the structure of those objects, differentiating between the simpler and the more complex; for all this is accompanied by corresponding sensory shifts. In this manner we are able to establish the so-called laws of nature; for a law describes the succession of certain phenomena but requires no knowledge of their causes. An excellent illustration of the above is the example of modern computers. A computer can solve a complex problem requiring us, for instance, to determine the optimal conditions for some technological process—despite the fact that the numbers made up of ones and zeros with which the computer opprates, and the objects involved in the technological process, share only a purely formal logical similarity.

All our reasoning is based on the notion of sensations being caused by sundry objects existing outside and apart from people. We have seen that this view, though making it possible to study the laws of the external world, leaves the essence of objects impenetrable to the human mind. Were we to assume that there is no essence beyond sensory impressions, we would be entering the domain of subjective idealism, for it would then follow that the object is entirely a product of human senses. Paradoxical as it may sound, if we examine the statement made by materialists—"through our sensory organs, we perceive the world as it really is"—one possible conclusion would imply that the object is entirely exhausted by human senses.

Let us also note that any thinking and unbiased person harbors a subconscious craving for the essential, a dissatisfaction with being limited to sensory impressions alone, and the never-satisfied urge to penetrate beyond the world of impressions.

On the other hand, those who have never given a thought to the entire subject put great faith in their perception, and it takes a great effort to realize the difference between the sum total of sensations and their object, between discernible phenomena and the undiscernible essence.

Let us look at some additional examples capable of undermining excessive faith in sensory perception. The plainest example demonstrating the impossibility of verifying people's sensations is the following. Two, three, ten, any number of people, as they look at a rose petal, will say: red. They will say the same when looking at a drop of blood, or a ruby crystal. From this we can definitely infer that each one of these people receives an identical visual imput from the rose petal, the blood, or the ruby. Yet there neither is nor can be any way of proving (whoever doubts this should try it himself!) that at least two of these people experience identical sensations from the objects they unanimously refer to as red. We would be equally justified, without lapsing into any kind of inconsistency, in presuming that these sensations are either perfectly identical or completely different. Obviously, in the latter case there can be no misunderstanding between people, since each person has once been taught the term "red" by his mentor, absorbing it in conformity with the mentor's individual sensations, and through him with those of the rest of mankind. Thus, by means of labeling, the perceptions of all people become superficially equivalent.

By now it is clear that a person has no means of comparing his sensation with the sensation given the same name by another person, be it even his own brother.

As our next example, we might consider the way the world is perceived by the blind. This does not mean a blind man who lost his sight at some stage in his life, nor a congenitally blind child of seeing parents. What we have to imagine is some sort of a special breed of people, blind from generation to generation, and having no contact with the rest of humanity. No doubt such people would have adapted in some way, and would manage not only to survive in the surrounding world but also to study it.

However, it is clear that their perceptual notions of the world would have little in common with our own; while we, whose minds are literally jam-packed with a huge amount of visual images, would be hard put to conjure up even a remote approximation of the world as perceived by the blind. Yet the most important implication following from this example is that the people in question, whatever devices they may resort to, whatever subtle analytical techniques they may apply, would never manage to discover the existence of the sense of sight, let alone form a concept of the nature of this sense—for the mind cannot reproduce a sensation it has never experienced, and which does not constitute a combination of other, familiar sensations.[2] What grounds, then, do

---

2. In considering this example, we must exclude the possibility of inheriting memory of visual sensations from remote ancestors with normal sight.

we have for being so conceited in asserting that our senses exhaust every possible kind of perception; in excluding the possibility of another way of perceiving inaccessible to us, which we can never discover, let alone attain? (Perhaps we could learn about this alien world if we could meet and communicate with its inhabitants; yet even then we would be unable to comprehend their perceptions.) Indeed, one sensory perception cannot be translated into the language of another. Try, for example, to describe a taste experience without resorting to any gustatory concepts—salty, sweet, sour—while free to use any concept pertaining to sight—color, brightness, perspective; or hearing—loudness, timbre, and so on.

Consequently, even an actual meeting of the sort mentioned above would fail to modify or enhance our picture of the world.

Here it might be appropriate also to touch upon the issue of the number of spatial dimensions—an issue that has been widely discussed with the appearance of non-Euclidean geometries and the relativity theories. Many of the views put forward in the course of these discussions appear to have been misguided; yet there were also some that could cause people at least some uneasiness and doubt about the validity of their sensations. Indeed, we perceive space as being three-dimensional, and this corresponds to the structure of the organs of equilibrium—the semicircular canals which reproduce the rectangular triaxial system of coordinates. Allegedly, there exist some species of higher organisms in which one or even two semicircular canals are underdeveloped, and as a result they behave as if the world were not three-dimensional but, rather, flat or even linear. If this reasoning is taken further in the increasing order of dimensions, it will lead to the inevitable conclusion that we might be perceiving only a three-dimensional cross section of an n-dimensional world where the full reality of objects and phenomena is inaccessible to us because of the lack of appropriate sensory organs.

To be sure, this path of reasoning is rather incomplete, since the sense of spatial dimensions is formed not only by semicircular canals but by the organs of sight, hearing, and so on. All in all, the existence of a world possessing more than three spatial dimensions is apparently as impossible to prove as to refute. What is important for us is to realize the extent to which our conception of the world is determined by the specific features of human perception.

One of the key issues is that of the perception of time. It seems to be more accurate to talk of the "sense of time," and to view it as a kind of function pertaining to all sensations, insofar as man forms the initial idea of time by subdividing his sensations into those that are happening now and those that have already taken place and are stored in memory only—that is, the idea of time is based on our concepts of the "present" and the "past." Hence, by way of inference, we construct the nation of the "future." On the other hand, an essential feature of the idea of time is the notion of continuity, which appears to be an inherent property of sensation.

Finally, the notion of time constructed in this manner is mentally projected upon the objective world. Of course, such a projection is quite hazy and vague; what is more, here too one cannot help interposing himself, subconsciously at least, as an observer perceiving the subject.

Many are discomfited by modern technology, in the sense that its continous advance seems to prove the objective nature of human concepts and knowledge of the world, providing the basis on which machines and instruments are built. Incidentally, this is not the last time we will have to deal with the false worship of technology in all of its various aspects. Now, after all that we have analyzed so far, we can plainly see that the fact of technological advance does not prove anything either. The best would be to recall our example of the computer, where external objects and phenomena are placed in an equivalent correspondence with numbers and numerical operations. Yet since translation into the language of numbers takes place as the initial data is entered in the computer one way, and as the outgoing results arrive in reverse, the computer's performance proves to be quite satisfactory. Just so with man's technological endeavors. In his mind, the external world is translated into the language of sensations. With his knowledge of the laws of sensory interconnections, which, as we have seen, correspond to the laws of the interconnections of objective phenomena, man reflects, draws certain conclusions, and finally calculates, designs, and builds some machine or other, while making a reverse translation from the language of sensations. Obviously, however subjective (in the human sense) those sensations are, this will have no bearing on the quality of the machine's performance. If additional proof and illustrations regarding the issue of technology are required, more than enough are available: the two-way translation from one language into another and back: the two-way reflection of a light beam, and so on. The following example may be cited: we constantly translate sensations into words that have absolutely nothing in ccmmon with sensations, bearing but an abstract correlation to them; we manipulate words in various ways, and translate the resulting verbal patterns back into sensations.

Resuming our analysis of sensations, we might observe the following: ultimately our senses can perceive not the objects themselves but only the phenomena involving the objects. Indeed, visual perception, for instance, is possible only when an object reflects or emits light. The sense of taste is possible only when matter is dissolved in saliva, and enters into chemical interaction with taste receptors in the tongue.

Some doubts may arise in respect to the sense of touch; yet a closer examination shows that here too the same holds true: tactile sensation is possible only during interaction between one or another part of the subject's body and the object.

Physicists, in setting up their experiments, strive to reduce to a minimum the disturbance caused by gauges and measuring devices to the object. In our experiments, aimed at gaining knowledge of the world, we never observe an undisturbed object but only interaction between the object-subject pair. Hence, sensations provide us with information on what happens, under this or that set of conditions, to the object (in other words, the way sensations shift, or the object influences other objects). Summing up our sensations, we can tell how the object will behave in various circumstances. However, no matter how great the number of components in this summary, the end result will never capture the object's essence, for essence refers to what the object is, and not the way it behaves. The most thorough and comprehensive knowledge of the conduct of a given object does not reveal its real nature. Naturally, being unable to grasp the essence with our senses, we are forced to construct our speculations in the form of negations. In other words, we can quite justly assert that a given view does not express the essential, without being able to produce an alternative view that does. An understandable predicament, for the essence is transcendent, irreducible to sensations, stretching beyond the ordinary limits of human reason which is based on senses.

Unfortunately, deprived of the ability to touch the essential with their senses, people have long settled for substituting the manifest for the substantial, growing accustomed and reconciled to the substitution. Any natural science is founded on a number of such counterfeit definitions of the essence of objects.

Let us take the science of electricity. Here the key concept is the charge, which is defined as an entity exerting a certain mechanical force on another entity, or else as something generated by friction brought about in a certain manner.

Let us turn to biology. Its key concept—the living organism—is defined as something possessing the functions of feeding, reproduction, and so on.

The science of optics defines light either as the cause of visual perception or as the cause of photochemical decomposition, or else as the exciter of the photoeffect—that is, in all cases as the exciter of certain phenomena. One hardly needs detailed explanations to see how far removed those and similar definitions are from expressing the essential.

Confining ourselves to the above-cited examples and illustrations, we may summarize: our perception of the world can be considered as subjective or as objective as we wish. Linked to the external world through our senses alone, we have no means of verifying them. The very act of questioning the objectivity of sensory perception would be legitimate only if we assumed the existence of a nonhuman arbiter. The materialists, however, not content with the vague notions pertaining to the subjectivity or objectivity of human perception, categorically declare: "We perceive the world as it really is." Oddly enough, were one of them to take this idea a step further to its logical extreme, it would necessarily presuppose an arbiter who could positively determine what the world "really is," measuring human perception against the ultimately known, authentic view of the world.

Thus it only takes some consistent reasoning to realize that one of the underlying assumptions of materialism leads to the idea of God. As we can see, materialism implicitly carries its own contradiction within itself.

Let us now examine certain results of natural sciences, a field seen by materialists as such an unbeatable trump card, such a powerful ally in the fight against idealism. Let us weigh the true value of the words "science has proved" that have such a magical effect on today's general public. In doing so, we need not waste our time examining such pearls of primitive atheism as, for instance, the claim that the launching of satellites into space has "put to rest" the idea of "God" by failing to find Him in the heavens where He is supposed to reside. (Then again, the idol-worshiping crowd might just find this very type of argument convincing.)

In our days, when all natural sciences have reached an incredible complexity, frequently employing cumbersome mathematical machinery, sprouting terms and concepts, branching into ever-growing areas of research, we are witnessing two diametrically opposed developments. First, the common crowd, as well as amateurs dabbling in science, are filled with increasing admiration for natural sciences and unquestioning faith in their omnipotence. The very sight of volumes crammed with mysterious and puzzling formulae has a bewitching effect. Belief in the power of science is fueled by the flood of popular articles, magazines, and books. This is comfortable, cozy belief, lulling the spirit, fostering passivity and mental apathy, while causing no harm to one's self-respect.

Secondly, the topmost shoots of science are increasingly stymied by insurmountable contradictions and ambiguities as scientific data grows less and less tangible and intelligible. Some of the best minds, relying on results obtained in their respective fields of expertise, spontaneously arrive at the idea of the unknowable nature of the world and recognize the necessity for rejecting determinism and the kind of simplistic materialism that has dominated science since the last century, when everything looked so clear and simple and researchers seemed so victorious in their onward march.

To the modern man in the street, natural sciences appear as a resplendent towering edifice, radiant and all-powerful. What is more, the average man cannot tell the difference between knowledge and knowhow, between studying and comprehending nature, on the one hand, and putting natural phenomena to use, on the other. Thus his blind faith in science is further strengthened by the "wonders of technology." All of this—the endless pages covered with jumbled formulae, the exploration of distant galaxies, the discovery and study of subatomic particles—all of this has such an overwhelming effect on the average man that he would go into raptures but for his deep-seated indifference to anything except the workings of his digestion, reproductive glands, and so on. At any rate, he regards nature as a submissive housemaid, completely humbled and dominated by the priests of science. If you as much as mention God, the philistine will douse you with the ever-handy bucket of derision and condescending pity.

What then is science actually capable of? Will natural sciences, even in the remote future, be able to provide us with the knowledge of the world? Having posed this question, it is essential to begin by clarifying once more what it means to know (or comprehend) the world. Comprehending any object means answering the questions (1) what is this object? and (2) whence, how, and why did it come into being? Moreover, these questions must be actually answered, not dismissed — answered in a way that would settle them once and for all. That is the yardstick we will apply to determine the ability of natural sciences to provide real knowledge.

As we have already mentioned in passing, any branch of natural sciences rests on a number of cryptic and obscure definitions and premises. Next, by means of formal logic clothed in verbal or mathematical forms; by means of experiments interpreted in the light, and within the context, of the initial premises and definitions; by means of endless layers of terms, categories, and concepts piled one upon another, a highly complex system evolves — one that certainly requires talent, sophistication, and expertise. This system looks imposing indeed; yet it obviously cannot yield any knowledge beyond that upon which it has been based. And its foundation — as we have said from the start — contains not an ounce of knowledge. Of course, this would be best explained through an example, by taking a specific science, and tracing the chain of interlinked categories down to the lowest link, to see it helplessly suspended in midair.

We have already introduced the science of electricity. Let us come down from its heights to the foundation. Starting from relativist electrodynamics, through Maxwell's equation, we will reach the simple concepts of potential, current intensity, and so on. This stage can still provide us with answers: currency is the flow of charged particles; potential is the energy contained in a single charge; and so on. However, this is the last rung (counting from top to bottom) where things are neat and tidy. The next question — "What is a charge?" — is met, as we have seen, only by helpless mumbling about some sort of entity acting on a similar entity with certain force.

Thus on the topmost rung of science all is well: complex notions are explained through simpler ones; the nature of complex objects is decomposed, broken down into the more basic units. Yet if the analytical process is not stopped in time, we arrive at the ultimate essence, which is unknowable. As we have already seen earlier, phenomena and regular patterns are quite accessible to study, providing the very material addressed by science in its uppermost reaches. Here the ineffable nature of reality is not apparent, for objects are so multilayered that their essence can be decomposed time and time again, reduced to more elemental entities, before reaching the ultimate core which is irreducible and, like any essence, intangible.

Mechanics, once you have managed to squeeze through the systems of nonlinear differential equations, will be reduced to the concept of the motion of a material point, which, it appears, is located outside of us, or, as materialists put it, "constitutes objective reality manifested through our perception." Once again the ultimate reality is impenetrable, inaccessible to knowledge. As to motion, it is defined either as the action of changing position in some sort of absolute space, or at best as the changing position of a given body in relation to others. It is plain to see that the latter definition also hinges on the notion of space. In spite of the numerous volumes devoted to the idea of space, it is comprehensible to humans only in reference to their own actual or mental motion—up and down, forward and backward, right and left.

The psychology and the physiology of the central nervous system are rather impressive when explained by such terms as "excitation" and "retardation" in the cerebral cortex; yet it is obvious to all that the essential meaning of concepts such as "thought," "consciousness," and "sensation" will not be revealed when they are replaced by other, more palpable-sounding names. As a matter of fact, it is the materialists themselves who vehemently deny that thought is an electrical (or any other kind of physical or chemical) process in the brain, insisting that the two are only connected or interrelated in some way.

Still, a yawning gap lies between determining a correlation or correspondence between two objects, and comprehending their essence. Words, loud-sounding terms difficult to digest, hide the truth from sight. People on the whole are easily impressed by terms and labels, especially obscure and high-flown ones. The number of ultimate, irreducible, and unknowable essences may be said to include the living organism, the beginning or the end or the infinity of space, the beginning or the end or the infinity of time, and finally the entire universe as a whole.

That all ultimate essences actually exist, that they are not a figment of imagination, follows from the acceptance of the objective reality of the world.

One could cite a virtually endless list of scientific arguments and theories, seemingly lucid and filled with profound meaning, until the moment they touch on one of the ultimate essences, when their apparent clarity and meaning begin to dissolve, to fade away. While meditating upon these subjects, man sub-consciously, intuitively, senses the presence of the intangible essence, but he is powerless to unveil it. Whenever man reflects on any one of these elusive entities, struggling to grasp its essential core, to capture its fleeting shadow, he invariably experiences a recurring sense of frustration, of knowing that in order to capture the nebulous substance, he would have somehow to overstep his own boundaries, overcome his limitations—and that it is an impossible feat. The inevitable recurrence of this feeling at the end of thought processes converging from various points of departure forces the conclusion that all ultimate essences are the domain of the Supreme Being, not of man. Eventually, shedding the false pride of materialism, one is compelled to admit that ultimate reality is known by God and can never be known by man.

Thus we have come to realize that if the entire world is not to be regarded as a subjective concept—that is, to be viewed through the prism of subjective realism, it is necessary to acknowledge the unknowable nature of ultimate essences, and hence the unknowable nature of reality as such.

The significance and objective of natural sciences assume, in the light of all we have discussed so far, a purely utilitarian form. What these sciences provide is not knowledge of the world but information on processes occurring therein, and prescriptions for the rational observation and utilization of these processes. Since "science" is a lofty-sounding word, definitely associated by most people with knowledge in the sense we have defined it, it would probably be more appropriate to use the term "scientific craft." Such a name would emphasize both the utilitarian angle and the fact that sciences, especially mathematical ones, are similar to professional crafts in demanding natural talent, extensive training, and perseverance.

We have still to examine the recent development whereby scientific crafts, in the course of their evolution, demolish an ever-growing number of pillars supporting the idyllically untroubled materialistic picture of the world.

The best-known examples are taken from physics. Heisenberg's uncertainty principle, as well as studies of the microcosm on the whole, gave rise to a wave of discussions whereby materialist philosophers waged a frantic and demagogic battle in defense of the principle of cognoscibility, while physicists became increasingly indifferent to this principle, content with workable observation of experiments and theories, and mental images of nuclear structures, with little concern for their hidden meaning. Whenever some physicist or other was persuaded to comment on the philosophic implications of the latest experimental results, the most prominent ones invariably reacted by referring to the unknowable nature of basic reality.

Furthermore, in our days almost no physicist or astronomer would talk any more about the infinity of the universe in space and time. Scientists even go as far as to cite the amount of matter in the universe as a significant factor. Based on observation of receding galaxies, on various gravitation theories, and so on, science derives identical numerical values, estimates the age of the universe, and often draws conclusion concerning its impending end.

Materialists, in order to salvage the notion of infinity so crucial to them, put forward various conjectures claiming that our universe is merely one of an infinite number of universes that comprise the world, but that because of the curvature of space, which follows from the general theory of relativity, no signal or light beam from another universe can reach our own. Oddly enough, what they seem to overlook is that they are thereby cutting the ground from under their own feet: for their argument is nothing less than a sermon on the unknowable nature of reality.

It is worth mentioning that in our days materialist science tends to accept the existence of telepathy, although so far it has been unable to come up with any sort of a satisfactory explanation for this phenomenon.

Also noteworthy is the acknowledgment of immutable genes as carriers of hereditary characteristics.

It is quite intriguing that, given the grandiose extent of modern technical and financial potential, to this day science has failed to find the intermediate missing link between monkeys and humans, essential for confirming Darwin's theory of evolution pertaining to man's origins; nor have any alien civilizations been discovered.

All of the above are but a handful of brief illustrations out of the great number of possible ones.

Thus we have demonstrated the unknowable nature of the world so far as comprehending the ultimate essence is concerned. We have also shown that reflection on the limits of knowledge brings one to God, regardless of whether the world is asserted to be knowable or unknowable.

We have come to realize that the essence of objects is hidden from us. Can we then refer to knowledge at all? Yes we can, but in one sense only. Knowledge consists of constructing a consistent picture of the world; of drawing precise lines between what is accessible and inaccessible to man; of arriving at appropriate guidelines for man's conduct in life; of acknowledging man's role in the scheme of things; of appreciating the bliss and wonder of the world; of finding God. It seems that to succeed in achieving these goals, one would need, in addition to reasoning skills and logic, intuition and imagination as well.

7

What Do We Really Know about the World?

What can we say about our world? We do not know what it is, nor what it is made of, nor whence or to what end. We are not equipped to answer these questions. What we do know is that existing outside and apart from us is a boundless, infinitely diverse world of which we are a tiny part. This world is ruled by elegance, beauty, harmony, and wisdom. We sense, perceive, recognize an untold profusion of phenomena obeying laws which, though highly complex, are open to human analysis and understanding. Our soul contains the other, inner world, corresponding to the outer one insofar as, even though we are unable to determine the exact correlation between the two, our actions in the outer world, ruled by thoughts representing a part of the inner world, lead to intended and expected results.

For us the exterior world exists solely through the mediation of the inner world of sensations and subsequent thoughts, through the mediation of the soul. Without our soul we are incapable of perceiving the world, even though we can mentally acknowledge the fact of its existence.

As long as we remain confined within the bounds of rational thinking, we do not and will not know where the world comes from, why it exists, and what it is, just as we will never know who, what, and why we ourselves are. Yet even given these limitations, we know that the natural world exists beyond, within and above us in all its splendor, inexhaustible variety, complexity, boundless magnitude, and harmonious order. We perceive the existence of nature—unified, omnipresent, and infinite—and through its medium we absorb and savor the joys of living. This knowledge, elevated to utmost clarity and palpability, is the highest summit accessible to the rational mind. True greatness lies in accepting one's limitations; true power, in keeping a clear distinction between the possible and the impossible; true pride, in recognizing the sublime wisdom of the world; true ecstasy of knowing, in sensible, realistic perception of the world.

Those are the brief conclusions following from the above analysis.

8

Opening the Book of Books

And now let us open the Book of Books, and immerse ourselves in the texts of *Shabbat* and festive prayers. We will realize before long that until now we have been forcing open doors, and that the fruits of our mental exertions have long been anticipated, and what is more, anticipated with a profundity, style, and language we dare not even dream of. Here we will read that God is one, omnipotent, incorporeal, infinite; that God is the source of all sources, Alpha and Omega, the beginning and the end of everything under the sun; that God is the cause of all causes, the law of all laws. We will read about the splendor and ultimate wisdom of the world, about the boundless joy of beholding this world, the boundless bliss of savoring it with the body, and the yet greater bliss of savoring it with the soul, and the inexpressible gratitude and adoration we feel before the Almighty.

Further we will learn about the moral, intellectual, hygienic, and social codes which derive from the primary knowledge.

However, there is hardly any point in a clumsily worded retelling of the contents of these Books. After all, they are wide open to everyone. All that is needed is the willingness and the ability to tap their wisdom. Even genuinely great thinkers wrote in a cumbersome and convoluted manner. Truly simple writing is found in the Book of Books alone. Still we have to admit that with the ages the arrogant and meager human brain has become less and less capable of taking in this simplicity. It is possible that the deeper man loses himself in the jungle of scientific craft, the less hope will there be for his brain eventually to purify itself, enabling man to regain the profound wisdom of simplicity.

9

Between Knowledge and Idolatry

T he picture of reality and our knowledge of it, whose outline I have endeavored to provide to the best of my ability, constitutes, as we have seen, the only possible one, since all other descriptions either are self-contradictory or, when their premises are consistently and scrupulously brought to their logical conclusion, have resulting concepts identical to those presented above.

Perhaps the truest path to knowledge runs through errors and disappointments. But it is definitely not the shortest and the easiest path. The key step is to overcome the belief, instilled over the present century by the school and the press, that "our age, the age of science and technology, must be the age of free thought alone."[1] Only after overcoming this hurdle will a person become capable of free, unbiased analysis and spiritual creativity. Therefore, we should return once more to the question concerning the limitations of scientific crafts, the extent of their potential or impotence, the views, ideas, and aspirations of the "free" contemporary crowd.

Today's scientific craft undoubtedly requires a great deal of talent, skill, and diligence. Yet, does its requirements consequently make it any different from the craft of a skilled engraver or weaver?

---

1. Whereby "free thought" is taken to mean atheism.

They are truly one and the same, both in essence and aim. In fact, the work of ordinary, unassuming craftsmen is always beneficial, something that cannot be said about the zealous efforts of scientific craftsmen.

What is also certain is that the pursuit of scientific crafts can be a more satisfying occupation, and that it can be both noble and commendable. The creative joy felt by glassblowers, ironsmiths, architects, musicians can also be felt by an experimenter getting a new and interesting result, or by a theoretician successfully solving an equation. Yet the halo created around the scientific craft carries danger and the threat of the total impoverishment of humankind. If nothing else, its danger lies in attracting those who may have been born with the potential for seeking the true knowledge. Of what possible worth, for example, is the life of some – no matter how stoical – scientific craftsman who, through feats of cunning and exertion, discovers a few elementary particles, or invents a bomb no less, when compared to one who devotes his life to learning from the Book of Books?! All that remains to the former is to admit, just before his end, that the so-called "great minds" eventually leave this world still mystified by the incredible complexity and enigma of reality – a reality that mockingly reveals dozens of new puzzles behind each bend of the road traveled by the seeker of imposing formulae. In his pride he had not even managed to savor the taste of natural life, since he viewed the sun as an object for experiments, and not as a God-given blessing.

The latter lives in harmony, with a clear sense of his place in the world, enjoying wisely and calmly the life of the body, and deriving his ultimate bliss from the flight of the all-embracing and all-comprehending thought, made mighty by the clear knowledge of its power and powerlessness and of the limits of its potential. The former ceaselessly chases after something that bewitches him with promises of happiness, satisfaction, peace of mind. He is always hopeful for tomorrow and empty for today, like a philistine dreaming of a pot of gold – and that goes on until his dying day. The latter rejoices in contemplation of the universe, in the present moment. His happiness is granted him today, a happiness that does not have to be invented, that grows deeper with time, yet remains essentially the same.

Speaking of scientific craft, it can also be noted that, even if we applied tangible utilitarian benefits as the measure of its value, we would still have to acknowledge its steady relative decline. Indeed, how could we possibly compare the benefits brought by the greatest discovery of ancient times – fire – with those caused by the greatest discovery of modern times – the unleashing of atomic energy?

Once again let us stress: the most important, most harmful, most saddening phenomenon is the idolatry of scientific crafts. Whether the object of worship is a stone idol or the fetish of modern science makes no difference whatsoever. In both instances what is being worshiped is the product of human craft.

It would seem that we cannot and must not hope to find a way out of the dead end humanity has managed to blunder into over the millennia. It is unlikely that human reason is even capable of pointing the way out of stone dungeons filled with poisonous vapors back to the grapevine and the wholesome smell of ripening wheat, away from the grinding mental millstone of scientific cant to the serene lucidity of contemplation. All we have to understand is, first, how meager are the benefits and how great the calamities and abominations bestowed by scientific crafts; and second, that there is no difference between ordinary artistic, and scientific crafts; and thus to shatter the halo conferred by the crowd on the high priests of science, a halo the creation of which they themselves, whether out of cupidity or naïveté, have done a lot to bring about. We must realize that in his pursuit of illusory material gains, man resembles a dog chasing its own tail. He first gives rise to the craft of science and then loses control over it and begins to idolize it, believing in its omnipotence, its supreme merit, without feeling deceived in any way.

We have to see the wave of oblivion steadily devouring man's true purpose— that of contemplation, reflection, understanding. The more the human crowd follows the urges of the stomach, the greater the tribute of mindless adoration paid to scientific craft.

It is to be stressed again and again: we make no attempt to do away with one single letter, one single formula belonging to scientific craft—the pride and idol of "enlightened humanity." All we must do is admit, honestly and unequivocally, that scientific crafts share absolutely nothing in common with knowledge, which should be sought in immediate perception of the world, in contemplation, in analysis of ordinary interactions between man and the surrounding world, and above all, in the inexhaustible revelations of the Book of Books. Immediate perception of the world comes the closest to its ultimate essence; the pinnacles of scientific crafts, sunk in the tangled and convoluted jumble of phenomena, is the furthest. The ancient, lucid words in the Book of Books express a wisdom which every man must struggle to attain within his soul. Intricate scientific books provide the means of reaping greater or lesser benefits from the physical world; yet these books conceal a trap. Carried away by the pursuit of these benefits, one is liable to lose irretrievably the main benefit potentially granted to man—the gift of possessing and savoring knowledge.

Over the last two or three millennia, as people became much more skillful on the whole, they have also become, to the same if not to a greater degree, much more primitive. Adroit hands are hardly superior to the mind! Sophisticated, and at times disobedient, toys are hardly superior to knowledge! The final and absolute purpose of existence became the quest for the means of existence. Given this tendency and these aspirations, people need an idol. Thy are so desperate to have some convenient, undemanding, soothing idol to worship that, as soon as their old idol is taken away, they immediately invent a new one. Primitive and, more important, lazy minds find their ideal mainstay in their object of worship. It is so simple, so primitive and accessible; with an easy heart, people can pass on to it the heavy yoke of responsibility, while they themselves can drift with the current in blissful serenity. People can relieve themselves of the burden of doubts and questioning, retaining only the most simple and soothing pleasures: a full belly, sexual gratification, and . . . self-importance.

The idols of ancient times were undisguised. Back then people were only entering the first grade at the school of hypocrisy and still largely called things by their proper names.

In the course of centuries, these big children eventually grew tired of their old and tattered dolls. It was precisely at that time that they came across some crumbs of knowledge based on the Book of Books, as well as the ancient people it belonged to. However, this knowledge proved to be too complex, demanding, and burdensome for them. They had only enough spiritual strength to patch up the idol and wrap themselves as well as they could in the odds and ends of hypocrisy and verbiage. The idol remained an idol; life did not become more complex; man was not saddled with additional demands. The next two millennia were of definite benefit only to the fatty tissues of human brain.

Finally came the time of the idols of science, bearing a far too heavy resemblance to their ancient predecessors. Once again specialized branches of idolatry came to replace universality. Yet what heights of importance and brilliance they have reached, and how cozy and peaceful living with them has become! It would appear that this time marked only the moment of mankind's enrollment at the university of hypocrisy; the process is far from over, and scientific crafts are not the final achievement of idolatry.

In ancient times man's soul—naked, sensitive, spontaneous—felt nature, reacted to it, and tried to comprehend it.

Thousands of years went by; people grew more cunning and refined. But the pores of human spirit have clogged up. The soul put on the motley rags of categories and notions invented by humans themselves and lost the ability to feel. People have become completely submerged in ranks, positions, titles, duties, rights, rules, formulae, distinctions, punishments, permissions, fashions, authorities, profits, losses, power, weakness, honor, contempt, and countless other trivialities and phantoms.

From childhood onward, people learn to make sense of it all, to be excited, inspired, disappointed by this illusory reality, while their natural instinctual knowledge withers, dwindles away, becomes as extinct as the keen sense of smell or hearing. That a forest animal perceives smells and sounds a thousand times better than man may not be such a setback, as this sensory ability can be compensated by appropriate equipment; but the lost gift of sensing nature is irreplaceable. Here we cannot help admitting that man has become hopelessly inferior to animals, who to this day definitely preserve in some unique form the original "sense of nature." Man, however, retains only the most primitive vestiges of this sense, manifested occasionally in the effect weather has on the mood, or the inspiration gained by some poets and artists from landscapes. Yet the ability to be moved by the miracle of a blade of grass, the sweet caress of a warm breeze, to engage in reverie and contemplation; to let the mind gingerly brush against the innermost depths, the highest peaks of the spirit, and to feel the melting and startling tremor ripple through your entire being during that instantaneous realization and acceptance of the world and your place in it; all that is gone. The sensitive soul, the free uncluttered mind unpolluted by vulgar materialistic primitivism—those have been blunted, rendered insensitive.

Watching the soundless burst of color ushering in the new day, lost in breathtaking anticipation of the familiar yet ever new moment when the sun pours down its golden shower upon the earth huddling under its misty covers; contemplating the going down of the enormous fireball of the setting sun, lingering in the thickening darkness soaked in the heady fragrance of wild grass under the boundless star-studded firmament, ancient man would tremble, brimming over with joy and admiration, his soul transported by awesome rapture, resounding with thousands of tender strings attuned to the slightest movement in the kingdom of nature. He sensed (sensed is the word to use) the inconceivable and overwhelming grandeur of nature, his own insignificance in the enormous and astounding world, and the immeasurable happiness of inhabiting this world, as well as the pride of being able to perceive it.

The soul of contemporary man has become hardened and unkempt. Even while basking his body in the sun, he regards it with the same arrogant and calculating eye, the same dull, cold and avaricious expression, with which he would consider some garish plate hung in his room for respectability's sake. He is preoccupied with petty thoughts about tomorrow's business, and filled with sluggish faith in scientific views on the structure of the world, the solar system, and the sun itself, quite satisfied with the scraps of knowledge retained by his memory from school days. He fancies himself to be a masterful and superior specimen. Yet how measly and pitiful he is, stagnant and depraved in his princely presumption! And, compared to him, how great was ancient man in the clear knowledge of his insignificance!

Not only have our contemporaries squandered the wisdom of their ancestors, but they are also discarding its every remaining trace, indignant at any mention of it. The trouble is, their notions of this vanishing knowledge are founded not on the genuine sources of wisdom and spirituality that are unattainable to them, but rather on different versions of distorted substitutes. Having blasphemously defiled fundamental ideas of true monotheistic religion and offered to the masses such a distorted, impoverished, idolatrous version of it, thinking individuals of succeeding generations began to associate religion with a miserable children's tale. Motivated by a thirst for knowledge, these individuals hastened to turn their faces away from religion instead of plumbing its depths. This was only to be expected, for anyone taking the inward path would have to struggle through layer upon layer of stupidity and hypocrisy, and that demands the kind of endurance that even the most persevering are unlikely to have.That is why even the best minds took the straight path to modern-day idolatry, which seemed to promise more breathing space and freedom of thought.

The majority of contemporaries come across as merely indifferent to anything that lies outside their bodily "self." Indifferent people are hopeless people.

The man who has gone astray can be redeemed; his soul can be reshaped; whereas the indifferent one is shapeless. He slides down the useless, meaningless pathway of his life, leaving no traces. Despondency is his sole traveling companion. Indifference is contagious, spreading the fastest when passed down from parents to children. There should be a law depriving the indifferent of their parental rights, as it is done in cases of insanity, alcoholism, and perversion. Naturally, a discussion dealing with the issue of life's calling must exclude indifferent people, for it is impossible to argue with a person whose invariable reaction is "What do I care?" Such a person is dead, and his life is but an illusion.

The intuitive conclusion following from all of the above is that the search for knowledge is immeasurably superior to any other human occupation. However, the appeal to intuition does not in itself constitute proof. This appeal carries the least conviction in the eyes of the rationalist, who can immediately counter with the following objection: the man whose heart is set on knowledge finds in it his happiness and meaning, just as the money-grubber attributes the same qualities to money, and the glutton to food. Viewed in this light, everything may be reduced to saying that tastes differ, to each his own, everyone finds his happiness in the things he likes, as long as they are attainable.

Yet there is at least one consideration that should be sufficiently convincing even to the rationalist: the money-grubber is satiated with constant success; his soul grows insipid and stale, whereas failure is liable to drive him to insanity and suicide. His life is unlikely to take any other course, provided that for him money is truly the goal and not the means. The depraved debauchee squanders his strength, eventually falling into ruin or disease. The glutton's fate follows the same pattern. Yet has anyone ever become sated with sunrises? Has anyone, after experiencing even once the rapture of looking at a blade of grass or a green leaf, grown tired of fields and forests, or lost his ability to savor sweet fresh air? No such person exists. All the more ludicrous, then, is the claim that an excess of knowledge (unless it is false knowledge) causes one to be repulsed by additional knowledge, to feel an aversion for the challenge of discovery, understanding, intellectual curiosity.

If we peel off the shell of pompous verbiage usually worn by speculations on the meaning of human life, we will uncover the following. All the commonly argued premises eventually come down to people's desire for maximum pleasure. The only difference between various points of view is that one person says, "I wish to live so as to derive maximum pleasure from life"; another wants "maximum pleasure for all"; while a third excludes himself, only desiring "maximum pleasure for the rest of humanity."

True, it is impossible to deny that the last statement expresses the already familiar motto, "to live for the sake of humanity." However, we too could approach the issue of the meaning of life in a rational manner, with the principle of maximum pleasure as our starting point. We have already seen that only the quest for knowledge can provide supreme and lasting happiness; thus, to say, "The ultimate purpose of man's life is the pursuit of knowledge" is, from the rationalist's viewpoint, equivalent to saying, "The ultimate purpose of man's life is to derive maximum spiritual pleasure." Of course, when viewed in this light, the struggle to provide all people with conditions necessary for unimpeded enjoyment of the fruits of knowledge becomes an important and noble cause. The only peril to be avoided in this struggle is that of confusing the means with the end.

Let us now consider, through the example of a modern youth, just how tortuous and thorny the path to knowledge is in our days, and how unlikely such a youth is to eventually reach the true goal of his life.

To begin with, let us assume that our young man has not succumbed to indifference, that he has retained his spirit of inquisitiveness. Full of youthful fervor, armed with a fresh mind and an excellent memory, he will spend five to ten years, the best years of his life, mastering some portion of the huge monolith of modern natural science, physics, or mathematics. Perhaps by the end of that time he will have achieved something, solved some recalcitrant differential equation or, through some ingenious modifications in testing conditions, succeeded in tracking down a hitherto undiscovered phenomenon. Accordingly, he is full of ambitious designs and plans.

Thoughts of new experiments, new mathematical computations are more or less closely intertwined in his mind with musings about future appointments, academic titles, the girl he loves or will love, and once again brilliant presentations at conferences to come, trips and flights, discussions, debates, triumphant victories.

In another, less frequent version, the young man may be predominantly motivated by selfless commitment, altruism, dreams of discoveries and the benefits they will confer on mankind. Yet even in such a case he is filled with faith in his scientific craft, its sanctity, significance and power. He is therefore lost to knowledge.

But let us suppose that our young man proves to be one in a hundred, one in a thousand, and driven by a thirst for knowledge inherited from dozens of past generations, moves onward. The quest for origins, ultimate ends, essential truths inflames his mind and heart. Gingerly and alertly, he descends from the giddy heights of science to the bottom floors, and from there to the basements, where he discovers a gaping void instead of foundations, the same void we have talked about earlier, hidden to those gazing down by the impenetrable thicket of categories, terms and tenets. He is now facing the unknown and the unknowable. If he had been motivated by idle curiosity alone, he will hurry back up to the safety and security of the summit, where only at times, in harmless debates, he will crush his opponent with caustic comments on the unknowable nature of reality. However, if he has a sensitive and candid nature, a difficult, forbidding stretch of days and years lies in store for him, during which he will be tossed this way and that, stern and distant, with no place to rest, no ray of hope. Everything will seem dismal and pointless. He may end up in a lunatic asylum; or else, having lost the gift of simplicity, he may seek the truth in obtuse philosophical theories steeped in mysticism, sophistry, and symbolism. Yet it is just possible that his youth will assert itself, and he will intuitively reach for the sun, the fragrance of the fields, the life-giving instinct, as the only authentic values available to him. And maybe, just maybe, he will go further yet, and his soul, refreshed by deep meditation, will flourish, shedding the age-old crust accumulated by generations long dead, and, until then resigned to blindness, he will suddenly see the light. However, he will be immediately assailed by the old feelings, instilled in childhood, of contempt for religion and the fear of being perceived as a believer. Only after a long and arduous battle with himself, a long inner search, will he finally regain his sight once and for all.

By counting the number of "ifs" and "maybes" dotting our young man's path to knowledge, we will realize how small the chances are for finding such an individual within the mass of contemporary youth, either beset by indifference or sunk in idol worship.

10

The Eternal People

H aving clarified, to the best of our ability, the general philosophical issues, let us turn our attention to certain specific problems related to our people.

It does not require much effort to realize that the entire course of this people's history, fate, and evolution is profoundly and substantially different from that of any other nation. This fact has been acknowledged both by friends and by the most bitter foes. The most stable and remarkable feature that sets this people apart is its invincibility, resilience, continuous rebirth from ashes and dust, the ever-recurring bursts of spiritual and physical revival. Neither a professional historian nor a layperson could point to any other people whose history represented anything even remotely similar. An untold number of minor nations throughout history were devoured by voracious global predators. Whenever this happened to a nation, it would be partly destroyed, partly dispersed, and in two or three generations it would vanish without a trace. Part of it would be enslaved, digested in the predator's bottomless belly, losing its identity, its language, turning into yet another drop in the well-mixed homogenous blood of the huge organism.

How many giant nations, having reached the peaks of might and power, suddenly began to decline and totter—as a result of either insatiable expansionism or internal tension, rivalry, tyranny; or, finally, because of spiritual and bodily bankruptcy and surfeit. In the course of decades, sometimes centuries, the giant nation would crumble into pieces that no longer bore any resemblance to the original parts that had gone into forming its unity.

And only the eternal Jew, so hated and so essential for rendering minor and major services, would resurface in every millennium, every age, every decade, rising again and again from the fire and smoke, with the same smile on his inimitable face. He was loathed and badly needed, tolerated when he put his heart and soul into others' fields made fertile with the ashes of his ancestors, when he was ready to move heaven and earth for a passing stranger, and then he was suppressed once more, used to quench the overpowering lust for blood.

He was too much of an embarrassment—this eternal Jew—to the philistine. He made for an irksome sight, working a tiny piece of his beloved land, pouring loving care on the fruit of his vines, while giving the highest regard to omnipotent and incorporeal thought, attaching the highest value and esteem to the spirituality of his every act, the purity of his soul and body, and ridiculing the nice and tame idols worshiped by the philistine wallowing in the miasma of sloth and sleep.

Yet the eternal Jew was even more of an embarrassment when, sharing the same roof with the philistine, he kept up his eternal and incomprehensible prayer. And whenever the philistine's discomfort and unease became too much to bear, he remembered that he had a sharp knife and a burning coal guaranteed to bring easy and swift relief.

The philistine's problem is easily solved—what with the knife and the coal. But what about the philosopher, the sociologist, the historian, the economist? Their embarrassment is even stronger than that of the philistine. The eternal

Jew does not fit into any of their elegant theories, the eternal Jews disrupts, by the very fact of his existence, the magnificent edifice of the scientific system. This system had been working without fail. The history of any nation, the rise and fall of any civilization, brightly illumined by the system's piercing light, became simple and crystal clear; facts and events arranged themselves in a precise chain of causes and effects. Yet suddenly the system gasped and ground to a halt, with its gears, bolts, and springs flying off in all directions. The system has choked on the eternal Jew, and its triumphant light has gone out.

The sheer obstinacy of this eternal Jew knows no bounds! At the very point where, by every law of materialism and political economics, he is supposed to disintegrate and scatter through separate countries in separate and disconnected branches, he unexpectedly regroups to form a single entity. Where the sociologist predicts, as plain as day, complete assimilation, the eternal Jew survives for centuries in the inviolable world of his own. At the very moment when, in the racist's view, the eternal Jew, weeping in fear, is supposed to lay his head voluntarily on the chopping block, he spits in the executioner's face and leaps onto his trusty charger.

Oh yes, the eternal Jew is quite an embarrassment to the men of learning! Nor do they have a knife or a coal handy. Well, a pen may not be such a bad instrument either! The soul of the man of learning cries out in the voice of a teenage bully who has found a way out of a ticklish situation, "Let's kill him!" while the relieved pen writes the words "There is no eternal Jew; there used to be once, but not any more . . . " And his heart purrs with pleasure and contentment. The theories sparkle; all systems run smoothly, arranging facts and events on labeled shelves.

This is a premeditated lie, not a misconception; so any argument is pointless. Yet where should we look for causes and explanations? A little logic could be of help. We have seen that the history of our people follows a course that is completely different from that of any other people. We have seen that the essential issue that must be solved is the issue of tenacity, of immortal endurance. Yet a unique phenomenon must be the consequence of a unique cause. What, then, is that unique feature distinguishing our people from all others? Let us try to examine a number of possible explanations.

There are some people who view superiority of race or blood as the underlying cause. These people are guilty of immodesty, even indecency. True, accusing them of immodesty means offering a merely ethical argument, not an actual rebuttal. A much more convincing objection is this: blood is a legacy distributed equally among all the individuals comprising a nation. Were endurance an attribute of blood, it would have to be a component feature of every separate individual, even of those completely removed from collective national identity.

However, we know of a countless number of defectors and renegades who deserted without sapping the people's eternal strength. If the quality of blood were the explanation, it would be impossible to account for entire large groups breaking away and losing all spiritual ties with the preceding generations, while preserving the original racial purity. Thousands of examples convince us that defection always starts in the spiritual sphere, and purity of blood does nothing to prevent it.

Others are of the opinion that the indestructible nature is inherent in a unique psychological makeup. However, in the first place, psychological makeup is once again a feature of the individual, whereas endurance characterizes the collective. The people retains its endurance despite the withdrawal of individuals or entire groups. Moreover, psychological makeup is nothing but a veiled term for the same quality of race or blood discussed in relation to the first explanation.

To be sure, we are not to rule out the possibility that certain features of physical and psychological structure constitute one of the factors facilitating the nation's survival. However, accepting these features as the cause would mean founding the explanation being sought upon an indemonstrable hypothesis, as a result of which the entire explanation would remain as it were suspended in thin air. After all, to actually prove that this people's genetic and psychological makeup is less responsible for its assimilation and disappearance than that of other peoples, we must necessarily cite the fact of its indestructibility. Yet here we are obviously entering a vicious circle: we presume something to be the cause of a certain phenomenon, and prove the existence of this "something" by pointing at the demonstrable existence of the phenomenon hypothetically accepted as the effect.

This tells us that we have gone astray. After all, the goal we have set for ourselves is to find tangible existing features specific to this people, which could have been the cause of its unique vitality; instead we have engaged in erecting arbitrary suppositions.

Another opinion holds that the hostility of surrounding nations and the constant persecution are the underlying cause in question. This view appears quite plausible. Numerous examples are cited that demonstrate, in a rather convincing manner, how outbreaks of persecution stimulate national self-identity, bringing about its intense revival and growth. And yet the example of certain ethnic groups—for instance the Georgians, who, though spared any carnage for two thousand years, managed to remain remarkably united and faithful to ancient traditions—shows that even persecution is not the cause but rather an attendant circumstance.

We could undoubtedly cite a number of other theories, but those can be refuted in an analogous manner.

There is but one feature that makes us truly unique: we are the bearers and keepers of the Book of Books. This is what sets us apart; therein lies our exceptional nature, and nobody – neither friend nor foe – can encroach on this proud truth.

The one entrusted with bearing and keeping the eternal Book can and must, by virtue of his appointed purpose, be eternal. Besides, thought and metaphysics, as well as corporeal existence according to the spirit of the Book, rule out apostasy and desertion. That is as clear as day.

Thus we have identified the one genuinely unique determining factor, and have seen convincing proof that it actually bears a causal relationship to the phenomenon in question.

In the Book of Books we can find the key to what it is that makes us truly unique. The Book of Books revealed to our ancestors the majesty, wisdom, and beauty of the universe at the time when other peoples lived in total ignorance of even the first principles of knowledge, fully content to blindly worship their stone idols; and also at the time when the false glitter of scientific crafts held absolute sway (as it continues to do to this day) over the dazzled crowd, which saw in these sciences a host of new all-powerful idols ripe for undemanding adoration.

From a young age, each new generation was taught by the Book of Books the noble ideals of justice, the supreme virtues of mercy and kindness toward one's neighbor.

The Book of Books is an inexhaustible source of morality, of the chastity of soul and body. No wonder our ancient predecessors described the Book of Books as radiant with light, a dazzling all-pervading light that eclipses the sun.

Having realized all this, we can briefly summarize the preceding arguments: the true uniqueness of our people stems from its possessing the gift of light and the capacity to experience and appreciate it. Our people journeys through the ages along a brightly lit path. This path has not been trodden by anyone else, and so nobody's past or future history resembles those of our people.

Let us also note that it is the only nation which, throughout its history, never converted to another religion. This is an unparalleled example. Other nations converted to a different faith at least once; more often than not, such conversions were numerous. In the best case, the departure from one faith and the acceptance of another were a gradual process, with the conversion involving separate individuals motivated by experience and deep reflection. Alas, it was more often the case of a cynical, mercenary-minded pastor, impelled by ambition or some other selfish consideration, who would drive the obedient herd of his followers to the feet of a new idol.

Finally, let us consider the phenomenon in question from another angle by posing the following question: is the survival of this people really necessary? Throughout the preceding analysis we have tacitly assumed that a nation's permanence constitutes a virtue. Yet do we really have well-grounded reasons for making such an assumption?

To be sure, many noble and passionate nations will be deeply offended by the very fact of posing such a question. They will probably object by citing, above all, their sense of dignity and honor. But that is a flimsy argument that may be appropriate to a heated face-to-face discussion but not to a dispassionate study, especially at the present time, when pride and dignity are held in a much lower esteem than feasibility.

The adherents of ageless national continuity present the two following reasons meant to bring assimilationists to their senses.

First, they call on them to take a look back; to see how for thousands of years the sacred national banner, borne unblemished and unscathed through the cordons of inquisitors of all ages, countries, and creeds, was passed from generation to generation; and to feel ashamed at the very thought of deserting this incredible relay race, of dropping the banner in the mud, consigning it to oblivion.

This is certainly a very powerful, very impressive image. Yet its impact, though unquestionably enormous, acts on emotions alone and patently lacks any argumentative power. It impresses but does not necessarily convince. To make this clear, suffice it to cite the following retort used by the skeptics: true, hundreds of generations have fought for the safety and purity of this banner, by subjecting themselves to inhuman suffering, sacrifices, deaths. This has certainly become a time-honored tradition. But for the sake of what?

Is it not time to sever at last, and as soon as possible, this endless chain, to put an end to senseless suffering, to leave the stifling circle of the eternally besieged for the wide-open spaces of the world outside, offering carefree pleasure and ease?

Although fundamentally these skeptics are definitely wrong, their objections sound plausible. Traditions must be maintained in the name of something; yet references to ancient past and selfless sacrifice do not give sufficient grounds for these traditions, do not provide justification for further sacrifices.

The other argument, frequently used by the adherents of national survival, does not appeal to emotions at all; on the contrary, it is purely utilitarian, catering to the deserters' sense of self-interest. "Go on, betray, assimilate, change your names," they say to renegades. "Whatever you do, in leaving us you will never be a part of them either. If not you personally, then your children and grandchildren will be reminded of their inferior origins, and their groveling servile souls will be spat upon."

However, after an objective analysis we will be forced to dismiss this argument as well, for it is clear that if the main objective were to escape abuse and persecution, it could be successfully achieved in the fifth, or the tenth, or the umpteenth generation by means of deliberate blending with other nations.

Therefore, however beautiful the sentiments of pride, dignity, respect of traditions, and past ideals may appear, however reasonable the rationalist arguments may seem, we must dismiss all these considerations and state that the sole genuinely compelling rationale for preserving for ages to come the priceless gift of learning and knowledge is that abandoning our mission would be intolerable and impossible. This mission was entrusted to us by a higher power, and it requires us to carry the treasures of the spirit over the oceans of spiritual void, to keep the light burning through the all-pervading darkness, to serve God, acknowledging our devotion to Him and our striving to experience His divine presence.

And perhaps there is wisdom in the belief that, for as long as each generation has at least one man carrying the Book of Books in his soul, the endless thread linking the people with its past will never break, and the people will remain indestructible and eternal.

As to this mission, what can serve as better proof of its reality than the image revealed before our mind's eye, looking back at our people's past history – rows of fires from which, together with smoke and sooo, there issues forth and soars up to heavens the piercing, undying cry:

SHEMA YISRAEL! HEAR, O ISRAEL!

Only having gained a firm grasp of these rationally formulated irrational causes, can we proceed to determine our life's objectives, based on the law of our nation's immortality, a law that remains valid regardless of the conduct and views of separate individuals.

Indeed, all the so-called "laws of nature" are based on experience, on its evaluation and description – that is, on the past, which, in view of its stability and recurrence, is automatically transposed onto the future. It is by following this course that we arrive at the law of our immortality and the conclusions regarding our higher purpose. Whether each given individual lives and acts in accordance with this preordained law depends entirely on his free will.

Century after century, thousands of our people's offspring abandoned their mission, but the nation carried on; thousands were exposed for the faint-hearted turncoats that they are, but the heart of the people remained steadfast and pure; thousands abandoned themselves to vices, but the people remained undaunted and immune to the false dazzle of the alien life. For thousands of years, our people's history was constantly buffeted by these contradictory forces; and even though an entire generation may have given rise to a mere handful of individuals fit to carry the people's banner, its history endured and will continue to do so in ages to come!

11

Our Treasures

L et us now examine the subject of our prayers, rituals, and traditions. Before we do, however, we should naturally mention the language of prayers and sacred books. From the outset, this language was designed to express philosophical concepts, to evaluate and communicate the profound essence of the world. Its words are incredibly poignant and rich with meaning. Other languages were originally intended for everyday use, and only later were they supplemented by a jumble of words and terms, in an attempt to adapt them for vague description of abstract concepts. Their vocabulary was limited, solid, and flat. It could be used for paving the surface of the man-dominated portion of the world, but it can hardly be an appropriate tool for breaking out of the two-dimensional space, for constructing a building with a panoramic view to catch a glimpse of the universe. This requires words filled with spirit, a vast spirit concealed in the modest symbolism of scant words and permeating the magnificent spaces of the world.

Such a word is not merely understood, it is felt by one's entire being, absorbed gradually and ever deeper. An accurate translation from this language is impossible, for no complete equivalent can be found for its words in another language. That would be tantamount to equating an object with its shadow.

The spirit of our prayers is universal, transcending national boundaries. The only individual element they contain is gratitude. The word "I" appears only in expressions of reverence toward the world's splendor, of gratitude for the great gift of perceiving and comprehending the world. The prayer bursts out, flooding the soul in a tidal wave of boundless gratitude.

All the wishes, entreaties, and hopes expressed in prayer represent universal ideals. Prayers guide, prayers educate. Some separate individuals, at the cost of a lifetime of searching, eventually find a philosophy of their own, the joy of a fulfilling and meaningful life. Prayer, on the other hand, brings into the soul of each man—even the most unsophisticated and plain—both philosophy and the joy of living, and does so in a simple, unembellished, and vivid language. Yet that is only the first step, the point of departure, the initial forward thrust toward independent thought and action.

Rituals and injunctions, despite their forbidding numbers, are more than just the "wall around the law," more than a powerful protective tool. To a no-lesser degree, they also constitute a comprehensive hygienic code setting the rules of bodily and spiritual hygiene, the rules of collective national living. Yet their greatest significance probably lies in infusing spirit into the prosaic routine of everyday life.

Suffice us to recall even the simplest blessings pronounced over bread and wine, or fruit. They serve as a means of adding the sublime imperishable joys of spiritual life to the temporary corporeal ones. Eating a succulent fruit is a delightful but short-lived pleasure. The enjoyment of admiring that fruit, though longer-lasting, is probably less strong. To behold and savor that fruit with full awareness of the splendor of the world—that is a pleasure boundless in its depth, power, and duration.

One can simply bask in the sun—or, while basking, experience and absorb the warmth, multiplied thousandfold, of perceiving the ravishing beauty of the world.

Rituals are also necessary for keeping people in a spiritual state befitting the occasion. Simple observation shows that only rare individuals are capable of tuning their attention, at times even in pronounced defiance of the surrounding mood, so as to enter into a certain frame of mind. In such people, disposition and spiritual state are functions of their consciousness. For most people, however, they are largely tied to material factors, their bodily state, and, to a yet larger extent, imitation. All of these elements are exploited by the ritual, which ensures relativr emotional uniformity in individuals of more or less refined sensibility.

Unquestionably, the ritual helps emotional natures as well to absorb the word of God in a more intense and profound fashion, and possibly with a considerably smaller expenditure of spiritual energy (raising, as it were, the efficiency rate of the soul).

Finally, transmitting the ritual intact to future generations is simpler by far than passing on views and ideas, which are easily distorted, adulterated, or lost.

What is more, the ritual is vital to us, if for no other reason, than by virtue of the fact that for millennia it served as a protective wall, a living manifestation of our people's devotion to the Book of Books—that is, our major means[1] of survival. Obviously, anyone who agrees with all this, and yet, citing the difficulties involved in observing the ritual, considers himself no longer bound by it, is, first, a hypocrite, and second, suffering from an excess of self-importance, thinking himself to be above the wisdom of his forefathers.

The simple and mindless act of excretion appears so effortless and natural; whereas the observance of even a fraction of the intricate and formidable ritual practice, literally involving every smallest movement, at first seems an impossible task.

---

1. Here the emphasis is on the word "means," to avoid confusing it with the cause, which has already been discussed.

However, eating and drinking, sex and even sleep, as you well know, quickly lead to surfeit. The body, only recently dissolving in physical rapture, is filled with a sense of dejection and emptiness; not to mention various maladies, aches, and pains—which only increase with age. Meanwhile, ritual practice is a reliable protection against any kind of excess. . . . However, its main value definitely lies elsewhere. The person observing the prescribed ritual, and thereby infusing spirit into his every action, continually partakes of the highest joys, perceiving them not through his stomach or the respective glands but by means of his soul. Every physical pleasure he experiences, even the smallest one, is preceded by the overwhelming joy of perceiving yet again, in yet another manifestation, the full glory of the world, of experiencing once again, with his entire being, the inexpressible gratitude for the privilege of beholding, sensing, perceiving, thinking, admiring. The seeming monotony of movements and repeated words is but a technique of the ritual discipline. In actual fact, the process of development, maturity, even aging is accompanied by an ever-deepening understanding, as the weakening elements of bodily perception are replaced by steadily growing spiritual insights. This undertaking precludes overindulging and satiety.

There is also the issue of those who perform the ritual mechanically, without thinking and without groping for inner meaning. For such people there remains, first of all, the restraining and ennobling function of the ritual. Their and their children's moral integrity is ensured. Second, and most important, they are the durable links, the intermediaries connecting the more profound among their ancestors with their sometimes remote offspring. They transmit from generation to generation their lifestyle, traditions, behavior patterns, humbly carrying precious material into the future, where it will eventually and inevitably go toward shaping the most resplendent and profound individuals. The continuity of these chains is the key to immortality.

And what about the one who breaks the chain? He is too insignificant to undermine the nation's preordained immortality. All he does is voluntarily forfeit the only treasure in his possession. He consigns to perdition and oblivion the hitherto unrevealed germs of future generations he carries within himself.

Suicides have never been the downfall of any nation. They are robbing themselves alone, and if they choose to turn a deaf ear to the moans of their forefathers who had carried their link through fire, let them go, indifferent to the agony of the unborn great-grandchildren. We, the survivors, watch them depart with dry eyes. They are ridiculous and revolting to us.

To think of the mountains of paper expended on enlightening the humankind sunk in the pits of bestiality, on erecting moral ideals, on meandering through the maze of philosophical exploration of the nature of human motives and destiny! All the righteous rage, all the exhortations, all the brilliant mental effort spent in the excruciating search for rules of conduct and interaction.

Meanwhile, a handful of people, through generations, was living a life where the only values recognized as genuine were things pertaining to the spiritual or the inspired; and for each of these people, as long as he did not desert the alliance, it was unthinkable to succumb to depravity, sadism, debauchery, decay—any of the infamous forms of human degeneration.

The sociology of the Book of Books also differs from all sociological theories in that its key element is the eternal human essence, undeviating in its endurance and noble impulses; whereas sociologists, being undeniably rational people themselves, replace man by naïve theories in their works.

Only through ritual, through language can a child attain knowledge and, thereby, preserve it within the bounds of the nation. As I have already said, a child's philosophy is that of childish materialism. A child begins by learning how to act, and only later begins to wonder why. Only by doing everything differently from the children of other nations would he be able to eventually find some positive way of applying his mind to the nature of this difference. Otherwise, by functioning in the material sphere of life shared by the surrounding environment, he will never reach this mode of thinking; it should then be considered a blessing if the outside world reminds him of his being unlike everyone else (in the sense of being inferior, of course), and thus cause him to be aware of his difference in a negative fashion.

Let us note that, by educating the child in the spirit of ritual observance, we can be reasonably assured, perhaps even certain, of guaranteeing his moral integrity, and purity of soul and body.

At this point it would be appropriate to take up once more the subject of our sacred books, and the interpretation of the historical material contained therein.

Without entering into a detailed discussion of this topic, suffice it to point out that the notorious "biblical criticism" has lost, in the light of the latest archaeological finds and discoveries, the last remnants of firm ground. This must be admitted even by contemporary atheists, provided that they adhere to logic and facts. Having failed in "biblical criticism," the zealous materialist rhetoricians regrouped to focus their attack on the cosmogony depicted in the Book of Books. Let us examine, however, the main points of this attack. As an example, it is sufficient to cite one of the most conclusive (in the author's view) arguments: how can you talk about the things made on the first days of creation, when at that time there was not even a sun to count the days by. This type of reasoning may sound convincing to all those who imagine God as a bearded old man without a watch, telling time by the sun and fashioning man out of clay the way a potter makes his pots.

As to cosmogony itself, the picture is as follows. Contemporary scientific craft is known to hold a number of hypotheses (hypotheses, and nothing more!)

concerning the origins of the solar system. According to some of them, the solar system originated from a nebula, from the primordial chaos reigning therein. This description bears a formal similarity to the account given in the Book of Books. However, the scientific crafts, as we have seen earlier, do not make any attempt to get to the bottom of things, to reveal the innermost core. Indeed, any cosmogonic hypothesis, even if it became a proven theory explaining the mechanism behind the origins of the solar system, would only put off the mystery, since there would immediately arise the problem of the origins of the galaxy, and so on, down to the ultimate question of the origins of the universe. And this last question cannot be answered, now or ever, by any scientific craft. The Book of Books, however, does just that!

Can any natural scientist be conceited enough to assert that man, in some future time, however remote from ours, will paint a description of the origins of the world more perfect than the one contained in the Book of Books?

A similar approach could be applied to the account of the genealogy of our people.

There still remains the issue of the recorded events that were incredibly propitious for our people, events that are referred to as miracles. To be sure, we have no rational methods for certifying their authenticity. However, in this respect we can point out the following: when each spring a seed gives birth to a plant that carries all the generic features of its species; when the buds dotting apparently lifeless branches sprout beautiful leaves bursting with life, this comes as no surprise or shock to anyone, with everyone nonchalantly muttering, "The law of nature." Yet when they are told about certain somewhat unusual events from the life of our nation, a nation which even its sworn enemies have always acknowledged to be different from all others, above all by virtue if its endurance and indestructible nature, those same people react with a disdainful wave of their hand and the skeptical "I can't believe it!"

Thus it would appear that a frequently recurring miracle, such as a green leaf, is admissible, while a rare event from our people's history is inadmissible precisely because of its rarity and the fact that it was not witnessed by today's observers. A logic that is strange, to say the least! And what do we do with the very fact of our people's continuous survival, an equally unexplainable phenomena unique to our nation? Do we dismiss it as impossible? In fact, that is precisely what people occasionally attempt to do.

However, we have been distracted by particulars, whereas what is important in the Book of Books is not the facts, which basically serve as illustrations alone; and not the apparent contradiction in these facts, if such can be found; but the cohesive unity and consistency of philosophical ideas, and above all the idea of the omnipresent Supreme Being. These ideas are extremely complex constructs rendered in a language accessible to common humanity.

12

Our Future

We do not seek to set ourselves apart from or above all other nations. It is none of our concern to know on which rung of the ladder we are placed by others, for we ourselves do not strive to occupy any particular spot on this vertical ladder. Nevertheless, we are firmly aware of our mission, our calling; we recognize and embrace our destiny with the full knowledge that it is this destiny that makes us indestructible; without it we are mere dust.

With joy and gratitude we embrace our wonderful fate, and we are in no way compelled to measure it against the fate of others. We are immensely proud of having received this gift, and fully cognizant of the extent of our obligations. We know that unwavering devotion to our predestined path is the guarantee of our permanence. At the same time, we also realize that permanence is our primary duty, the necessary condition for carrying out our mission. We have no need to parade our qualities, our innate virtues. Whatever characteristics we possess were created with the express purpose of serving our mission. The more we consciously develop these positive qualities in ourselves, suppressing negative temptations, the more we succeed in creating a harmonious fusion between our lifestyle and our mission, the happier will our existence be.

Our ancient history supplies us with countless examples of the magnitude and variety of evils caused by the unbridled impulse of investing in a way of life alien to our preordained fate, by the temptation to savor the benefits of this life, to follow it along a path leading us away from our road, our goal, our destiny.

We know nothing of the destiny of nations that surround us. That is their concern, not ours. All we are ready to do is meet respect with respect, friendship with friendship.

Just as in the life of an individual the satisfaction of physical needs is but a means to spiritual creativity, the same should hold true for the life of a state. The exclusive pursuit of a prosperous state system as an end in itself is quite similar to an individual's single-minded preoccupation with the smooth functioning of his body, something that arouses repugnance in the majority of people who consider themselves civilized. Yet the overriding concern with a prosperous state system is somehow viewed as the summit of noble aspiration, and for the most part does not touch off any warning bells. We must realize that our people will apparently never create a powerful state apparatus, while the most powerful spiritual force has been its birthright since time immemorial, and will be to the end of time.

Just as all through the ages each physical, bodily function, every common-place act was refined, elevated to a higher order of thought, revelation, awe at the splendor and wisdom of the world, with sensory satisfaction relegated to a secondary plane—so it should be in regard to the state. After all, we are the people of the Book.

We crave warmth and comfort. We crave tranquillity. We crave pleasure and entertainment. We crave wealth. We crave physical beauty and strength. Yet if the prerequisite to gaining all these benefits is "free thinking," then we would rather starve in the everyday sense of the word. No price is too great for forging an inseparable link between our soul and the Book of Books.

Let shabby rags be worn over a flourishing soul filled with faith and searching. Let features furrowed by suffering conceal a vital memory and indomitable will. If such an alternative indeed exists, we prefer to store our power not in bulging muscles but in souls filled with virtue, moral purity, wisdom, veneration, and total commitment.

13

Boundless Gratitude

The world into which we have all been born is a magnificent place. It overflows with soft and exciting colors, enticing scents, caressing sounds. Sweet are the fragrances of fruit floating from forests and orchards, heady the juice of ripening berries, inviting and unspoiled the carpet of grasses and flowers.

Solicitous and tireless is the sun that nurses all life—golden and languid at noon; smiling and twinkling through the morning dew; dreamy, a little pensive in the evening, as it slides over the green face of the earth, drawing nectar from flowers and emerald glitter from leaves.

Cool, sprightly, and balmy are the fluttering breezes; lovely and crystal-pure the sparkling springs.

Love and birth in the radiant world.

Washed by rain, roused by the generous sun, swooning under nature's lavish caresses, the earth brims over in luxuriant growth. Buzzing from flower to flower, the bee carries the miracle of a new life hidden in yellow pollen. The sounds of wooing birds fill the air. Fearless is the female watching over her cubs in the forest lair. It is a glorious world, breathtaking, awe-inspiring. Infinite is the wisdom of the Almighty. The feeling of gratitude for the privilege of witnessing this consummate beauty, for the joy of life and knowledge, floods the soul, pouring out in ecstatic prayer.

The youthful clamor of frenzied, impassioned spring is followed by fertile summer, replaced in turn by tranquil, dreamy autumn. The grass, the trees have completed their yearly labor and now have the time to enjoy a leisurely rest in the lingering rays of the sun before succumbing to the winter's slumber. Equally happy is the man who feels like the grass and the trees in the autumn of his life. Truly wretched is the one who has walked his road oblivious to life's real joys, blind to the divine splendor and harmony of the world, untouched by God.

Of all the pleasures granted to man, the greatest, the most lasting and exalted is the joy of inspiration. Borne by thought, it gives birth to thought and action. Animals, insects, plants rejoice in savoring nature's gifts, elated by the thrill of feeling themselves a part of it. Now man, who too has access to the same elation and delight, is also heir to an immeasurably more precious gift, the capacity to perceive the sublime majesty and higher purpose reigning in the world. He carries the potential for filling his soul to overflowing with the feeling of gratitude for this gift, for pursuing and passing on to his son the thirst for deeper, fuller knowledge, for striving to dedicate his life to this noble quest. Prayer is kindled in his soul. This awareness, this gratitude, this thirst, this striving, this prayer—these are the things that lie at the root of inspiration. The worldly routine, the human ties acquire meaning and grace when the person is moved by inspiration. Therein lies the seed of all seeds, the flavor of all flavors, the joy of all joys.

III

Fragments

III

Fragments

T he question is, how shall we use our soul's gift of awareness: to master and elevate to the spiritual plane our bodily appetites—or to indulge in hedonistic abandon? In the former case, humans are definitely superior to animals; in the latter, it would be unfair and insulting to the animal to be compared to this semblance of a human.

The greatest mistake made by the Tolstoyans and others like them is that they tried to force man to renounce the body altogether in favor of the soul. Such an act is impossible, since it contradicts human nature. Yet to elevate and redeem cravings of the flesh, to infuse spirit into each bodily function—that is entirely within man's powers. That is the lesson to be learned from the millennia-old history of our people. Herein lies the height of spirituality available to the ordinary person.

Curiously, after all the hue and cry about science "refuting" religion, today all sciences lead in the straightest possible line to the rudimentary truths of religious metaphysics.

What makes the scientific craft more dangerous and harmful than handicraft is the demand it makes on its devotees to sacrifice their spiritual energy, spiritual potential, making it impossible to exercise properly these invaluable, God-given powers. A reaper in the field breathing in the scents of ripening wheat is a thousand times more capable of genuine thought than the "learned" craftsman wasted by formulae and poisoned by the tainted laboratory fumes.

For thousands of years, all that has changed in the life of the human herd are the external trappings. Remaining immutable are all the basic essentials of man's corporeal existence: eating, sleep, the struggle for daily bread, sexual intercourse. Nor has there been the slightest change in the passions and urges driving and inciting this herd. Envy, greed, ambition remained unchanged. All that these changes apparently amount to is steadily growing hypocrisy and declining virtue.

Contemporary man is most susceptible and accustomed to the language of rules, habits, and conventions of social existence. Words in praise of God's greatness are absent from this language.

The scientific craftsman, crowing over the greatness of his achievements, is totally incapable of prostrating himself before the exalted wisdom of the Creator, the Maker of the very world of which this "man of learning" has managed to discern a tiny speck.

Everyone agrees that the entire complex system of our rituals was vitally important in the past — hundreds and thousands of years ago — and that without it we would have long disappeared. And then comes the arrogant "Yes, but now, in this day and age, this is clearly absurd!" What a bunch of puffed-up, conceited swell-heads, so smug in your ridiculous belief that the people who preceded you by a few generations were more stupid than yourselves!

You say: "It's silly always to wear a hat. For the life of me, I can't understand why this is practised and what it's supposed to do." What it does is perpetuate our existence. One look at the past would provide sufficient proof.

As to whether this is silly or not, I will answer you with a question: "Perhaps it may seem silly to you to stuff your belly with all sorts of rubbish a few times a day (and shamelessly too, in front of everyone!)? Or to become a comatose sleeping log for seven or eight hours daily?" And yet you somehow you seem to treat these functions very seriously, because they too are necessary for prolonged existence, and that on an individual, not collective plane. I guess you are still unqualified to judge what is silly and what is wise. After all, you know nothing about yourself, or about the world in which you live, or about your own people.

You do not ask why you eat, drink, or sleep. Such a question seems ridiculous to you: any child knows why—to live. On the other hand, the functions I have just mentioned cause immediate pleasure, and for that reason are probably not quite relevant to the following reasoning.

Still, let us take work. Often it is not only not pleasing but plain painful, and yet the majority of humans accept it as absolutely vital. To live, to survive!

Or let us look at the rearing and education of children—an aggravating and not infrequently thankless task. Once again, this is done in order to maintain life, to survive, but this time in a somewhat broader, generic sense. Or take the dozens of burdensome social and civic duties performed to ensure the survival of society or state. The honoring and meticulous performance of these duties is considered to be among the highest virtues; and only when it comes to the 613 commandments do you suddenly begin to doubt and question: why, whatever for? For the very same reason, of course! In order for our people to survive, to go on living!

True, these duties are somewhat different from the ones discussed before. The consequences of neglecting food or sleep are quickly felt and pertain primarily to the bodily aspect of human existence. Nonobservance of the commandments, however, may take its toll in a number of generations, and mainly endangers the spirit. Hence the Jew feels himself free to act, free to choose between observing or neglecting the commandments.

Either deep thought or refined intuition are required in order to comprehend the need for the 613 commandments. When neither is present, the situation can only be saved by habit, upbringing, tradition. However, when even this factor is absent, it will be a matter of generations before the given chain of individuals ceases to exist as part of a nation.

You think that all those old men go through mechanical motions, that they are incapable of comprehending the philosophical underpinnings of the acts. But has it ever occurred to you that they simply keep silent about this because for them it is all self-evident; that all the answers you reach by slow and tortuous reflection, are for them as obvious and clear-cut as the basics of life?

Try to prod one of those of old fogies, encourage him to speak out on philosophical matters. Hearing him talk, you are sure to suspect him of having read through all the ancient and modern "foremost authorities" on the subject. Well, that is definitely not the case. What happens is that the "foremost authorities," upon discovering some tiny sliver of truth, are so astonished that they begin to consider themselves incredibly wise, important, and superior, and so they write their weighty volumes as a towering monument to their stupendous achievements. In this they are very much like a rooster breaking into wild cackling over a grain found in a garbage heap. Our old men, however, know the essential, fundamental truth; yet they also know that they are only human, ordinary people, even though blessed with knowledge.

––––––––––––

One of the crucial tasks at hand is to prove that in two thousand years people have not only failed to become more perfect but, on the contrary, have largely lost their former breadth of mind, their power, their thirst for transcendental knowledge. We should begin precisely by exposing the abomination of opinionated conceit, of people's self-complacent belief, instilled in childhood, in their impeccability, in the superiority of the "twentieth century" over all the preceding ones, in the omnipotence of science and technology, praised to the skies throughout the world by books, newspapers, and electronic media.

We must realize what a pitiful state the modern man is in, isolated from God by countless self-imposed barriers of objects, notions, theories. Dazzled by these graven images of his making, he kneels before them, exactly like a savage fascinated by the idol he has carved out of wood. However, to give the savage his due, he at least does not lose the sense of his insignificance. Not so the latter-day pagan, who admires not so much his idol as its maker—that is, himself. There lies the end result of this ultramodern religion, if I may use the term.

Self-worship, self-adoration—that is the order of the day! As a result, even the brightest minds—disastrously scarce nowadays—who are cognizant of the eternal restlessness of man in the quest for ultimate reality; who search for the source and destiny of objects and living creatures; who are choked by tears of gratitude and adoration in their awareness of the world's wisdom and harmony; even they have been poisoned by this "auto-religion" to such an extent that they are too hesitant, too embarrassed to address God directly, opting instead to veil their true feelings and thoughts coquettishly in vague speculations regarding "nature."

This "auto-religion" is polytheistic, teeming with idols of all sizes and shapes: man himself and various products formed by his hands and soul, including the terminological fetishes that exert such a potent influence on the imagination of the modern pagan. High-sounding terms inflame the idol-worshiper. Terms also have an immediately soothing effect on him, without explaining anything. The more flowery and incomprehensible the term, the more unfailing its impact. For instance, the well-known facts of thought transference cause certain misgivings in our pagan's mind, shaking his cozy and serene brand of religious faith.

Yet the moment he lays his hands on a popular brochure bearing the scientific title "Telepathy," he immediately regains his peace of mind.

Similarly, the problem of the gender and nature of a future child appears simple and easily solved as soon as the field is taken over by dazzling terms like chromosomes, genes, data transfer, genetic code, DNA, and so on. And no one seems to be bothered by the fact that none of the basic questions such as "why?" or "how?" has been answered. Is it so difficult to understand that, from the gnoseological point of view, there is absolutely no difference between saying "it's a girl" and "it's a girl because the ovule linked up with a spermatozoon bearing a female genetic combination"? Moreover, from the cognitive view-point, the latter statement is less informative; for while the former case allows the question "why is it a girl?" the latter permits at least the following three questions:

1. Why did the ovule link up with this particular spermatozoon?
2. What are an ovule and a spermatozoon?
3. Why does the joining of this particular type of spermatozoon and the ovule result in the birth of a girl?

A similar analytical procedure could be applied to any cosmogonic theory. Once again, the statement, "the earth came into existence," is preferable to "as a result of the condensation of nebulous particles which were initially in a state of turbulent movement, the planets came into existence." However, in the latter case the savage receives a generous dose of intoxicating scientific cant, and that makes him calm, proud, and satisfied with himself.

The word "nature" now—there is another term, formally incorporated into the language of the modern pagan. Its use is considered legitimate. Yet a direct and sincere reference to God triggers hysterical howling. No wonder—for this immediately undoes the cozy tenets of "auto-religion"; worse yet, this gives rise to the notions of moral duty, human obligations, and various injunctions. And that is totally unacceptable to the adherent of "auto-religion," to whom everything is permitted, since "all things are in man, all things are for man."

If only punishment and reward were the inexorable, immediate, and unequivocal consequence of sin or virtue respectively, then people would naturally behave in an ideal fashion. Indeed, a potential criminal would refrain from committing a crime if certain of inevitable and swift retribution. Yet in such a case human beings would be no different from animals. What makes humans human is their having freedom of choice. On the other hand, punishment is still inevitable, but this inevitability is veiled by time, the passing of generations, and so on. The same holds true for recompense. This point is amply illustrated by numerous examples from our history.

Materialistic excess and philosophizing lead to the dismissal of human nature, of its eternal desires, passions, and aspirations. From the example of the corrupt modern world, we can see the consequences of ignoring those things and relying exclusively on materialistic reasoning.

Significantly, the further some modern individual is removed from science, the more assertive he is in his claim that, given the latest scientific achievements, it is no longer possible to maintain the beliefs held by people two thousand years ago.

Science's gravest error has been to replace the pursuit of knowledge by the search for chains of deterministic causality.

All faiths had emotion as their primary source. The worship of the idols of science is the first faith founded entirely on lassitude, and apathy, and requiring absolutely no spiritual effort from man.

To realize and accept the helplessness of science where true knowledge is concerned, and then to break with materialism—that is the first step toward religion, yet probably the easiest one. Further progress is liable to prove more difficult. For instance, what a Herculean effort it takes to overcome the skeptical scorn, instilled by upbringing and education, toward the time-honored sacrificial rites, and to realize the true worth and significance of this practice. It takes a great deal of determination and self-discipline for the soul to become a harmonious whole.

A typical representative of the gray mass constituting today's majority, when faced with any form of religious expression, gives a puzzled shrug and says: "How can we tolerate this in the twentieth century?" Yet ask him point-blank: "What do you know that makes you different from a person living two thousand years ago?" Incoherent mumbling is all you will hear in reply.

The fact is, what impresses this sorry excuse of a spokesman for the twentieth century has nothing whatsoever to do with the contents of what is known as science: he worships the covers of books he has never read, the conventional authority of newspapers and popular-science magazines, the loud names of academies and universities, academic titles and degrees. . . . And furthermore, belief in these idols is so comfortable, so uniquely suited to the ingrained sloth of his submissive spirit!

The so-called "biblical criticism" bears a strong resemblance to the Chinese trial. Both of them use the presumption of guilt as their starting point. Every "critic" begins by assuming that the Bible is a legend. Having mounted his high horse of conceit, he begins to select and shuffle facts, historical records, archaeological finds, interpreting them so as to fit a preconceived atheistic mold. He concludes his sleight of hand by making an overt or tacit reference to the authority of contemporary science, which "has ruled out any possibility of supernatural phenomena."

Why not turn this whole issue right side up by admitting the existence of a coherent and harmonious view of the world and endeavoring to comprehend the surrounding world and human history in the light of this view?

A conscientious researcher, instead of trying to explain religion through science, as Christianity attempts to do, should, on the contrary, examine the output of science through the prism of religion. Religion does not have to be "saved" – it is quite secure. It is science that needs saving – and that can be done by its being assigned its true role and value within the range of human activities. Then it will be recognized for what it is: a craft; no matter how complex, or even useful, it is still only a craft among other crafts. Even the consummate expert in the art of shoemaking would never go as far as to try to explain the world by means of his craft. The scientific craft, alas, presumes to do just that.

The recent years of scientific development provide excellent material for understanding the true role and value of science.

About a hundred years ago, science appeared to be on sure ground; everything was safe and sound, with determinism holding absolute power. During that serene age of unqualified scientific supremacy, which spanned the time from Newton to Maxwell, it seemed that everything could be explained and even predicted. Then this balmy period came to an end. The neat and tidy edifice, from whose top the adherents of science shouted their defiance at God Himself, began to crumble and collapse. Determinism gave place to uncertainty, to statistical means of describing natural phenomena. The ossified theories of Galileo and Newton were replaced by the deformed notions of Einstein, Heisenberg, Bohr. . . . However, the problem lies not so much in the complexity and flexibility of new theoretical concepts as in the unstable nature of theories and concepts themselves, varying and replacing one another at a dazzling pace, inevitably thwarted by limitations and inconsistencies.

Take, for instance, the series of cosmogonic theories, bursting like soap bubbles. A telling example is the belated acknowledgment of the finite nature of the world, of the necessity for a prime mover, and so on. Also deserving of note is the path of biological science, the theory of evolution, genetics. Experimental research, applying ultramodern technology, repudiated the idea of intelligent life existing on Mars. Also ruled out was the possibility of life on Venus. In science magazines, inveterate materialists argue the issue of terrestrial intelligence being the only one in the universe. Experiments in telepathy are being analyzed. Archaeological and paleontological discoveries demolish, one after another, the theories concocted by arrogant and self-serving archaeologists and paleontologists. Occasionally, what seems at first like a modest and insignificant result may make such a gap in atheistic fortifications that they can never be patched up again. What could be recalled in this connection is the report on the possibility of synthesizing oil in the bowels of the earth. This, when the theory of oil originating from the remains of ancient sea organisms constitutes one of the key links in the general paleontological theory. This naturally begs the question: could it be that other "irrefutable" paleontological truths are equally "binding"; in which case, would it not be advisable to synchronize the time intervals in world genealogy with the Torah?

Possibly, the two primary issues of Jewish philosophy are the creation of matter out of absolute void and the coexistence of the freedom of choice and predestination.

Undoubtedly, it is very difficult for a man of science to come to the realization that the study of such phenomena as human interaction, the interconnection between the divine soul and the animal soul within man, the influence of humans on one another, the impact of parents on their child, the link between man and God, life, creation *ex nihilo,* and man's higher purpose can be conducted in an integral fashion only, without bothering with trivia, with scrupulous attention to petty details so common to scientific crafts. This type of studies is not only most important to mankind but also the most complex. The man of science, however, views them as primitive, blinded as he is by equations, symbols, terms, diagrams, and sophisticated technology.

"I don't want my son to marry a non-Jewish girl! That would be terrible!"

"In that case, why don't you think it also terrible that he eats nonkosher food and desecrates *Shabbat?*"

"That's a different matter. Those things are impossible to observe in this day and age, and they're pointless anyway."

"Well then, to continue your train of thought, it may so happen that tomorrow it will be pointless to prevent your son from doing what he intends to do. And by the way, why exactly don't you want him to marry a gentile?"

"Why, I want him to be a Jew!"

"Forgive my saying so, but he is not a Jew already. It is now Shabbat eve, and your son, if I am not mistaken, has gone with his friends and girlfriends to a restaurant. What exactly do you mean when you say 'a Jew' "?

"?!?"

"The trouble is, you should have thought about this before."

"It makes me laugh to look at you—the way you are praying, rocking! How can anyone do this today, in the age of interplanetary travel?"

"And it makes me laugh to look at you—the way you sit there and admire yourself. The only difference is, I have hundreds of generations of our shared ancestors on my side. You, however, can only depend on your contemporaries, who have turned the world into a kingdom of violence, bloodshed, and sin."

Today it has become quite fashionable to search for relevance and meaning in God-given commandments from the rationalistic positions. This approach is used in the fields of hygiene, medicine, sociology, and so on. In this fashion, the idea is gradually introduced of the commandments being a product of human mind and experience and not imposed from on high. Certainly, none of the commandments is inconsistent with medical and hygienic considerations, with the conditions required to maintain a healthy society and the mental stability of its individual members. Moreover, the commandments take into account the abilities and needs of the average human, accommodating his every physical and spiritual function. At the same time, the ultimate meaning and the ultimate purpose of the commandments are transcendental. Absolute rationality as defined by human reasoning pertains exclusively to products of human mind. The commandments, however, serve to fulfill the divine decree; hence, they will always contain an enigmatic element surpassing human understanding—the transcendental aspect.

The process of illumination to be followed by a man of science, a man with a modern view of the world, may be outlined as follows:

1. Recognition of the fact that science deals merely with interconnections between phenomena, whereas it is powerless before the infinite.
2. Realization of the greatness and wisdom of the Creator, the maker of the harmonious universe and the preserver of its continuous existence.
3. Veneration of the Creator.
4. Acceptance of the Torah as the vessel of all that gives purpose, justification, and meaning to existence.
5. The deepest and most joyful knowledge of all—simple faith.

He is merely a link in the chain. Hence he should feel responsible for his link, and realize that the meaning of his life lies in keeping the chain intact.

The chain leads to ultimate bliss. Disjointed links are swallowed up by the whirlpool of suffering. The single seed reaches the future along the unbroken length of the infinite chain. For this seed to preserve its life-giving power, only one thing is needed: the safety of the chain. In spite of all the odds, in spite of the temptations, in spite of the unbearable suffering.

The search for God is common to all people, regardless of time and place. Only the abject worm, grown fat in self-satisfied complacency, is deprived of this gift. Thirsting and not knowing how to slake their thirst, the majority of humans invariably resorted to primitive comforting fetishes of their own making. Christ was one of those fetishes.

To venture conjectures regarding the motives for creating the living world and man would be wrong and unfeasible for numerous reasons. To begin with, even to formulate the question of motives already presupposes some degree of personification and attribution of human qualities to the divine. Moreover, to claim understanding of these motives would mean putting oneself on the same footing with the Creator. We can discuss phenomena and natural laws, and classify them. But motives—that is altogether outside our sphere of competence.

All of humanity's zealous scientific exertions are no more than classification techniques. We are skilled in isolating and grouping objects and phenomena in conformity with shared human perception of their qualities. Usually each of these groups (belonging to the numerous groups within the classification system) is based on one of the primary, indissoluble essences, hopelessly beyond the grasp of human knowledge. Next, through more or less complicated reasoning, objects and phenomena are found that our mind perceives as similar, in one way or another, to the given ultimate essence. As the sequence unfolds, the reasoning process grows increasingly intricate and sophisticated, as a specific analytical apparatus takes form. This is the way any specialized branch of science is born and shaped.

Previously we have shown how clear-headed reasoning can help us descend from the dizzy heights of science to the bare essence. That was analysis of science. Now we can see its synthetic manufacture. We can see the most common tool of this synthesis—the device of classification.

This device could indeed prove quite useful where utilitarian benefits are concerned. By determining the similarities and differences between phenomena, it points out ways of utilizing them. Yet who would dare assert that putting reality in neat pigeonholes is the way to enlightenment, that the most extensive inventory or catalogue can be equated with genuine knowledge?

It would be quite interesting to trace and compare the benefits conferred on humanity by:

1. the discovery of fire—and the discovery of atomic energy;
2. the invention of writing—and the invention of computers.

Anyone still unconvinced that humanity has been on a downward course of decline must himself have declined to an extent where he has lost the ability to see the obvious.

Reasoning alone is unlikely to prove that abstinence is superior to indulgence. This may be felt, intuitively known, but admittedly cannot be demonstrated by philosophical argument. However, it appears that this could be easily achieved by empirical means; what is more, by using the evidence of the senses—that is, the language understood the best by adherents of sensual gratification. Indeed, any pleasure of the flesh culminates either in satisfaction or in pain (for example, as a consequence of overeating, sexual excesses, or drunkenness).

Let us consider the best outcome—satisfaction. First of all, this state is short-lived; furthermore, and that is the main point, it immediately begins to make forceful and ever-increasing demands for more. Hence, in neither of the possible instances do bodily pleasures bring appeasement. This is an empirical fact, requiring no proof.

Now let us consider the case of a man who abstains from excess, and not for the sake of abstinence but rather in the name of some ideal which he views as superior and worthy of attainment. Let us say that it is someone who observes *Shabbat* in spite and in defiance of all the hostile external circumstances. In order to achieve his ideal, he may be forced not only to relinquish potential pleasures but to make literal physical sacrifices: to brave the cold and foul weather while walking long distances, to abstain from hot food, and so on; and occasionally, when worse comes to worst, to risk his well-being and even life. And yet each minute lived through in this manner carries within itself a most profound sense of satisfaction with duty fulfilled, with the hard-won victory over oneself and the external world. The enjoyment this person experiences at such a moment does not clamor to be repeated, does not awaken thirst for more and stronger pleasures, for it restores harmony once and for all. This pleasure is always complete and fulfilled, in contrast to gratification of bodily cravings, ever longed for, never satisfied because of their illusory nature.

The entire history of this people is the field of an ongoing battle between the spirit (duty) and the body (temptation). Generation after generation, the body gains triumphant victories, and yet in some mysterious way the mission of the spirit reaches the next generation, kindling the minds of its best, though precious few, representatives.

All right, fine, so you don't believe in this. But there must be something you believe in—unless you have a hole in place of a soul! What do you believe in, then?

In spite of everything, the inherited ideas still manage to survive through millennia, preserved by the commandments: the concepts of compassion, generosity, virtue, duty, and so on.

How long can this momentum last without reinforcement? And what will happen next?

Why is everyone so convinced of the necessity for the survival and continuation of humankind? For the sake of what? For the sake of immortal blind matter? Yet there is a quite humane and painless way to put an end to mankind through birth prevention! The fact that this is not being done, not advocated by even the most "enlightened" contemporaries, definitely testifies to the existence of a latent religious sentiment.

If, after all, we were to look for the physiological basis of our people's "uniqueness," natural talent, and vitality, the primary focus would be on the laws of cleanliness, specifically those concerned with sexual relations and food. Indeed, limiting conception to particular times and practicing abstention during certain periods cannot help affecting the fetus directly, and indirectly through influencing the vital functions of the woman's body as a whole. In any case, the highly esteemed natural sciences in their modern guise are absolutely powerless to refute this hypothesis. Humanity's entire activity is geared, directly or indirectly, toward procuring food. Any sincere person will admit that nourishment, food, is man's most valuable asset—with only children as the possible exception, and even then probably not for most people. Once this fact has been acknowledged, we can immediately see the self-evident logic and profound moral significance behind the ritual of offering cattle, grain, and wine in sacrifice. Our contemporary, however, steeped as he is in self-delusion and hypocrisy, accustomed to using the language of terminological labels, no longer able to think in plain, natural terms, will never understand and accept this simple truth.

It is hard to get even an approximate idea of the extent to which man's soul has been eroded by a century and a half of education in the spirit of "free thought" and the worship of science with all its technical jargon and formulae. Religion is inaccessible to him precisely by virtue of being simple and straightforward, untranslatable into the "scientific" language he understands. What will be required is a totally isolated generation of some sort, so as to regain the lost innocence and mental clarity.

"How can you bear spending eight hours at the synagogue on Rosh Hashana?"

"And how can you bear spending eight hours at work every day, earning a living of some sort? I, at least, gain peace of mind and inner calm, and not just for one day—not to mention the fact that I am simply satisfying the need to express my appreciation for the joy of living and the beauty and harmony of the universe."

"Why do I need all that trouble and hustle about kosher meat, when I can get perfectly good meat at the store for a ruble eighty?"

"You tell me, then, why this daily bother, when your grandfathers themselves could have done away with it once and for all?"

"You consider the unique destiny of our people to be a result of haphazard coincidence, on the one hand, and the survival of our nation as the supreme objective, on the other. At the same time you attach the highest value to our people's worldly prosperity. How are these to be reconciled? Why pay the price of incredible privation and hardship (that is, sacrifice one of your main ideals) in order to preserve at all cost the result of a coincidence?"

"You claim that you are raising your child on emotions and culture. How will you do it, how many times a day? How will you decide what is more important: routine activity or an edifying lecture? What lessons are you teaching him today, right now? Whereas I know exactly what, when, for how long, with a particular lesson prescribed for every day of the year!

"A child learns above all from routine, daily activities—and those are the very things that should be imbued with spirit!"

"The main driving force and guarantee of endurance is discipline. What would happen to discipline if everyone began to discard the commandments at will?"

"What reasons do you have to consider yourself more advanced, intelligent, and wise than your ancestors?" Here is where we arrive at the necessity of admitting the boundless conceit of our contemporaries, their blind worship of the idol of science. Yet is not the reign of Hitler the best proof that the people who could allow this abomination to take place are more animal-like, more preoccupied with gratifying their gluttony and lust than ever before?!

Another vivid illustration: to draw a parallel between a modern "philosopher" and any ancient thinker; moreover, we should begin such a comparison not from the scientific but from the moral aspect, that of simple integrity and honesty.

The impossibility of finding a rational explanation for most of the commandments, their transcendent nature stems from their Divine origin.

A man bogged down in the life of the flesh is incapable of understanding and experiencing to the full the supreme joy of existence and the bliss of the righteous.

A task of overriding importance is to thoroughly discredit the folly inherent in the self-importance of modern people, to expose the glaring absurdity of the popular sentiment: "Given the latest advances in science, culture, civilization, all of this looks like barbaric mumbo jumbo."

Illumination may begin at a certain stage of mastering scientific crafts, but that is where the positive role of science comes to an end. The success of further progress hinges on the ability to reject the sciences as a path to knowledge, to cast aside not only their contents but their methods as well. It is highly dangerous to attempt to combine faith with science, to expect the scientific crafts to verify religious insights, and worst of all, to apply the reasoning and argumentative techniques derived from science to transcendent knowledge. One must realize not only the paucity of these sciences' cognitive content, but also the naïveté of their seemingly brilliant systems, proofs, elaborate chains of terms and categories, when contrasted with the genuine brilliance of apparently simple yet infinitely profound and all-embracing truths and laws to be found in religion. One must realize that the problem of God and man is immeasurably broader and deeper than, for example, quantum mechanics.

The Pentateuch contains relatively little specific, detailed information that constitutes the object of scientific scrutiny. Yet what is significant is that none of that information, after thousands of years, has become incompatible with scientific facts of the sort that is subject to immediate, palpable, and unequivocal verification.

The world rests on the bedrock of immutable laws that are permanently maintained by God, and are only altered on the rare occasions when the fate of the people hangs in the balance. It is such instances that are commonly known as miracles.

Hellenism is the cult of the body, of the carnal instincts. All of literature is in effect nothing but licentious wallowing in sensual promiscuity elevated to the pedestal of art by self-admiring authors intoxicated with their ability to produce well-turned phrases.

"A rabbi was wrapped in a Torah and burnt alive, while a scoundrel survived. Where is justice?"

"Yet it could be that one single day lived by the former was fuller and more beautiful by far than a hundred years lived by the latter. The rabbi's soul dwelt in the highest and purest spheres, bathing in heavenly delight, while the scoundrel spent his entire life in frantic searching, constantly frustrated by his failure to achieve anything, to enjoy anything."

Why get entangled in the meshes of causality? All the voluminous works put together will still not yield one drop of knowledge. How can analysis of the physical structure of wood, examination of its chemical composition and biological aspects possibly bring about that awe-inspiring, breathtaking rapture of looking at a grove of silver birches? How can the ability to classify stars into groups, and the knowledge of their types and distinguishing features, ever replace direct perception of the starry sky, purified by thoughts of its Creator?

The greatest error of modern man engaged in scientific pursuits, an error that calls for pity rather than scorn, is that by perceiving the world through the distorting lens of school-inculcated sophistry, through the mesh of formal definitions and classifications, man irretrievably loses the awareness of the true value and meaning of things, even though he still preserves lingering traces of that value and meaning. Thus, for example, the moon is associated in his mind with a textbook diagram that depicts a globe of certain dimensions situated at a certain distance from earth. The flights to the moon finally removed any vestiges of mystique it still retained, as newspapers declared it to be a rocky, barren waste. A sufficiently educated person may recall the chemical composition, the so-called fossil age, the intensity of the magnetic field, and so on. Yet does this in any way reflect man's fascination with the moon? Can all these figures and formulae have any possible relevance to the enchantment flooding the soul on a moonlit summer night? And are not various physiological functions directly affected by the lunar cycles?

Can the solar science, with its hundreds of insipid books and research papers, ever match a single delightful moment of what is known as "basking in the sun"? Can knowing the chemical composition of water or the fact that it is a structurized liquid ever quench a thirst? The world was created for man; it shapes his state of mind and regulates his physical functions—and therein lies the purpose of all animate and inanimate nature, whatever its composition and inner structure.

The crucial goal is to ensure—whatever the ratio of time devoted to prayer, observance of the commandments, and Torah studies, on the one hand, to the time spent in activity related to survival and sustenance—that life's main focus and sole meaning remain imbedded in prayer, the commandments, and the Torah. To perform one's religious duties in a casual manner, in one's spare time, to treat them as merely another "hobby" that adds value and zest to life—that is absolutely inadmissible.

In point of fact, the expenditure of time and energy on this "daily activity" derives its sole *raison d'être* from providing man with the means to live and order his existence in accordance with the precepts of the Torah.

Our world was designed by God in such a fashion that the material, bodily aspect veils the spiritual essence of things, the divine vital current coursing through all living things, and constantly maintaining their reality as entities created from a void. The body of an object, its perceived exterior, is accepted by man as self-evident and self-sufficient. Yet if a veil is drawn around the emanation of the Divine Light inherent in all things and underlying its ultimate existence, an immeasurably greater mystery conceals from the eyes of man the divine force which enfolds our world and penetrates its every pore, ultimately immanent in all things yet transcending them all by virtue of possessing a degree of purity and refinement that is incompatible with base matter. To put it in more-easily-comprehended mathematical terms, the two entities reside on various planes of existence, or better yet, in different dimensions. However, this all-permeating divine force is certainly but the end-result of a downward chain of numberless reductions, infinitely removed from the absolute and unreachable Supreme Being dwelling above and beyond the created universe.

Now man, utterly incapable of realizing and absorbing any of this, insists on viewing the corporeal world as a self-supporting, substantial, and self-perpetuating reality.

The Holy Torah and its commandments are the sole vessel capable of providing, in spite and in defiance of the natural order of things, a direct link between the Jewish people and God. The commandments are God's will clothed in a form intelligible to man. They constitute the outer skin, the attire by donning which man communicates with God. The Torah is God's sublime wisdom, the only source of knowledge available to man, whose mind, by embracing this wisdom, comes in direct contact with God, drawing light and life from higher realms, and rechanneling them to enrich our entire world.

Man as a representative, though the highest one, of this lowest of all worlds—our world—is hopelessly incapable of comprehending concepts pertaining to the highest of all created worlds. Turning once again to examples from physics and mathematics, man could be defined as a being existing in three-dimensional space and irreversible time, and thus unable to imagine a world with additional dimensions, let alone comprehend God, who transcends time and space, for whom there is no division between past and future, and so on.

And only the Torah can bridge the abyss separating God and man; only the keeping of the commandments can lift us above our world; only God's mercy can inspire the chosen with the strength and wisdom to comprehend the higher realms.

If spirit were not obscured by matter, if the divine force infusing and enveloping the world were patently visible to man, there would be no freedom of choice, and earthly life would not constitute a test to be passed by man. Yet God's will, as our sages tell us, is designed precisely so that man, while living in this gross material world, may escape the snare of this world's misleading self-importance, overcome the temptations of primitive bodily life, triumph over his animal nature, and ascend to the spiritual heights, beckoned by the divine source inherent in every Jew. Like the burning flame of a candle, man must strive to break free of the wax and the wick which, though feeding the flame, are completely alien to it in their crass corporeality.

Man's most redeeming feature lies in the victory of virtue over sin, the taming and subjugation of his animal nature, the quelling of the thirst for illusory pleasures.

The pleasures sought by man's animal nature are far from being exclusively of the kind attracting hedonists or libertines. Sensual intemperance may don the quite respectable garb of science or poetry; gratification of the senses may require supreme inventiveness and mental effort; so that it is quite easy to overlook the simple truth—namely, that ultimately all of it is rooted in vanity, self-adoration, aggression, and the hunger for success.

Our ancestors were limited in their mobility within physical space; yet their minds possessed a cosmic reach, transcending the corporeal world.

Present-day pygmies, on the other hand, may travel at the speed of tens of thousands of kilometers an hour, or land on the moon; but their mind lies safely and smugly entombed in matter. They cannot even conceive of the need to differentiate between motion in this lowest of all worlds, whose essence, to put it in terms you can easily grasp, is invariable in respect to any set of coordinates—that is, identical on earth, the moon, or the farthest star—and motion that carries thought beyond the confines of this world, transporting it to the highest spiritual realms through the power of the mind.

What possible further proof do you need, besides the fact that your progenitors, through hundreds of generations, from the age of two, when they could barely speak, reverently uttered the name of Moses, invariably adding the highest title of "Our Teacher," preserving this solemn awe into their venerable old age of unsurpassed maturity and wisdom. What new discoveries, then, what depths of borrowed knowledge can be boasted by the last two, three, or four generations that considered themselves superior to both Moses and their direct ancestors who worshiped him; generations that have casually betrayed their forefathers' mission and sacred quest for the sake of indolence and apathy, for the sake of what they term "the benefits of progress"—whereby, artificially placing themselves in an environment totally inimical to man's physical and spiritual nature, they frantically pursue the surrogates of natural joys, or not even surrogates but simply a breath of fresh air, a drop of clean water, a glimpse of sunshine.

Finally, leaving all higher matters and philosophical debates behind, let me pose a very simple question. Would you not want children to become children again instead of their parents' tormentors; wives to become mothers and custodians of their homes; parents to win back their children's respect; the notions of honesty, virtue, faithfulness to regain their original meaning; people to rise, to begin with, at least to the level of animals who are free of overindulgence and perversion, be it in food, drink, or sex? Instead of proffering theories and arguments, let us but turn to the unadorned past, whereupon we shall be compelled to admit: all of that existed only when we lived in accordance with the *Shulchan Aruch*.

Start observing the commandments, and you will taste their flavor and acquire a taste for them. Give it a try! Indeed, if you had never eaten bread in your life, the best teachers in the world would not be able to communicate its taste in words.

Regardless of how long people sift through the multitude of interconnecting material phenomena, this attempt will only lead them away from the realization that they are delving only into primitive, crude matter. The more cumbersome and complex the analysis, the more it obscures the object being analyzed. They will never understand that rummaging through our material world with material tools and thoughts confined to matter precludes any possibility of transcending the boundaries of this world, of attaining the vision of higher realms. To express this in a language you are accustomed to, I could use the following illustration: with a three-dimensional apparatus for perceiving space, researchers may use three-dimensional instruments to study the properties of three-dimensional space for as long as they wish, without coming the least bit closer to understanding space that is four-dimensional, and in relation to which three-dimensional space is but a cross-section.

Or let us take another example. As a being locked in time and moving along a one-dimensional temporal axis, man perceives only the given moment – that is, the point transversed by the temporal axis he is moving upon. No physical device will enable him to see the entire axis. Yet God rules over the world not only by supporting the existence of all things contained therein, but also by exercising absolute dominion over this world as a whole, from unquestionably higher worlds. It is from those higher worlds, circumventing the natural order of things, that the Torah was passed down directly to the Jewish people, as the sole immediate link between the highest and the lowest worlds. Therefore, the deeper man penetrates the mysteries of the Torah, the stronger the inner voice of the supraconscious consciousness rising above the mundane corporeal world. And the first step on this upward path is made by arraying the soul in the vestments of the commandments, the same that are worn, despite their common earthly form, by the divine spirit. It is here that man begins to draw closer to God, to partake of His divine power, more potent and sublime that the one conferred from on high to maintain his existence.

Look into your heart, and you will find, hidden deep under the mound of layers accumulated by countless generations, the glimmering spark from the fire consuming the souls of our forefathers, the fire of adoration for the Creator and Protector of this breathtaking world of ours, of the love for one's fellow beings, of the thirst for the light of knowledge.

Before embarking on a study of the Book of Books, try to ascertain, meticulously and honestly, whether your intentions are pure, whether you possess the right degree of nobility and moral integrity. For, after all, you cannot help admitting that it is these very qualities that must characterize a genuine human being and a genuine Jew, which you aspire to be. If, however, you have not yet acquired these virtues, then try to develop them in yourself, help your good nature triumph over the bad. Only after attaining this victory over yourself, which may prove to be a far from easy task, will you have earned the right to be initiated into the monumental store of Jewish knowledge and faith, and become capable of understanding and assimilating our code of laws.

Therefore let us not make any further references to your possible shortcomings. Henceforth let us assume that you are honest and pure of heart, that you soul is wide open and receptive. You have a fervent desire to become a Jew, a genuine Jew. However, through no fault of yours, you have not yet learned anything, have not drunk a single drop from the boundless ocean of our Teaching. Hence you are ignorant as to what constitutes a Jew or determines the Jewish destiny. You try to breach this ignorance with all sorts of superficial, externally imposed views regarding this momentous issue.

You, alas, picture the genuine Jew as a naturalist, a musician, a poet, a politician, and finally a warrior. Nothing could be further from the truth. You should bear in mind that what set the first Jew—Abraham—apart from the rest was the fact that his acts and intentions were devoted solely and exclusively to the cause of carrying out God's will. Our sages liken Abraham to a chariot unquestioningly obedient to the rider's will. This and this alone constitutes the Jewish essence passed down through generations.

Alas, our people's history has witnessed frequent occasions when a large or small fraction of Jews, tempted by the artificial dazzle of an alien way of life, would voluntarily surrender their spiritual legacy, succumbing to the cult of physical gratification. Nor did this always happen in the literal sense of Hellenistic body-worship, hedonism, and dissipation. More often than not, this escape would wear the refined guise of advancement in natural sciences and literature, or political rivalry. Moreover, many of those who chose this path were not motivated by self-interest but acted out of honest though mistaken beliefs, for the world that we inhabit is ordered in such a way that its every tangible and visible aspect is perceived as self-evident reality. The bodily form of objects eclipses their "spirit," the divine emanation that fills them, maintaining their existence, in an endless process of renewed creation *ex nihilo*. It is the spirit alone, refined and ennobled by the continuous work of perfecting itself, cleansed of all impurities, painstakingly strained through the cleansing sieve of observing the commandments, that awakens to the glory of God suffusing all things. Then one's eyes will be opened to the truth that our world is not only permeated by God's radiant light enlivening all of creation, but also encompassed by the sublime manifestation of the divine essence, transcending human understanding, beyond the notions of time and space, whose sole identifiable attribute can be said to be its absolute detachment from all that is earthly, in other words its divinity.

For the Jewish people, the most disastrous period of abandoning their duty and appointed mission began about a hundred and fifty years ago, with the advent of the so-called golden age of science and civilization. Led astray by the false glitter of success enjoyed by natural sciences, confusing the notions of "knowledge" and "knowhow," "science" and "craft," the Jews displayed incredible zeal and enviable energy in their eagerness to erect a new idol for themselves and the rest of humanity, one that was credited with omniscience and omnipotence, and awarded the title of science.

Years passed, and the initial euphoria began to fade. By now, all right-minded natural scientists have realized that true knowledge and the activity to which they have devoted themselves are different things; that the study of interconnections between objects and phenomena will not bring them a bit closer to an understanding of their essence; that ultimate reality, when viewed from atop the tower of Babel of their intricate mental constructs, does not draw nearer but recedes. . . .

The best among these scientists have already understood that, when it comes to essential and ultimate truths as opposed to connections between temporal objects and phenomena, the sole authority is the Holy Scripture—its literal meaning, its allegorical imagery, its edifying and profound lessons, whose multilayered richness is accessible only to those of a noble mind and a pure soul.

They may have realized and understood all that; but their apathy, their lack of the sense of duty lost over generations, prevent them from taking the next step—to resume the formidable tasks and obligations required of a Jew; and so they retain their attitude of moralizing hypocrisy.

Our sages say that the soul of every Jew combines two natures, two spirits—the divine and the animal. The extent of the victory achieved by the former over the latter is what determines the degree to which each man fulfills his destiny on earth.

Our sages teach us that God fashioned the material world out of pure spirit. Consequently, the task of every Jew lies in turning matter back into spirit, refining and spiritualizing the gross physical world.

God's greatness lies precisely in that He (His emanation) has the power to infuse spirit into the crudest matter; and this is done through the mediation of the Jews, whose chief task is to release the divine spirit trapped in base earthly forms, to sublimate all physical functions through observing the commandments.

Is the theater audience more concerned with the way the props have been arranged than with their psychological impact? Would their experience be more rewarding for the detailed knowledge of paints and cardboard used in making the decorations?

Similarly, the essence of the moon, of stars, of candlelight is due more to the effect they produce in man than to their composition and structure.

To seek the rationale behind the commandments is a difficult, and perhaps even unnecessary, task. They were ordained by God, and in their observance lies our sacred mission, and thereby the content and guarantee of our life, our continuous existence as individuals and a nation. It is not enough to understand this by reason alone. This must be grasped with the heart, so that the flame of love for God burning within it, of the love toward one's neighbor as one of God's chosen, would yield the strength for carrying out the divine commandments.

About the Author

Herman Branover is the Lady Davis Professor and head of the Center for Magnetohydrodynamic Studies of Ben-Gurion University in Israel. He received his Ph.D. and D.Sc. degrees, as well as the rank of full professor, in the former Soviet Union. In 1957 he began his struggle for the right to leave the Soviet Union and settle in Israel. After fifteen years of refusal, harassments, and imprisonments, he was released in 1972. He was the first Soviet Jewish professor permitted to emigrate to Israel. During the years of refusal Professor Branover made the transition from atheist to Torah-observant Jew and follower of the Lubavitcher Rebbe. Dr. Branover has served as a professor at Tel-Aviv University as well as at New York University and Argonne National Laboratory in Chicago. He is a member of the Russian and Latvian academies of science. In Israel he founded the organization SHAMIR, which provides Jewish education to Jews from the Soviet Union and has published more than 350 Jewish books translated into the Russian language. He established the magazine *B'Or Ha'Torah* on Judaism and the modern world, and has published 18 books and 250 scientific articles on physics and energy engineering, as well as numerous books and articles on Torah and science.